THE LAW OF
THE COVENANT

THE LAW OF THE COVENANT

An Exposition of Exodus 21-23

James B. Jordan

Institute for Christian Economics
Tyler, Texas

Printed in the United States of America
Library of Congress Catalog Card Number 84-080954
ISBN 0-930464-02-8

Unless otherwise indicated, Scripture quotations in the body of the commentary are either the author's own, or are from the New American Standard Bible, copyright 1971 by the Lockman Foundation, and used by permission.

Published by
Institute for Christian Economics
P.O. Box 8000
Tyler, Texas 75711

To my wife, Brenda, with love.

PREFACE AND ACKNOWLEDGMENTS

The style of this work is different from that of some other
modern Bible commentaries. This is because I have written it as a
Christian addressing other Christians, rather than as a scholar
addressing other scholars. There is no true conflict between
scholarship and faith, but my primary purpose is to edify the
Church of Jesus Christ, and thus my scholarship is subordinate to
that end.

The passage with which I am concerned has been the object of
much higher critical analysis, and could become the subject of a
lengthy scholarly discussion.[1] This is not my purpose. While I do
not despise the place of sound conservative scholarship, my purpose in this book is to give a theological and useable exposition of
the first extended law code of the Bible. To this end I have
brought to bear in my discussion as much as seemed useful from
the work of modern scholars, while leaving much of the apparatus
of scholarship behind.

There is no extensive commentary on this passage of the
Bible, written from an orthodox, evangelical standpoint. Thus, at

---

1. The interested reader might procure Edward J. Young, *An Introduction to the
Old Testament* (Grand Rapids: William B. Eerdmans, 1960 [revised edition]); also,
in ascending order of scholarly detail and precision, Roland K. Harrison, *Introduction to the Old Testament* (Grand Rapids: Eerdmans, 1969); Oswald T. Allis,
The Old Testament: Its Claims and its Critics (Phillipsburg, NJ: The Presbyterian
and Reformed Pub. Co., 1972); G. Ch. Aalders, *A Short Introduction to the Pentateuch* (London: The Tyndale Press, 1949); and Oswald T. Allis, *The Five Books of
Moses* (Phillipsburg, NJ: The Presbyterian and Reformed Pub. Co., 1949 [2nd
edition]).

numerous points I have been put in a position of either saying very little, or else breaking new ground. The reader may well find peculiar or strained, for instance, my interpretation of the stipulation that the owner of a slaughtered beast be compensated five-fold for an ox and four-fold for a sheep (Ex. 22:1), or my discussion of the meaning of "thou shalt not boil a kid in its mother's milk" (Ex. 23:19), to take two examples. I only ask the reader's indulgence, that he or she carefully consider my suggestions. I may be wrong at one place or another, but then again, I may be right. What seems strange to us might not have seemed strange to an ancient Israelite.

I have tried to place modal qualifiers at relevant places in the book ("maybe," "it seems to me," etc.). Perhaps this book needs more such sprinkled throughout. Let me say here that I do not offer these studies as the *final* word on any subject, but only as a hopefully *helpful* word. These studies are dated: 1984 A.D. It is my hope that they will assist others to study these portions of Scripture more carefully, so that by the year 2084 A.D., someone can write a far more definitive work than this can hope to be.

These studies in Exodus 21-23 were originally prepared in outline form for a Bible class at St. Paul Presbyterian Church, Jackson, Mississippi. I should like to thank the members of that class for their support and encouragement.

A grant from the Chalcedon Foundation of Vallecito, California, enabled me to work on this book extensively while finishing my seminary training. A grant from the Institute for Christian Economics of Tyler, Texas, enabled me to finish it. I wish to thank Rev. Rousas J. Rushdoony and Dr. Gary North, respectively the presidents of these two foundations, for their encouragement and help. A gift from Mr. R. E. McMaster enabled the Institute for Christian Economics to publish this book, and I thank Mr. McMaster for his support.

I wish to thank Rev. Ray R. Sutton for valuable interaction over these studies, and Prof. John M. Frame for reading the manuscript and making valuable suggestions, as well as for writing the introduction. Much of what is of value in this book comes from others, but its infelicities are mine alone.

The translation of Holy Scripture used in this work is at many points my own. For the remainder, the New American Standard Version has been used (usually taking the literal marginal reading rather than the text reading). I am grateful to the Lockman Foundation, holders of the copyright on the NASV, for granting permission for its use.

Last but by no means least, this book is dedicated to my wife, Brenda, without whose encouragement and support I could not have accomplished this task.

James B. Jordan, Th. M.
March, 1984

TABLE OF CONTENTS

Preface and Acknowledgments vii

Introduction, by John M. Frame xvii

I. The Bible and the Laws of God 1
   The Law is God-Centered   1
   The Bible is Covenantal   3
   The Bible is a Book of Life   8
   The Law of God is Unchanging   11
   Old and New Testaments   17
   The Laws of God Have Multiple Equity   18
   The Law of God is General and Particular   19
   The Uses of the Law   24
   God Gives Laws to the State   26
   The Binding Nature of the Law   28

II. The Law and the Redemption of Israel 30
   The History of the Seed People   31
   Redemption and Vengeance   36
   God and Pharaoh   39

III. The Book of the Covenant: Its Context 46
   Redemption and Covenant   46
   The Law Before Sinai   50
   Godly Civilization   52
   A Renewed Creation-Covenant and Fall   55

IV. The Ordinances: Structure and Characteristics 61
   The Arrangement of the Ordinances   63
      I. Laws Concerning Slavery   64
      II. Laws Concerning Violence   64

   III. Laws Concerning Property and Stewardship 65
   IV. Laws Concerning Marriage and Faithfulness 65
    V. Laws Concerning Witness-Bearing 66
   VI. Laws Regulating Time and Rest 66
  VII. Epilogue: Exhortations to Obey God
         and Conquer Canaan 66
  Characteristics of the Case Laws 68

V. Slavery 75
  Male Slaves 76
  The Circumcision of the Ear 78
  Female Slaves 84
  Slavery in the Bible 87
  Practical Observations 90

VI. Violence 93
  The Nature of Violence 93
  Capital Offenses 96
    I. Premeditated Murder 97
   II. Accidental Manslaughter 97
  III. Striking Parents 103
  IV. Kidnapping and Slave Trading 104
   V. Repudiating Parents 105
  Assault 109
    I. Fighting or Dueling 100
   II. Slave Beating 112
  III. Bystanders 113
  IV. Retaliation and Recompense
      (The Law of Equivalence) 115
   V. Equivalence for Slaves 121
  The Goring Ox 121
    I. The Rebellious Beast 122
   II. The Incorrigible Beast 124
  III. Ransom 125
  IV. Appropriate Punishment 125
   V. The Price of a Slave 127
  Hazardous Property 128
    I. The Open Pit 129
   II. Ox Gores Ox 130

VII. Property 131
The Importance of Property 132
Theft 134
  I. Restitution 134
  II. Self-Defense 136
Pollution 137
Safekeeping 140
Borrowing, Neighborliness, and Rent 142

VIII. Faithfulness 145
Seduction 146
Spiritual Adultery 152
The Defenseless and the Poor 155
  I. The Foreigner 156
  II. The Helpless 156
  III. Interest 158
  IV. Pledges 159
Loyalty to God 161
  I. Cursing God 161
  II. Cursing Rulers 162
  III. Tithes 163
  IV. The Firstborn 163
  V. Holiness 165

IX. Justice 167
Justice and the Witnesses 168
Personal Adversaries 169
Justice and the Judges 171
The Sojourner 175
Judicial Procedure 176

X. Sabbaths and Festivals 181
Sabbaths 182
Festivals 184
  I. The Feast of Unleavened Bread 186
  II. The Feast of the Harvest 189
  III. The Feast of the Ingathering 190
The New Covenant 192

XI. Conclusion 194

Appendix A: Old and New Covenant 196

**Appendix B: The Case Laws Correlated with
the Ten Commandments** 199

**Appendix C: Tithing: Financing
Christian Reconstruction** 207
The Melchizedekal Tithe   208
The Levitical Tithe   209
Education   213
Medicine   216
Advisors to the State   216
Worship   217
The Foundation of Society   217
Should the Tithe Always Go to the Church?   219
How to Tithe   221

Appendix D: State Financing in the Bible 225
The Mosaic Head Tax   225
The Meaning of the "Atonement"   226
The Circumstances of Collection   227
Use of the Tax   230
The Temple Tax in the New Testament   233
The Prince's Tax in Ezekiel   235
Nehemiah's Head Tax   237
Implicit Teaching   238

Appendix E: Salvation and Statism 240

Appendix F: Proleptic Passover: Exodus 4:22-26 243
A Survey of Interpretations   243
A Suggested Interpretation   251
Addendum on the Circumcision of Abram and Sarai   260

Appendix G: Four and Five-Fold Restitution 261
Four-fold and Five-fold   263
Sheep and Oxen   266
Oppressing the Poor   268
Revolution   269
Conclusion   270

Appendix H: On Boiling a Kid in Its Mother's Milk 272

Index of Hebrew Terms Discussed 279
Index of Persons Cited or Referenced 281
Scripture Index 283
Subject Index 299

Introduction

John M. Frame

Jim Jordan, though by years only a babe in the household of the theological profession, has already published an extraordinary amount of material—articles (both scholarly and popular), newsletters, reviews of literature, music, and films. He has dealt with exegetical, theological, historical, and practical topics, and all with an extraordinary amount of originality, interest, cogency, and usefulness. So to many, those familiar with the "Christian Reconstruction" movements which have published his articles, Jim needs no introduction. It is my privilege, then, to say a few words to the *rest* of you, as you read, or think about reading, this Jim's first published book.[1]

Jim was born on Dec. 31, 1949, in Athens, Georgia, where he grew up. His grandfather was a Methodist clergyman, following a tradition of several generations. His father, for many years head of the Modern Foreign Languages Dept. at the University of Georgia (specializing in French literature), was a staunch Christian believer, churchman, and Sunday School teacher in the Lutheran Church in America. His mother taught piano while raising the family. Jim went to the University of Georgia on a scholarship acquired through the National Merit program and graduated in 1971 with a degree in Comparative Literature. His studies also included intensive work in music history and political

---

1. I had better write fast, or it may not be the first after all. Jim has at least three other books in various stages of preparation: *Food and Faith*, *Trees and Thorns*, and *Slavery and Liberation in the Bible*.

theory. He spent four years in the Air Force with the rank of Lieu-
tenant, first as an Administration Management Officer, and then
as an Air Force Historian. Then came seminary training at Reformed and Westminster Theological Seminaries, earning
M.A.R. and Th.M. degrees from the latter (thesis topic: "Slavery
in Biblical Perspective"). He serves as an elder in the Association
of Reformation churches and as Associate Pastor of Westminster
Presbyterian Church, Tyler, Texas, where he writes and teaches
for Geneva Ministries. He is married (Brenda) with two sons
(Dale, 8, and Douglas, 6).

Jim was one of the most interesting and able students I ever
taught at Westminster Theological Seminary. In my mind I've
sometimes compared his personality to two other interesting
characters with southern accents: conservative commentator Pat
Buchanan (CNN's "Crossfire") and Larry Hagman's portrayal of
J. R. Ewing ("Dallas"). Jim reminds me of Buchanan chiefly in
the quickness of his mind, his ability to produce cogent "instant
analysis." At first, I thought Jim was almost too fast, perhaps too
glib, needing to spend more time and effort before categorizing
things. But the more I meditated on his ideas, the more his instant
analyses seemed to hold up to scrutiny. I still take issue with him
sometimes (see below); but I have developed a great respect for
the intellectual gifts God has given him.

And J. R. Ewing?? Well, of course Jim's moral standards are
the precise antithesis of J. R.'s! But antitheses often reflect one
another in ironic ways. Jim shares J. R.'s view of life as warfare, a
warfare requiring total effort and maximum ingenuity. Jim fights
for the Lord, not for the devil as does J. R.; but Jim often cannot
resist a sly laugh (very Hagman) in contemplating God's triumphs.

The present book, I think, is very important. I am not an Old
Testament specialist, so I cannot vouch for all of Jim's exegetical
proposals. Most of them do seem sensible to me. But if only, say,
three-quarters of them hold up, this book will still be one of the
most helpful commentaries on the market. The Book of the Covenant, Exodus 21-23, is one of the most important parts of the
Bible. The Pentateuch is the heart of the Old Testament, and the

Ten Commandments are the heart of the Pentateuch. Within the Pentateuch, the Book of the Covenant is the most concise, the most fundamental exposition of the Decalogue. Yet most Christians today are entirely ignorant of this part of the Bible. The laws in this passage (like others in the Pentateuch) are rather mysterious to modern readers. Jim clears up many of these mysteries for us. Why is a son executed for cursing his parents? See pages 105ff. What does the Bible say about street-fighting? See page 111. What does Ex. 21:22ff. say about abortion? See page 115. Why are dowries important? See pages 146ff.

This is, of course, of more than academic interest. Jim is one of these "theonomists" or "Christian Reconstructionists" who believes that these mysterious biblical laws are still binding, even upon New Testament believers. This position is controversial today, and I cannot hope to give an adequate analysis of the issues here. The introductory chapter of this book deals with those questions quite ably. But if that doesn't satisfy you, don't give up on the book. The most persuasive argument is the exposition of the law itself. When you see how much sense it makes to your Christian mind, you will *want* it to be binding today; and when you reach that point you are already 80% theonomist.

Jim knows that Israel's situation is different from ours, both culturally and redemptive-historically. But he insists, as we all must, that these differences be formulated as Scripture does, not as we might like them to be. That loyalty to Scripture, not the "theonomy" or "reconstructionist" label, is the important thing. Therefore, I think that many of us who prefer to avoid such labels and to avoid identification with such movements, will find this book remarkably illuminating and edifying.

Besides, "theonomy" as Jim expounds it may not be at all what you were expecting. Here is a theonomist who denies that there is a corpus of civil laws in the Bible (p. 242)! This theonomist tells us that "the death penalty is not mandatory in all cases where it is prescribed by law. It is the maximum penalty" (p. 148f.). Further, he is rather flexible about the role of government — warranting government intervention even when such intervention is not expressly mandated by Scripture, if that is the only way to get the job done (pp. 138ff. the quotation from Gary North). There is a kind of common-sense flexibility here that many people do not associate with theonomy (although such flexibility has always characterized the movement at its best: pp. 138ff. do, after all, come from North's writings). Clearly, Jim is much more interested in what Scripture says than in maintaining some stereotypical image of "the theonomist." His distinctions provide opportunities for serious discussion between those who accept and those who reject the theonomy label.

You can learn so much here — from theoretical insights on the "multiple equity of the law" (pp. 18ff.) to practical advice on what to do when your child breaks your neighbor's china (pp. 143f.). I found especially helpful the discussion of the "uses of the law" (pp. 24ff., Appendix E), the correlation between the Book of the Covenant and the Decalogue (pp. 63ff.), the discussion of tithing (pp. 207ff.), and the analysis of Israel's Exodus from Egypt in terms of the slavery laws (pp. 39ff.).

At some points I have problems with Jim's discussion. His distinction between "Old" and "New" covenants (pp. 55ff., 196ff.) does not seem to me to do enough justice to Heb. 8. Also, I have my doubts as to whether the Hebrew pleonasm really furnishes us with "two witnesses" (p. 96, note 5). Sometimes the fertility of Jim's mind still exceeds his self-discipline.

On the whole, however, the book is a tremendous contribution. There are fresh insights on nearly every page. It raises the discussion of biblical law to a new level of precision and cogency, because it deals with the law in such detail. It is the most practical piece of biblical theology I've seen in a long time. It has changed my thinking on a number of matters. So I encourage you to read it in gratitude to God and in anticipation of more from this gifted young author.

Westminster Theological Seminary in California
March 16, 1984

1

THE BIBLE AND THE LAWS OF GOD

Because modern Christians are often confused regarding the usability of "Old Testament Law," this chapter is intended to set forth general canons for a Biblical theology of law, before moving to a detailed exposition of the passage. I can hardly hope to be exhaustive here, or to defend every single point. Footnote references direct the reader to more elaborate treatments of the various themes.

The Law is God-Centered

The modern tendency is to read the Bible only to find out what it says to men as individuals. The Scripture is consulted only to find out what the Bible says to *me*, about *me*, for *me*, and so forth. Clearly there is nothing wrong with this in itself, but it produces a warped view of the Bible if this is the *only* way it is read. The Bible, God's written revelation, speaks not only about individual matters, but also about social and cosmic (creation-al) matters as well. This is because the Bible, while it is man-*oriented*, is God-*centered*.

The Bible was written for mankind, and thus everything it says is relevant to humanity. Man's chief purpose, however, is to glorify *God* and to enjoy *Him*. Fallen man glorifies himself and enjoys himself, or tries to do so. What does it mean to glorify someone? Basically, two things. First, it means to praise him. When a person brags about himself, he is glorifying himself verbally, with his words. When we sing the praises of God our Creator and Savior, we glorify Him verbally. Second, it means to do things to

1

please him or to honor him. We spend most of our time trying to please ourselves and to honor ourselves. The Christian's labor, however, is to be accomplished for the pleasure and honor of God. When we glorify God, through life and lip, we find that we enjoy Him, and that we enjoy life. This is only natural, since God is the Author of life and the Creator of the world. When we do things His way, we cannot help but prosper in the long run.

God is a Person. He is interested in everything He has made. God is love, and He loves everything He has made. Thus, we are told in Matthew that God feeds the birds (6:26) and that not one little bird dies but that the Father takes note of it (10:29). God even cares for the grass of the field (6:30). God has a *personal* interest in these things, and thus so should His image, man. This should teach us to treat God's world with care and respect, for we shall have to answer for it if we do not.

In His law, God has protected the trees[1] and the birds.[2] If we take a man-centered approach to these laws, we might say that the purpose of this legislation is *only* to ensure human prosperity. Such an approach to the law of God misses the most basic point. These

---

1. "When you besiege a city a long time, to make war against it in order to capture it, you shall not destroy its trees by swinging an axe against them; for you may eat from them and you shall not cut them down. *For is the tree of the field a man, that it should be besieged by you?* Only the trees which you know are not trees for food you shall destroy and cut down in order that you may construct siegeworks against the city that is making war with you until it falls" (Dt. 20:19, 20). Notice that the argument God gives, which we have emphasized, calls attention to the place of trees in *His* scheme of things, and the value *He* places on them. Just as God regulated Adam's use of the trees of the garden of Eden, so He continues to regulate man's use of trees.

2. "If you happen to come upon a bird's nest along the way, in any tree or on the ground, with young ones or eggs, and the mother sitting on the young or on the eggs, you shall not take the mother with the young; you shall certainly let the mother go, but the young you may take for yourself, in order that it may be well with you, and that you may prolong your days" (Dt. 22:6, 7). While the ecological benefits of this law would indeed have the effect of prolonging the life of man, in itself such a rule would have only slight effects. The import of this law is that it tells us that God will bestow life on those men who respect the life He has given to other creatures. It is *His* concern with the birds, as well as with men, which lies behind this legislation.

laws show us God's own genuine personal care for His world, and as such these laws cannot be altered by human whim. To be sure, the Bible is man-oriented, and thus obedience to these laws will improve human life; but the laws are God's, and cannot be changed by man. Thus, as we examine the laws in Exodus 21-23, our first concern must be the glory of God, not whether these laws *seem* right to us sinful men. If we start with God, we will soon see how these laws also improve human life.

The Bible is Covenantal

The term "covenant" is frequently used in Christian theology, but with various shades of meaning. I shall be using it to identify the personal, binding, structural relationship among the Persons of God and His people. The covenant, thus, is a *social structure.* To understand this, we must consider the doctrine of the Trinity. God, according to His Word, is a Person, and He is also three Persons: the Father, the Son, and the Holy Spirit. The three Persons have a *personal relationship* among Themselves: They love each other, and they communicate with each other.

Each Person of God is morally perfect, of course. Also, the relationships among the three Persons are always morally perfect. If we could describe the personal character of any one Person of God, we should then have a description of a morally perfect person. In the same way, if we could describe the inter-personal relationships of the three Persons of God, we should then have a description of a morally perfect society. The Bible shows us both what a moral person is like and what a moral society is like. Principally this description is found in the law and in the Proverbs, but the whole of the Bible is "profitable for doctrine, for reproof, for correction, for instruction in righteousness, so that the man of God might be mature, thoroughly furnished for every good work" (2 Tim. 3:16f.).

Man is created in the image of God (Gen. 1:27). This does not mean that man is part of God, or an extension of God, or has some "spark of divinity" within himself. Not at all. Man exists completely outside of God, created by God outside of Himself.

Man *depends* on God for Life, but man does not *participate* in God's *existence*.[3] At the same time, however, man was created to participate in social *fellowship* with God, to enjoy the life of God in this way. Man was to have a *community of life* with God, though not a community of essence.

According to Genesis 1:27, "God created man in His own image, in the image of God created He him (singular): Male and female He created them (plural)." What this says is that *man is a copy of God.* Man's capacities, his personality, and his morality are copied from God. Also, the fact that man is a social being is copied from God. Each individual human being is an image of God, but also *each human society is an image of God.*[4]

Now, to get back to our original question: What is the covenant? We may say, in part, that *the covenant is the personal structural bond among the three Persons of God.* The only time that bond was ever broken was when the Lord Jesus Christ went into hell (separation from God) on the cross, crying "My God, My God, why hast Thou forsaken Me?" (Matt. 27:46). This is a great mystery.

The inter-personal relationships among the Persons of the Trinity constitute a covenantal bond which involves Persons and a structure. This bond is simultaneously *personal* and *corporate*. God's personal relationships with men are therefore also covenantal. When God created man in His image, man was incorporated into this covenant among the three Persons of God. This relationship was not only personal, however; it was also *structural*. There

----

3. It might be worth calling attention to the fact that the Bible continually symbolizes man's dependence on God by means of food and water. God is Giver of both. Man does not have life in himself, and must have them to live. From the Tree of Life in the Garden to the Holy Eucharist of the Church, God's gift of life to man is signified through food. This is particularly prominent in the wilderness experience of Israel (Exodus - Numbers), but it can also be seen in the very description of the promised land as a land of milk and honey. See James B. Jordan, *Food and Faith* (forthcoming).

4. A more extensive discussion of covenant and of man's imaging of God is found in James B. Jordan, *Trees and Thorns: An Exposition of Genesis 1-4* (forthcoming).

were *rules* which defined what perfect personal and social morality was to be like. When Adam and Eve broke these rules by rebelling against the structure God had given them, they broke the covenant, and were subsequently cast out of the presence of God, into an earthly wilderness which eventually will become hell.

The covenant is a personal-structural bond which joins the three Persons of God in a community of life, and in which man was created to participate. On the cross, Jesus Christ descended into hell as a substitute for His people, and as a result, His people are reunited into the covenant. We call this work of Christ *redemption*. Redemption is the doorway back to the garden of Eden, back to the covenant fellowship of God.[5]

Were we to make a transcription of the moral character of any one Person of God, or of *the* One Person of God, we should have a description of a morally perfect man as well, because man is the image of God.[6] This would show us what *individual morality* consists of.

Were we to make a transcription of the moral character of the covenant relationship among the three Persons of God, we should have a description of perfect social life for man. This would show us what *social morality* consists of.

God is no more One than He is Three, and no more Three than One. In the same way, the social life of man is no more important than his individual life, and his individual life is no more

---

5. "I do not ask in behalf of these alone, but for those who believe in Me through their word; that they may all be one; even as Thou, Father, art in Me, and I in Thee, that they also may be in Us; that the world may believe that Thou didst send Me" (John 17:20, 21).

6. "With regard to the doctrine of the Trinity, Van Til denies that the paradox of the three and one can be resolved by the formula 'one in essence and three in person.' Rather, 'We do assert that God, that is, the whole Godhead, is one person.' " John Frame, "The Problem of Theological Paradox," in Gary North, ed., *Foundations of Christian Scholarship* (Vallecito, CA: Ross House Books, 1976), p. 306f. The point is that we cannot address "God" in prayer unless the Oneness of God is personal; otherwise, we should only be able to address one of the Three Persons in prayer, never simply "God." Thus, we can speak of man as an individual as an image in general of the One Person of God, even though human nature most closely seems to image in particular the Second Person, the Son.

important than his social life. The Bible, thus, is concerned both
with individual and with social morality. When we say, then, that
the Bible is covenantal, one of the things we mean is that the Bible
gives the rules for social life, as well as for individual life.

How does this relate to law? The law of God is a transcription
of His holy character, both individual and social.[7] The law tells us
the structure of covenant life, but the law cannot guarantee our
personal involvement in that covenant life. It is grace which
brings us into personal involvement with the covenant life of
God.[8]

Modern man tends to contrast structure with personal freedom. The Bible never pits these against each other. They are two
sides of one coin, as it were — the coin of the covenant. Modern
man pits structure against freedom in his art, his music, his
politics, and even in his Church life. How many Christians feel
that a formal worship service will destroy freedom of worship? In
reality this is not the case, for formal structure in worship makes
for easier participation, and thus greater freedom. (Of course,
just as an overemphasis on freedom leads to anarchy, so an
overemphasis on form can be stifling. The point is that covenan-
talism provides such a balance.)

An example of a covenant relationship is marriage, which is

---

7. "The law reflects not only the *presence* but the *moral character* of God. 'We
know that the law is good,' says Paul (1 Tim. 1:8; cf. Rom. 7:12, 16); a good thing
can be produced only by that which in itself is good (Matt. 7:16-18; 12:33), and
God alone is good (Mark 10:18). In detailing what He requires of man the Lord
has revealed what is good (Mic. 6:8), and the Psalmist declared, 'Thou art good
and doest good; teach me thy statutes' (Ps. 119:68, AV)." Greg L. Bahnsen,
Theonomy in Christian Ethics (Phillipsburg, NJ: The Craig Press, 1977), p. 142.
Chapter 5 (pp. 141-148) of this book is an extended discussion of the relation of
the law of God to the character of God.

8. We should also say that the personal-structural relationships among the
Persons of the Godhead are not the result of submission to law, in the sense that
men submit to God's law. The whole point here is that the law of God is a revelation of His character to the creature. The sovereignty of God over the creature,
in the moral realm, is seen in the fact that God's personal character is the law for
the creature. The three members of the Godhead do not give law to one another,
for each is equal to the others.

called a covenant in Malachi 2:14.[9] If two people begin to live together, and sleep together, we call this fornication, not marriage. There is indeed a personal relationship, but there is no legal bond. On the other hand, if two people are legally married, but are separated, something is obviously wrong, since the personal aspect is missing (cf. Ex. 21:10). Thus, a true marriage covenant has both a legal bond and a personal aspect. Also, in marriage there is a structure within the covenant, with the man ruling and the woman being ruled. In this way we can see that law and structure are not opposed to personal fulfillment. Indeed, the fear and guilt that attends fornication is personally ruinous, while it is precisely the legal contract which makes the living liberty of marriage possible. The legal side reinforces and strengthens the personal side. The fact that structure is an aid to freedom has many implications for worship, for civil order, for music, and so forth.

In summary, the covenant has three aspects. There is a legal bond. There is a personal relationship. There is a structure within the community.[10]

God's law is a description of His own moral character. It shows us our sin, and it also shows us how to live righteously within the covenant. It cannot *empower* us, however. We are dead in trespasses and sins until grace comes to us and gives us new life. Grace not only raises us from the dead, but empowers us day by

---

9. " 'Yet you say, "For what reason?" Because the LORD has been a witness between you and the wife of your youth, against whom you have dealt treacherously, though she is your companion and *your wife by covenant.*' "

10. This structure is seen in the Trinity in that, though each number of the Godhead is equally God in the sense of His essence (the ontological Trinity), yet there is subordination of roles within the Trinity, with the Son under the Father, and the Spirit proceeding from both the Father and the Son (which ontological order is manifested to the creation as the economic Trinity). Thus, the intra-Trinitarian structure consists of economic relations. In that the Son is under the Father, in some sense, there is some parallel between God's structuring man's life by law, and the Father's "structuring" the life of the Son. It would probably be best, however, to reserve the language of "law," in its theological meaning, to the relationship between Creator and creature. We might say that the structural side of the God-man relationship is *law*, while the structural side of the intra-Trinitarian relationships is *order*, for we speak in theology of the *order* of Persons in the Godhead.

day. So, law gives us the standard; grace gives us the power. In
the covenant, law reveals the structure; grace enables the personal
involvement, both social and individual.

It is possible for a person to obey God's law in the temporary
power of the flesh. This is Pharisaism. Even Christians, when
they sin and stop depending on God for grace, can fall into lifeless,
Pharisaical obedience. Such obedience is legalistic, or law-
centered, rather than covenantal, or God-centered. It abstracts
the law from the Person of the Law-Giver.

The Bible is covenantal. That is, it is both personal and structural. It also shows us both grace (redemption) and law (covenantal life). Moreover, it is social as well as individual.

Finally, some say that the Old Testament is more social in its
orientation, while the New Testament is more individual. This is
in fact not really true, but even if it were true, would this change
the fact that God is Three and One, and that God is equally interested in individual and social life?

The Bible is a Book of Life

It is the task and privilege of the Church, and thus of churchmen, to proclaim and teach the Word of God. Because men tend
to be selfish and possessive, seeking to glorify themselves, there is
a tendency for churchmen to take the Bible as only a manual for
the Church, and not for all of life. The Bible becomes a collection
of preaching texts, some laws for individual morality, and a rule-
book for the Church, but nothing else. The Bible, they tend to
say, does not speak to science, medicine, history, politics, or law.

Dr. Francis Nigel Lee has coined the term "ecclesiocentrism"
for this phenomenon: "church-centered-ness." The ecclesiocentric
person speaks of the "regulative principle of worship," but neglects
the Bible's regulation of all of life. He speaks of the "Spirituality of
the Church," but fails to see that *wherever* the Spirit acts there is
Spirituality, including the home, business, and state. He magni-
fies what the Bible says about the Sabbath, while minimizing
what it says about the six cultural days of the week. This tendency
has cropped up over and over in Church history.

The result of this is a *restricted priesthood*. Only churchmen are *really* able to read the Bible. If anyone else wants to read it, he should read it in a "devotional" manner, seeking for an experience or some word of individual morality. But the "layman" should never read the Bible with an eye to his profession. Doctors must not read the Bible for help in medicine. Lawyers must not read it for ideas about law.

We have to repudiate this notion. The Bible is a book of life. It is for *all* of life, not only for sabbatical life (worship, the Church), but also for cultural life (work, business, family, government, medicine, etc.). We believe in *the priesthood of all believers*. A priest is a judge, and in whatsoever capacity a man is called to make decisions in that capacity he is to read the Bible. Doctors should read the Bible for medical clues. Lawyers should consult Biblical law. Historians should take the chronology of the Bible as their starting point. Geologists should consult the carefully recorded description of the Flood year. And so forth.

The Bible is a covenantal book, and the covenant is broader than the institutional (sacramental) Church. The Bible *is* a book of preaching texts, but it is *also* a book of life. When we reduce the Bible to a mere collection of "inspiring texts," we only hurt ourselves.

Often churchmen emphasize only the redemptive aspect of Scriptural revelation, stressing the various stages of redemptive history. The effect of taking an exclusively "redemptive-historical" approach to the Bible is often an ignoring of most of what the Bible says about covenant life. (No one ignores this completely, of course.) For instance, it is true that God caused His law to be written comprehensively during the Mosaic period of Old Testament history. The covenant law was inscripturated at a certain point in history, for reasons which shall be discussed later in this book. This fact does not, however, alter the nature of that revelation: It was *law* which was revealed, and law does not change.[11]

---

11. Being a transcript of God's character, the law in its essence cannot change. The word "law" is used in varying ways, however. Particular laws, being applications of the unchanging principles of God's law, do vary. On this whole matter, see Bahnsen, *Theonomy in Christian Ethics*.

The fact that the Mosaic inscripturation of the law has a significance in the history of redemption does not, or should not, obscure the fact that this law-revelation also has a significance for covenant life throughout all history.

Similarly, the fact that the Flood has a redemptive-historical significance should not alter the fact that it also has a geological significance. The records of the Patriarchs in Genesis 5 and 11 not only show us the (redemptive-historical) fact that Christ is a true descendent of Adam, but they also may possibly show us one of the medical benefits of the pre-Flood "waters above the firmament" (long life), as well as providing us with an air-tight chronology of the first 2500 years of the existence of the universe.[12]

The Bible is a book for all of life. It gives us accurate history. It also gives us law, for "what nation is there that has statutes and judgments as righteous as this whole law?" (Dt. 4:8). It provides touchstones for geology and benchmarks for medicine.

The Bible is a book for all of life. It is to be consulted by all priest-kings in their professional capacities for such guidance as it will give. It was a Bible-reading mariner, Matthew Maury, who discovered the ocean currents precisely because he had been assured by Psalm 8:8 that there are "paths in the seas."[13]

At this point I wish to enter a caveat. There is a proper "ecclesiocentrism" which recognizes that God has ordained His special officers to expound the Scriptures, and that particular heed is to be paid to those who "labor in the Word and in teaching" (1 Tim. 5:17). Moreover, the Bible is centrally concerned with matters of redemption and worship, for these are the foundation stones of all the rest of culture.[14] We shall see this as we examine

---

12. Cf. James B. Jordan, "The Biblical Chronology Question: An Analysis," in *Creation Social Science and Humanities Quarterly* II:2:9-15; II:3:17-26. The address of the Creation Social Science and Humanities Society is 1429 N. Holyoke, Wichita, Kansas 67208.

13. Cf. Jean Morton, *Science and the Bible* (Chicago: Moody Press), p. 119f. I am indebted to Dr. Henry Morris of the Institute for Creation Research for calling my attention to this.

14. There are, indeed, certain Calvinistic and also certain Anabaptistic writers who, in their enthusiasm for "all of life," downplay the centrality of the

God's arguments with Pharaoh in Chapter 2 of this study. The fact that the Bible is centrally concerned with such things, however, does not negate the fact that it speaks to all areas of life, in varying degrees of specificity. The chronology of Scripture, for instance, is always connected to the Seed-line, but this does not make it any less true, and any less valid as a statement of the age of the world; and as a statement of the age of the world, Biblical chronology is relevant to a host of disciplines.

The Law of God is Unchanging

Since God's law is a transcript of His personal character, it cannot change, any more than God can change. Jesus makes this point in Matthew 5:17-19: "Do not think that I came to abolish the law or the prophets; I did not come to abolish, but to fulfill (or, put into force). For truly I say to you, until heaven and earth pass away, not the smallest letter or stroke shall pass away from the law, until all is accomplished. Whoever then annuls one of the least of these commandments, and so teaches men, shall be called least in the kingdom of heaven; but whoever does and teaches them, he shall be called great in the kingdom of heaven."

Yet we know that there has been some change. We no longer sacrifice bulls and sheep, as the epistle to the Hebrews makes clear. If the law has not changed, then what has? It is the *circumstances* which have changed.[15] Let us consider some examples.

The law of God commands, "Husbands, love your wives"

---

throne-worship of God. Despite my appreciation for the work done by some of these writers, I cannot go along with the down-playing of sacramental worship which is found in some of them. See James B. Jordan, ed., *The Reconstruction of the Church*. Christianity and Civilization, No. 4 (Tyler, TX: Geneva Ministries, forthcoming).

15. Again, if we are using the word *law* to refer to the unchanging moral character of God, as we are here, then of course the law in its essence cannot change. When Scripture sometimes refers to a change in law, as in Hebrews 7:12, the reference is to particular laws or to the system of the law, which system undergoes a death and resurrection in Christ, becoming the New Covenant. Our point here is rather simple and non-technical: The unchanging essence of the law is a reflex of its source in God's own character; the changing manifestations of the law are a reflex of changes in circumstances relative to the creature.

(Eph. 5:25). This law is applicable in all times and in all places. Applicable — that is, *able* to be applied. If, however, a man is not married, then this law in fact does not apply to him. It is applicable, but because of *circumstances* it is not applied.

The law of God commands that we are not to have an open pit in our yard (Ex. 21:33f.), and that we are to have a rail around our roof (Dt. 22:8). If a man lives in an apartment, however, he will never have the opportunity to leave an open pit in his yard. As regards the rail around the roof, the houses in ancient Israel had flat roofs, and people frequently spent time on their roofs. In colder climates, snow threatens to cave in a flat roof, so roofs are sloped. This law would then not apply. It would apply, however, to a raised porch or balcony. Again, circumstances make the difference.

Thus far, the circumstances we have been discussing have been legal (marriage) or geographical (location). There are also, however, historical or temporal circumstances. As regards our topic, the major change in historical circumstances occurred during the first century A.D. There were four interlocked important events during that century which changed the way in which God's unchanging law is applied.[16] They were: 1) the sacrificial death of Christ, 2) the outpouring of the Holy Spirit in power, 3) the removal of the defilement of the world, and 4) the destruction of Jerusalem. These four events altered four aspects of Old Testament law, as regards the *way* it is applied.

First, *the sacrificial death of Christ replaced all the bloody rites of the Old Testament*. Such matters as circumcision, Passover, the Day of Atonement, the sprinkling with water mixed with ashes of a red heifer, the redemption price of the firstborn — all these had to do with blood or with death. They pointed to the coming death of Christ. Christians still keep these laws today, but because of changed circumstances, they keep them in a different manner. The Old Testament believer, when he performed these acts, put

---

16. Other theologians might list more or fewer than these. I have tried to cover all the necessary bases with these four.

his faith in God that God would save him from sin and death through some future act to which these rites pointed. The New Testament believer puts his faith in God in the same way, but he can lay hold *directly* on the death of Christ as his substitute and way of salvation. The same principle is involved in both cases, the same law is obeyed, except that the historical circumstances have changed.

Second, *the outpouring of the Holy Spirit gave to the Church more power than she had known before.* Because the Old Testament Church was relatively weaker than the New Testament Church, God made special provisions to protect the Church during her Old Testament infancy. This varied from period to period, and at some times we see very few such special provisions (as during Abraham's day). What we think of as the definitive expression of the Old Covenant, however, the Mosaic administration through the monarchy, does show such special provisions. During this time, God's protection took the form of tying the Church closely to a particular nation, with geographical boundaries, with a military force, with supernatural acts of protection and special supernatural guarantees. Moreover, since the people were to be holy, but since the Holy Spirit had not been poured out in power, God gave them many peculiar regulations as reminders of obedience. They were, for instance, to dress in a peculiar manner.[17]

In the New Covenant, all these reminders coalesce in the Memorial Supper, the Holy Eucharist.

Third, *the cleansing of the world means that men are no longer defiled by coming in contact with death.* Under the Old Covenant if a man so much as picked up a dead roach with his hand, he was unclean

---

17. "The Lord also spoke to Moses, saying, 'Speak to the sons of Israel, and tell them that they shall make for themselves tassels on the corners of their garments throughout their generations, and that they shall put on the tassels of each corner a cord of blue. And it shall be a tassel for you to look at and remember all the commandments of the Lord, so as to do them and not follow after your own heart and your eyes, after which you played the harlot, in order that you may remember to do all My commandments, and be holy to your God' " (Numbers 15:37-40).

until evening.[18] If he touched a human corpse, and then touched anyone else, that person too would become unclean.[19] Thus, he had to avoid all human contact for a set period. In this way he was cut off from the people.

These laws of cleanness, as we shall see in this book, signified life and death. Man's fall had defiled the world. Thus, clean persons, clean animals, clean land, etc., were the exception, only made clean through blood. In the New Covenant, all has been definitively cleansed (Acts 10, 11).[20] The death of an animal or of a person still *reminds* us of the curse on sin, but it no longer *defiles* us. The only place that remains defiled is the heart of man. The world is no longer defiled, but redeemed. Those men who refuse to participate in redemption, and remain defiled, will be removed from the world and sent to the lake of fire.

Fourth, *the destruction of Jerusalem, and thus of the Old Testament's culturally-tied Church system, changed the way certain laws are kept.* The epistle to the Ephesians speaks about this alteration in the way we adhere to Biblical legal principles in 2:11-22, referring to a category of laws which constituted a wall of division between Jew and Gentile. We may call these "boundary laws," for they were designed, in part, to set a visible boundary between God's people and the people of the world, in order to show that Israel was a priest to the nations. With the coming of the Spirit and the destruction of Jerusalem, these boundary laws were no longer to be observed in the same way. There are still, of course, moral and religious boundaries between God's people and Satan's, but there

---

18. " 'But all other winged insects which are four-footed are detestable to you. By these, moreover, you will be made unclean: whoever touches their carcasses becomes unclean until evening' " (Lev. 11:23, 24).

19. " 'Furthermore, anything that the unclean person touches shall be unclean; and the person who touches it shall be unclean until evening' " (Num. 19:22).

20. This is why consistent Protestants do not "consecrate" church buildings and other material objects. There is no need to do so. Indeed, to do so implies that Pentecost has not really and definitively cleansed the world, and thus obscures the Gospel. Setting aside buildings for a special use is a different matter, since the bipolarity of special/general is not the same as the bipolarity of cleansed/defiled.

need be no cultural boundary, as expressed in clothing and diet.

The relationship between Israel and the nations can be seen in Genesis 25:5, 6, 18. Here we see that Abraham set a difference between Isaac and his other sons. All his sons were covenant people, and we see later on that Moses' father-in-law, Jethro, a true believer (Ex. 18) was a Midianite, a descendent of Abraham. Abraham's other sons were situated "east" of Isaac. Symbolically, this put them at the east gate of Eden, at the east gate of the Tabernacle. Israel was the priestly nation, keeping the throne-sanctuary of God. The other nations were to gather at the east gate, and bring their tithes and gifts to God. Thus, Ishmael and his half-brothers settled in Havilah (25:18), downstream from Eden (Gen. 2:11). In Isaiah 60:4-9, these other sons of Abraham are seen returning to Eden, bringing their tithes and gifts (the sons of Keturah are mentioned in Is. 60:6, and the sons of Ishmael in 60:7). Thus, there was a God-ordained bipolarity between on the one hand the seed-throne people of Israel, who were particularly concerned to maintain right religion and worship as priests, and on the other hand the non-priestly true believers who lived during the Old Covenant period, who were particularly concerned with more cultural tasks.[21]

Another major change expressed in the destruction of Jerusalem was in the pattern or dynamic of the Kingdom. The Old Testament Church was strategically located at the crossroads

---

21. This bipolarity is expressed within Israel itself in the distinction between the Levites and the lay people (who might not enter the inner courts of the Temple). It was further expressed in the distinction between the Aaronic priests and the Levites (who might not enter the Holy Place). It was finally expressed in the distinction between the High Priest and the rest of the Aaronic priests (who might not enter the Holy of Holies). It is also worth noting that since all the Holy Land was apportioned to the sons of Israel (Lev. 25), it was not possible for any non-Israelite to be anything other than a sojourner in it, unless he joined some particular Israelite household. Thus, true believers outside of Israel were kept outside, because they were not called to *function* as priests. Note: From the standpoint of any inner circle, the persons in the outer circles are unclean, and cannot approach the inner circle. Thus, Cornelius (Acts 10, 11), though a convert, was still unclean. Similarly, an ordinary Israelite, though clean in one sense, was still too unclean to enter the sanctuary without defiling it (see p. 255, note 37).

of the world. Caravans from Europe to Asia, from Asia to Africa, and from Europe to Africa—all had to come through the Holy Land. Thus, in the Old Testament there were many laws designed to protect the stranger in the land. God brought the heathen to the Church. Now, after the Great Commission, God sends the Church to the heathen. More power is given for this task (the coming of the Spirit). The Church breaks all national ties, and becomes international (the destruction of Jerusalem). All revelation is inscripturated, making it easily portable and transferable (the completion of the Bible).

These four major changes are really a single package affair. The same laws which guarded against defilement also protected the weak Old Testament Church, and made for cultural boundaries with the nations. Were these so-called "ceremonial" laws (there were seldom any ceremonies connected with them) also moral laws? Yes, they were; just as much as the Ten Commandments, they revealed the perfect personal and social character of God.

We might summarize by saying that the Old Covenant law was given in a context of estrangement between God and His world, showing the possibility of reconciliation. In the New Covenant, however, the law is announced in the context of the reconciliation of the world, though the threat of estrangement (apostasy, hell) remains.

Are we still to keep these laws? Yes and no. No, in the sense that circumstances have changed and so they do not apply to us directly. Yes, in the sense that *we keep them in a form adapted to our new circumstances*. We put our faith in the shed blood of Christ. The Church is protected by church discipline. We confront the world through the power of the Spirit. There is moral enmity (boundary) between us and the world. We worship in the (heavenly) tabernacle-temple of God. We choose life over death.

Traditionally, theologians have spoken of the *equity* of the law. This means that a given law can apply to more cases than the one it particularly addresses. This is because there is always a *general principle* in any particular law. The Old Testament commands that we must not muzzle the ox who treads out the corn (Dt. 25:4).

The New Testament applies this to Church leaders and their salaries (1 Tim. 5:17). This is because of the general principle that the laborer is worthy of his hire. Similarly, we do not put rails on our sloped roofs, but we do put them on our balconies, because of the general principle that we are responsible for any hazardous condition on our property. In the same way, we still keep the general equity of the sacrificial laws, the cleansing laws, the protective laws, and the boundary laws, even though the precise *letter* of these particular laws no longer applies to our circumstances.

Old and New Testaments

How do we read any book? We open up to the first page, and begin at the beginning. Unfortunately, many people do not read the Bible this way. They begin with the New Testament, and downplay the Old Testament. This practice we may call "dispensationalism," with a small "d." Generally speaking, the hallmark of a dispensationalist is that he believes that whatever is not repeated in the New Testament has been dropped from the Old. The traditional Christian position is the opposite, that *whatever has not been principially changed in the New Testament still stands in force from the Old.*

First, the law does not change (Matt. 5:17-19). It is circumstances that change. Therefore, we expect continuity in the law of God, unless God tells us of some change in circumstances.

Second, seven-tenths of the Bible is Old Testament. Why should God have to repeat everything He has already said? The New Testament never claims to be anything other than the completion of the Bible, not some new and separate "canon" or Bible.

Third, the five books of Moses form a platform on which the remainder of the Bible is erected. All the basic concepts of the Bible are in the five books of Moses. The wisdom of Proverbs is there in germinal form. David wrote the Psalms from meditating on the Torah. The History Books show how the people of God obeyed or disobeyed the Torah. The Prophets called the people back to the old truth, to the Torah. The New Testament shows how Christ fulfilled the types and shadows of the Torah. In the light of that, *why should we assume that God starts all over in Matthew, chapter one?*

The Laws of God have Multiple Equity

In saying that the laws of God have multiple equity, we mean that each specific law implies God's law-system as a whole, and as a result, a given law will have applications in more than one area of life. Multiple equity means multiple applications, and even multiple principles. The Westminster Larger Catechism (Question 99, Section 3) puts it this way: "That one and the same thing, in diverse respects, is required or forbidden in several commandments," citing as proof texts Colossians 3:5, Amos 8:5, Proverbs 1:19, and 1 Timothy 6:10, to which we might add James 2:10.[22]

This means that more than one basic principle may underlie any particular command of the law. For this reason, some laws are repeated two or three times in the Torah, but in different contexts, showing that they pertain to different basic principles. For example, the prohibition on witchcraft occurs in Exodus 22:18, in connection with laws of adultery, since witchcraft is apostasy from the Divine Husband of Israel.[23] In Deuteronomy 18:10, the same prohibition occurs in a section on submission to authority, since witchcraft is identified with rebellion (1 Sam. 15:23, as demonstrated by 1 Sam. 28:7). Again, witchcraft is forbidden in Leviticus 19:31 and 20:27, where the context is the separation of life and death—part of the so-called "ceremonial" law. Thus, the sin of witchcraft is related to the 8th Commandment, to the 5th Commandment, and to the 3rd Commandment (to wear God's Name to good effect is illustrated by the laws commanding that life be preferred over death).[24]

This is what is meant, then, by asserting that the laws of God have multiple equity. The anti-witchcraft legislation has equity in the areas of adultery, rebellion, and blasphemy (as well as others). This fact explains why it is that the law codes in the Bible may

22. "For whoever keeps the whole law yet stumbles in one point, he has become guilty of all."
23. The clearest passages of Scripture showing God's marriage to Israel are Ezekiel chapter 16 and Hosea chapter 2. See Appendix F.
24. On the nature of the 3rd Commandment, see Appendix B.

seem to be arranged in a haphazard manner. It may look as if unrelated laws are just thrown together, but in reality this is not the case at all. There is a definite order to the arrangement of the laws. This is addressed in Chapter 4 and Appendix B of this study. The haphazard appearance is due to the fact that the particular laws are related in ways that we moderns would not immediately think of.

The Law of God is General and Particular

The doctrine of the Trinity teaches us that God is Three and One, and that He is no more One than Three, nor is He more Three than One. There is, in God, an equal ultimacy of the One and the Three. God's created universe reflects this perfect interaction of unity and diversity.[25] For instance, a man and a woman, in marriage, become one flesh (Gen. 2:24). We have seen that the law of God is a transcript of His perfect character and interpersonal society. As such, we must say that in the law the particulars are no more important than the generalities (universals), and the general laws are ultimately no more significant than the particular laws. It is important for us to see this, because there are those who object to the notion that the law of God is binding in all its particulars (all the "jots and tittles," Matt. 5:17-19).

Does the Bible present some laws as more general and some as more particular? Yes. In Matthew 5:17-19, Jesus makes plain that there are "little" commands as well as great ones. When He was asked to give the greatest commandment, Jesus did not hesitate to rank the laws in this fashion (Matt. 22:36ff.). Thus, there are indeed generalities and particularities in the law; yet, as Matthew 5:17-19 makes plain, *all* are binding.

Most would consider the Ten Commandments as very general laws, as categories around which the other laws of the Bible may be grouped. There is truth to this, in that the Ten Commandments are put in a special category by God, having been engraved

---

25. The finest treatment of this entire matter is Rousas J. Rushdoony, *The One and the Many* (Phillipsburg, NJ: The Craig Press, 1971); reprinted by Thoburn Press, Tyler, Texas, in 1978.

by His very finger (Ex. 31:18; 34:1, 28). Still, it should be noted
that, as they stand, these Ten Commandments are actually very
specific and particular. The Ninth Commandment, forbidding
false witness, has immediate reference to the law court. The
Second Commandment, forbidding any mediator other than
Jesus Christ, has immediate reference only to one kind of use of
visual depiction in worship. The Fifth Commandment, to honor
parents, means to provide for them financially in their old age, as
we shall see later in this book. Yet, we extend the equity of the
Ninth Commandment to include gossip and lying.[26] We extend
the equity of the Second Commandment to include all of God's
regulations regarding worship. We extend the equity of the Fifth
Commandment to include all respect shown to parents, and to
anyone in authority over us.[27] Thus, even the Ten Commandments have a particular and a universal aspect to them.[28]

Again, we might ask: How are we to distinguish the general
laws from the specific ones? The Jews considered that
Deuteronomy 22:6-7 was the "smallest" of the commandments,[29]

---

26. Except for times of war, when we may lie to the enemy, as in Joshua 2:3-5
as commented on by James 2:25. Note that Rahab was shown to be righteous by
sending the spies out *another* way, that is, a way other than that which she had
shown the soldiers. On this see Jim West, "Rahab's Justifiable Lie," in Gary
North, ed., *The Theology of Christian Resistance*. Christianity and Civilization, No.
2 (Tyler, TX: Geneva Ministries, 1982); and James B. Jordan, "Rebellion,
Tyranny, and Dominion in the Book of Genesis," in North, ed., *Tactics of Christian
Resistance*. Christianity and Civilization, No. 3 (Tyler, TX: Geneva Ministries,
1983).

27. The Westminster Larger Catechism, in its exposition of the Fifth Commandment, devotes the bulk of its space to the relationship between social
superiors and inferiors, not parents and children: Questions 124-30.

28. As Greg Bahnsen points out, Jesus put the case laws of the Old Testament
on a par with the Ten Commandments repeatedly throughout His teaching, so
that "when He quoted from the decalogue He could casually (and without explanation) insert a particular case law *along with*, and on a par with, the ten laws
(see Mark 10:19), where 'Do not defraud' from Deut. 24:16 in LXX — v. 14 in
English versions — is appropriately adduced in dealing with a rich young ruler
and placed on a par with 'Do not kill,' etc.)." *Theonomy*, p. 256. The LXX is the
Septuagint, the ancient Greek translation of the Hebrew Old Testament.

29. " 'If you happen to come upon a bird's nest along the way, in any tree or
on the ground, with young ones or eggs, and the mother sitting on the young or

but even this law is general in that it applies generally to all birds. Leviticus 22:28 shows that the same principle applies to other animals as well.[30] What is specific from one perspective may be general from another.

Modern man is willing to let God give him a few (unenforced) rules for his life, but modern man, and far too many modern churchmen, object to God's particular directives. *Generalities leave a lot of room for man to think as he pleases and to do as he pleases.* Specifics are humbling to the intellect and to pride. It is all right to say that God created the world, but surely one should not try to *date* creation by studying Genesis 5 and 11! It is true that stealing is wrong, but surely we don't need to start quoting any "Old Testament laws" about charging interest on a charity loan to a fellow believer, or about a six-year limit on charity loans. *Generalities leave room for a word from man.* The particularity of the Bible forces man to bow the knee.[31]

How are the laws of God arranged? There seem to be four levels of generality and particularity in the Bible. *First*, there is the Greatest Commandment, "You shall love the LORD your God with all your heart, soul, mind, and strength" (Dt. 6:5, Matt. 22:37). The command is: *Love God.* Since God is God, the command to love *God* means *submission* to God, and thus to His personal will or law. The command to *love* God means *willing and happy* submission to God and to His laws. The covenant has two sides: the structural (submit to the law) and the personal (willing and happy). This Greatest Commandment comprehends (includes) every other commandment.

---

on the eggs, you shall not take the mother with the young; you shall certainly let the mother go, but the young you may take for yourself, in order that it may be well with you, and that you may prolong your days.' "

30. " 'But, whether it is an ox or a sheep, you shall not kill both it and its young in one day.' "

31. I grant, of course, that someone who differs from my position regarding the age of the earth or the six year limit on charity loans may do so because he thinks that the particulars prove something else. Too often, however, modern Christians refuse even to treat such questions seriously, out of a disdain for particulars.

Second, there is the command to love our fellow man in the same way as we love ourselves (Lev. 19:18, Matt. 22:39). This commandment divides the Greatest Commandment into two parts: our duty to God and our duty to men. We should notice that these two Great Commandments are not found in any special place in the Bible, but are placed among the "small" particular laws of Leviticus and Deuteronomy.

Third, there are the Ten Commandments. The Ten Commandments break the Greatest Commandment into ten parts. Each of the Ten Commandments relates to God, and each relates to our fellow men, but some relate more specifically to God and others relate more specifically to man. The Ten Commandments are not to be divided up into two tables.[32] The two tables of the law refer most likely to *two separate copies* of the entire Ten Commandments. Such treaties were common in the ancient Near East. One copy was for the emperor, kept in the house of his god, and one copy was for the vassal, kept in the house of his god. In this case, the Lord is the Emperor, and so one copy went in His house, in the Ark of the covenant in the tabernacle. The vassal was Israel, and a copy went in the house of their God; thus, the second copy also went into the Ark of the covenant.[33] This is why it was called the Ark of the *covenant*.

Fourth, there are the case laws. The case laws of the Old and New Testaments break the Greatest Commandment into many parts. As we have seen, any given case law may be related to more

---

32. "So He declared to you His covenant which He commanded you to perform, that is, the ten words; and He wrote them on two tablets of stone" (Dt. 4:13).

33. This viewpoint is skillfully argued for in Meredith G. Kline, *The Structure of Biblical Authority* (Grand Rapids: William B. Eerdmans Publ. Co., 1975 [revised edition]), pp. 113ff. The two tablets of the ten words also form a testimony of two witnesses (Dt. 19:15; Rev. 11:3; etc.). Stones were used as symbolic witnesses by God, as we see in Joshua 24:26, 27 (and see the curse fulfilled in Judges 9:6ff.). There were also two witnesses against Israel's sin which were outside the Ark: The completed books of Moses were placed next to the Ark in the Holy of Holies (Dt. 31:26), and the creation was called as second witness as it heard the Song of Moses (Dt. 31:28-32:47). On the disposition of the two tablets of the ten words inside the Ark, see Exodus 25:16 and 1 Kings 8:9.

than one of the Ten Commandments, and so it would be an error to try to pigeon-hole the case laws under one Commandment each. In reality the case law as a whole comes under the Ten Commandments as a whole. Some case laws fit rather nicely under one or another of the Commandments, but most case laws seem to combine principles from several of the basic Ten.

It is possible to divide the legal sections of the Pentateuch[34] into sub-sections dealing with one or another of the Ten Commandments, and we shall do this in Chapter Four with respect to Exodus 21-23. (Also see Appendix B.) Even so, we must be careful of over-using category schemes. If we try to put the case laws under only one Commandment each, we likely will overlook some of the richness of the law, and miss some of what God has revealed. Rather, we must take each case law as it stands, and relate it to the other case laws, to the Ten Commandments, and to the two Great Commandments.

Case laws illustrate the basic principles in terms of specific cases. Studying these cases will give us wisdom in knowing how to deal with other situations not expressly provided for in the law. Pornography, for instance, is a phenomenon which follows upon the invention of the printing press. It was not found in the ancient world as any widespread social problem, and so the Bible says nothing about it. We shall have to study the case laws and meditate upon them, to find the wisdom to know what God would have us do about pornography when Christians ascend to power in our society.[35]

Frequently case laws take the most difficult, most extreme situation or case and show how the overall law of God applies in that extreme case. By showing how God would deal with the hardest cases, the Bible shows us how to deal with easier cases.

---

34. "Pentateuch" refers to the first five books of the Old Testament. The word is derived from the Greek word "penta," meaning five, and "teuchos," meaning work or book.

35. Pornography is a form of literature which advocates an anti-Christian religion, and thus comes under the prohibition on spreading idolatrous faiths, a capital offense. See R. J. Rushdoony, *The Politics of Pornography* (New Rochelle, NY: Arlington House, 1974).

Example: If we are not to muzzle the ox which treads out the corn, surely we are not to muzzle the preacher who preaches the Word (1 Tim. 5:17-18). If we are to execute openly rebellious and incorrigible teenagers, surely we are to execute incorrigible adult criminals (Dt. 21:18ff.).

The Uses of the Law

In its essence, the law of God is *revelation*. We have already discussed this at length: The law is a transcript of God's perfect personal and social character. As such, it is also a transcript of the perfect personal and social character of man, the image of God. It shows us what God is like, what we were created to be like, and what we shall be like through the redeeming blood of Christ the Savior.

Traditionally, the law is seen to *work* in three ways. These are called the three uses of the law. They are justification (which reveals the justice and judgment of God), sanctification (which reveals the character of God), and dominion (which reveals the purposes of God).

When man was created he was legally right with God, he was morally upright, and he had certain honors and privileges, the chiefs of which were sonship (Luke 3:38) and dominion (Gen. 1:26). Man was created just, holy, and glorious (Ps. 8:5). The rebellion of man made him legally guilty in the sight of God (unjust), morally sinful in his actions (unholy), and lost him his honors and privileges: He was cast out of Eden (dominion) and, while he is still a son of God by creation (Acts 17:29), he is no longer a covenantal son of God, and so must be *adopted* to be saved. This was his loss of glory. Salvation restores all three aspects of man's life—legal standing, moral standing, and dominical standing—and the law has a role in each aspect.

First, fallen man is *legally guilty* before the judgment bar of God's court. The sentence of condemnation passed upon him is the wrath of God. It is the law of God which man has broken, and which makes him guilty. The first use of the law, then, is to show man his sin. When God uses the law to show man his sin, He always puts pressure on man. This drives men either to hate God more (Rom. 7:9ff.), or to flee to God for justification (Rom. 3:19ff.).

The Lord Jesus Christ earned justification for His people by taking upon Himself the penalty for their sin, as their substitute. When a man places his faith in the sacrificial death of Christ, and in the God Who ordained this death, he experiences justification. The experience of justification has three stages. First, the law drives a man to Christ for *initial* justification. Second, day by day the law drives the Christian to his knees and to the cross, so that his confidence in God's justifying act is renewed and matures. This is a *progressive* aspect of justification, for an older Christian should understand more of God's saving work, and have greater faith and confidence. Third, on the last day, the Day of Judgment, the law once again condemns all men, but God declares his faithful sheep to be justified. This is *final* justification.

Second, fallen man is also *morally sinful* in the eyes of God. The law of God shows man what a holy life is like, so the law is the rule of holiness or sanctification. The Lord Jesus Christ earned sanctification or holiness for His people by living a perfect life for them. This perfect life is applied to the saints by the Holy Spirit. When a man places his faith in God, he is renewed and given new life; he is set apart to live a holy and righteous life in the midst of a sinful and corrupt world. This is the initial experience of sanctification: God counts him as morally holy in spite of his sin. The law is the moral rule of that sanctification from its initial inception, through its progressive development, until that final day when the saints are made perfect in righteousness. This is the second use of the law.

Third, fallen man has also forfeited *dominion and sonship.* Salvation restores men to dominion and to sonship by adoption. The Lord Jesus Christ, King of the Universe, lived a life in one sense devoid of dominion, with no place to lay His head and having no possessions, so that His people might be given the honors and privileges forfeited by sin. This is part of glorification, the bestowal of honors and privileges on the saints. Glorification also has three phases: initial,[36] progressive,[37] and final.[38] The law of God is the rule or guidebook of dominion. The law shows the saints how to exercise dominion, how to rule. Traditionally, this has been called the "civil" use of the law, but all dominion is part of this use or purpose of the law.

The law shows men how to rule the world. It shows fathers how to rule the home. It shows elders how to rule the Church. It shows masters (employers) how to rule servants (employees) properly. It shows the individual how to rule himself. It shows the civil magistrate how to rule the state. These illustrate the third use of the law.

God Gives Laws to the State

While most Christians are happy to get direction from the Bible for themselves, for their families, and for the Church, there are many who have reservations about looking to the Bible for judicial law. Yet, there is much judicial law in the Bible; or to put it more accurately, *all Biblical law has judicial implications*, and many of these implications are spelled out. Some of the objectives raised against deriving civil and criminal law from the Bible are these:

1. "This would mean *uniting Church and state*." No, not at all. Church and state are two separate institutions, but both should be ruled by God, and by His law, just as the family is separate from the Church, yet is ruled by God's law.

2. "This would result in a *Theocracy* (a Christian Republic, where God's law rules)." Correct. The question is: Shall we be ruled by man and his ideas, or by God and His?

3. "This would mean *intolerance for other religions*." This is somewhat true, but we do not tolerate child sacrifice today, even though child sacrifice and human sacrifice have been common

---

36. ". . . and whom He justified, these He also glorified" (Rom. 8:30).

37. " 'His master said to him, "Well done, good and faithful slave; you were faithful with a few things, I will put you in charge of many things. Enter into the joy of your master" ' " (Matt. 25:21).

38. Romans 8:17ff.

practices among the world's religions. We already are somewhat intolerant of other religions. (See No. 5 below.)

4. "But if we do not tolerate them, *they will not tolerate us.*" Well, according to the Bible we are in a war to the death anyway, and it certainly seems that in most places of the world Christians are not being tolerated. Even in America, Christian schools are under constant attack. Besides, who is our protector? Are we to trust God to protect us, or are we to enter into détente with non-Christians?

5. "*How can we evangelize non-Christians if we execute them?*" This is not a problem, since Biblical law does not require the execution of those who hold to other religions. Only if they actively promote their anti-Christian views and thus try to destroy the Christian Republic, does the Bible teach that action should be taken against them (Dt. 13:2, 6, 13).

6. "*Weren't these civil laws for the Jews only?*" No. As we shall see in our study, the "civil laws" were given long before Moses, and were known among the nations, even though the nations had departed from the faith.

7. "*Weren't Church and state tied together in a special way in the Old Testament?*" Yes. Well, doesn't that imply that these civil laws were designed for that peculiar situation? Haven't our *circumstances* changed? Yes, our circumstances have changed, but it is not primarily the state which has undergone the change; it is the Church which has been changed in structure. The Old Testament Church was for many centuries tied to one particular civil order (Israel) for protection, as we have seen. The Church is no longer tied to any particular place or culture. It is the Church that has been changed. God's laws show what a good social order will be like, whether or not the Church is tied to it in any special way. We should study the relationship between Church and state in the Bible, and see what relevant wisdom we can draw for a Christian society.

8. "*But some of these laws are so harsh. . . .*" Perhaps to our modern ears they seem harsh, but we must *be careful not to accuse God of sin.* He gave these laws, and regardless of whether or not we

should keep them today, surely they reflect His goodness. Doesn't this harshness serve to show us that we have too lax a view of sin? Also, have our modern loose laws done us any good? Modern humanistic law is soft on criminals and harsh on the innocent. Biblical law is harsh on criminals, and thus protects the innocent, the widow, the orphan, the poor, and the law abiding.

We have said enough to indicate that our position in this study is that the state is not exempt from the law of God. The reader is invited to consult Dr. Greg L. Bahnsen's *Theonomy in Christian Ethics* for an extended discussion of this matter.[39]

The Binding Nature of the Law

God is the Creator of all men, not only of Christians, and therefore His law is binding on all men, not only on Christians. As we have seen, people are bound to the law according to their circumstances. Not all of the laws apply to every person. Not all are bound to the laws for fathers, for not all are fathers. All men are, however, bound to the laws for individuals. Moreover, since all men are in the state, all men have some degree of responsibility for the laws of God for the state. The civil magistrate is directly responsible to obey God's laws for the state, but every citizen must work to see that God's will, not that of sinful man, is done.

By creation, the purpose of the *Church* was *worship*. After the rebellion of man, worship had to be reestablished on the basis of redemption. All men by nature worship something, but only the redeemed worship the true God, and thus only the redeemed are in the Church. *The sphere of Church power is limited to the realm of the redeemed.*[40] Ultimately, of course, all men will be held accountable for having or not having accepted the offer of salvation, but as a sphere of earthly power, the Church is restricted to its membership.

By creation, the purpose of the *state* was *order*. After the rebellion of man, order had to be established on vengeance.[41] Since all

---

39. See note 7 above, p. 6.

40. The power of the Church governmentally is sacramental; i.e., the power to bestow or withhold communion.

41. This is discussed at greater length in Chapter 2 of this study.

men, saved or not, are sinners, the threat of the sword of vengeance must hang over all men during their stay on earth. Thus, the sphere of state power is not limited to Christians or to non-Christians, but includes all men.[42] The Christian state imposes the law of Divine vengeance on all men, while the Christian Church imposes the law of church government only on its members.

Every state exercises vengeance in accord with some standard or law. The question is whether the state will exercise man's vengeance in terms of God's standards. Try as we may, we shall not find any third alternative.

Christians must confront the fact that God requires them to impose His law for the state upon all men, whether men like it or not. *The universe is not a democracy, but a Kingdom. If Christians do not impose God's laws upon non-Christians, then non-Christians will impose man's laws upon Christians.* Communism aptly illustrates what the latter situation is like, and as the influence of the Gospel wanes in America, there is more and more an attempt to destroy Christianity and Christian laws. Christian schools are under fire increasingly. Sabbath laws are virtually gone. Crime is rampant and unchecked by the penalties required by Biblical law.

Behold the wondrous works of man! What a boon to live in a "religiously neutral" society, where rapists, murderers, abortionists, and thieves are free to do as they please, and the innocent and Godly, the widow and the orphan, are hounded and persecuted! The law of God may seem harsh, but its strictness is meted out against evildoers. *The law of man bares its fangs of iron increasingly against the righteous.*

---

42. The power of the state is the power of the sword.

2

THE LAW AND THE REDEMPTION OF ISRAEL

The book of Exodus is the second of the five books of Moses. Except for a few annotations, such as the final chapter of Deuteronomy,[1] this entire section of Scripture was written by Moses, although he probably used earlier records in compiling Genesis under God's direction.[2]

In terms of the history of revelation, the five books of Moses constitute the basic platform on which all the rest of Scripture is erected. These books give us in detail God's directives for all of life, and are the most comprehensive revelation of the rules of covenant life. At the time of the exodus, God saw fit to put His Word-revelation into written form, thus ensuring its public preservation. As we shall see, the laws *recorded* in the Pentateuch had been, for the most part, *revealed* earlier. Because the traditional knowledge of God, passed down from Noah, was dying out, it was necessary to preserve the Word in written form. Also, at this point in history the seed-throne people (Israel) had reached sufficient number to be organized into a "nation," and thus the written recording of God's law was essential as a constitution of

---

1. Another place where a later Bible writer, under God's inspiration, seems to have inserted something into Moses' basic text is Gen. 14:17 (cf. 2 Sam. 18:18). Such identifying annotations do not imply in the least that the books of Moses were actually rewritten over and over by later "redactors," as certain modern critics believe. Cf. also Gen. 36:31; Ex. 16:35; Num. 32:34ff. The books listed in the Preface to this study can be consulted for more information, particularly Aalders, chapter 13, "Post-Mosaica and A-Mosaica."

2. See James B. Jordan, *Trees and Thorns: An Exposition of Genesis 1-4* (forthcoming).

that socio-religious order.[3]

The History of the Seed People

When God created man, He put him into a model environment called the garden of Eden. The essential characteristic of this garden was the presence of God, and His presence was what brought the model environment to pass. When man rebelled against God, he was driven out of this model environment into the wilderness. God, however, promised to raise up from the seed of humanity a Savior Who would crush the adversary and restore God's people to fellowship with Him. That restoration to fellowship would naturally entail as a consequence some kind of restoration of the Eden-type of environment.

God placed enmity (hatred) between His chosen people and His enemies. Humanity was divided between those whom God would save and those who would be left to go their own way. Right away, this hatred broke out into oppression and murder. Under pressure, Cain revealed his true nature and murdered his brother. God made it plain at the outset that there was to be a war to the death, a point too often forgotten by modern Christians.

The evil in the world deepened and matured until God destroyed humanity in the Flood, beginning again with a second Adam, Noah. After a couple of centuries, the truth of God that Noah had passed to his descendents began to be eclipsed again by the rising tide of evil. God then called Abram and his household

---

3. We must distinguish between the time when God reveals something and the time at which that revelation is recorded in writing. Not only is this the case with the Law, it is also the case with Wisdom literature. The Wisdom literature — Proverbs, the Song of Solomon (Canticles), and Ecclesiastes — was written and recorded during the reign of Solomon for the most part. This makes sense, for Solomon had asked for wisdom and had been granted it. Thus, he became an "incarnation" of wisdom, and a precursor-type of Christ, the incarnate Word-Wisdom of God. It was only fitting, then, that he should be the preeminent recorder of Wisdom literature. This does not mean that Solomon *wrote* all the Proverbs attributed to him; rather, he *collected* them under Divine guidance. They doubtless had been developing and circulating in Israel for a long time. Proverbs 17:23 is found in Exodus 23:8 and Deuteronomy 16:19, for instance.

to become the peculiar custodians of the truth, and told Abram
that the Savior would spring from his line.[4] Throughout the Old
Testament period we see that *God had His covenant people among
many families and nations* (e.g., Melchizedek, Jethro, Jonah's
Ninevites); there is no reason to think that God was parsimonious
with His saving grace during the Old Testament period. God did,
however, have *special dealings with the seed people,* Abraham's
descendents through Jacob.

When God established His covenant community-of-life with
Abraham, this meant that Abraham was restored, in essence, to
the garden of Eden environment. Thus, we are not surprised to
see that God guaranteed him *land.* Even though Abraham did not
formally own the land, he did exercise dominion over it, as
Genesis chapter 14 shows, and he did acquire a plot of it as a token
of his inheritance (Genesis 23). Abraham sent his other sons to the
East, to Havilah, thus establishing the bipolarity of seed-
sanctuary priests (Isaac) and the nations (Ishmael and the sons of
Keturah).

The history of the seed-throne people is a sermon to humanity.
Israel was to be a light to the nations, teaching them God's ways.
Thus, the history that God charted for Israel illustrates His principles (laws) and repeatedly portrays in various dimensions the
principles involved in man's fall and redemption.

Whenever God's covenant with men is reestablished, blessings
follow. This brings on the envy of the wicked, and renewed enmity.
We see this principle repeatedly exemplified in the history recorded
in Genesis. Thus we are told that God blessed Isaac, that Isaac
became rich, then richer, and finally very wealthy, and that as a
result the Philistines envied him and began to persecute him,
finally driving him out (Gen. 26:12-16). Similarly God blessed
Jacob despite Laban's attempt to cheat him, so that Jacob became
very wealthy, and Laban began to hate him, finally forcing Jacob

---

4. Between the Flood and the call of Abram were 427 years. See Martin
Anstay, *Chronology of the Old Testament* (Grand Rapids, Kregel, [1913] 1973).

to flee (Gen. 31).[5] The blessings to the Israelites in Egypt also brought down on them the envious wrath of the wicked, as we shall see.

It is significant that Laban's treatment of Jacob parallels in certain respects Pharaoh's treatment of the Hebrews. Although Laban *initially welcomed* Jacob, there came to be a *change* in Laban's attitude which resulted in Jacob's being reduced to an *inferior position,* bordering on slavery. This change may be recorded in Genesis 29:15, "Then Laban said to Jacob, 'Are you my brother, and should you therefore serve me for nothing? Tell me, what shall your wages be?' " A family member would not have worked for wages.[6] After earning his wives, Jacob labored six additional years (31:41), the period of slave service (Ex. 21:1). Jacob was oppressed (Gen. 31:39f.). God *saw* his affliction (31:12, 42), just as He later *saw* affliction of the Hebrews in Egypt (Ex. 3:7). In violation of custom (Dt. 15:12-15), Laban would have sent Jacob away empty-handed (Gen. 31:42). Even though Jacob had earned Leah and Rachel, Laban acted as though they were slave-wives given

---

5. We need to distinguish among envy, covetousness, and jealousy. *Covetousness* takes the attitude: "He has it. I want it. I will take steps to get it away from him." *Envy,* on the other hand, is not grasping, but destructive. It says: "He has it. I want it. I know I can never have it. Therefore, I will take steps to see to it that nobody enjoys it." On envy, see Helmut Schoeck, *Envy: A Theory of Social Behavior* (New York: Harcourt, Brace, [1966] 1970). While Schoeck's distinction between covetousness and envy is not made in Scripture, it definitely brings out some Biblical ideas.

Jealousy is a virtue, an attribute of God (Ex. 34:14). It is not other-directed, but self-directed. Jealousy says: "What's mine is mine. Don't fool with it without my permission." A man is properly jealous of his wife, and angry if others solicit her attentions. God is properly jealous of His rights and worship, and His jealousy protects His wife (the church) from the attacks of Satan. Human jealousy is never to be absolute, because "what's mine is mine" is only true under God. When men play God, the virtue of jealousy is corrupted by selfishness and egoism.

In modern English, 'jealousy' is sometimes used as a synonym for 'covetousness' and/or 'envy.' This unfortunate confusion of meanings means that the reader must always try to ascertain how a given writer is using these terms. This footnote identifies how I am using these terms.

6. Defense of this interpretation is well set out by David Daube and Reuven Yaron, "Jacob's Reception by Laban," *Journal of Semitic Studies* 1 (1956): 60-61.

The Law of the Covenant

by him to Jacob and so should not go free with Jacob (Gen. 31:43, Ex. 21:4). Pharaoh makes the same claim later on (Ex. 10:10f.). Jacob was not a slave, but Laban tried to reduce him to slavery. As Daube sums it up, "No doubt the general scheme, God helping his protégé out of danger and distress, is independently common to both. So is a good deal else. The falling into slavery or a sort of slavery abroad; the falling into it owing to an arbitrary change of attitude on the part of the host; the ambiguity in the conduct of the master who wishes at once to be rid of the dangerous subject and to keep him for the benefit he derives, and who tries to recapture him when he finally runs away with considerable wealth; the interposition of God by force or the threat of force; the defeat of the master's gods (in Jacob's story, the theft of the idols indeed provides an additional ground for pursuit). . . . Above all, the application in both stories of laws and customs governing the release of slaves or captives is fully explicable from the situation. Thus Jacob's negotiations about his wives and children, corresponding to those in Egypt, can cause no surprise."[7] Daube also remarks that "in both the exodus story and the Jacob one God advises the subject as to a method of extracting liberal provision from the master."[8]

Oppression, slavery, deliverance—these matters come to a climax in the exodus; but at the end of the book of Genesis, it does not appear that such a deliverance is needed.[9] The settling of Israel in Goshen brings the book of Genesis to a rounded conclusion. The book opened in Eden, and closes with the people of God returned to an Eden of sort—Goshen—a *stage* in the restoration of Eden which is the design of God.[10]

---

7. David Daube, *The Exodus Pattern in the Bible* (London: Faber and Faber, 1963), pp. 69f.

8. *Ibid.*, p. 70.

9. The pattern of oppression in a strange land, defeat of the oppressor by God, false charges against the Godly, and the emergence of the Godly with wealth, is repeated several times in Genesis: Abram and Pharaoh (Gen. 12), Abraham and Abimelech (Gen. 20), Isaac and Abimelech (Gen. 26), as well as Jacob and Laban (Gen. 29-31). It is also the theme of 1 Samuel 4-6.

10. The conversion of Pharaoh (Gen. 41) and his honoring of Jacob (Gen.

Goshen was a separate and distinct section of Egypt, a land which itself is compared to the garden of Eden (Gen.13:10),[11] and Goshen is repeatedly noted as the *best* part of Egypt (45:18; 47:6, 11). Goshen was further separated from the culture of Egypt due to the fact that the occupation of the Israelites was repugnant to the Egyptians (46:34). Of premier importance is the statement in 47:27, "Israel was fruitful and multiplied," precisely the same words as were used by God in the original Edenic mandate of Gen. 1:28. Additionally, we are told that Israel acquired property or possessions in Goshen — that is to say, they were about the business of fulfilling the Eden mandate for dominion.

Sometime after the death of Joseph and the birth of Moses, the attitude of the Pharaohs changed from friendliness to enmity toward Israel, and Israel began to be persecuted.[12] The persecution of Israel is understandable. The Hebrews were much blessed of God in numbers and wealth (Ex. 1:7), while the Egyptians, being slaves of sin, had been reduced to outward serfdom by the Hebrew vizier Joseph (Gen. 47:13-26). Egypt retaliated. Israel's capacity for dominion and for multiplication was reduced (Ex. 1:10-22). They were thus impelled to recall that *Goshen was but a temporary Eden,* their promised destination being Canaan.

Israel had been taken out of Canaan in order to separate her from pagan influences (Gen. 34 and 38). In Goshen, they were

---

47:7ff.) provide a third stage in the fulfillment of the Abrahamic promise of Genesis 12:2, 3. Joseph saves his people, and he also saves the world; the leaders of the world are converted; etc. Previous fulfillments of the blessing to the Gentiles are in Genesis 21:22ff. and 26:26ff.

11. "And Lot lifted up his eyes and saw all the circle of the Jordan, that it was well watered everywhere — this was before the LORD destroyed Sodom and Gomorrah — like the garden of the LORD, like the land of Egypt as you go to Zoar."

12. Theologically, the apostasy of Pharaoh is a recapitulation of the Fall. Recapitulations of the Fall are seen in Genesis 6:2 (the Fall of the Sethites), Genesis 9:20ff. (the Fall of Ham), Genesis 25:28 (the Fall of Isaac), and the several falls of the sons of Jacob in Genesis 34; 35:22; 37:26. See Chapter 3 of this study on the Fall of Israel after the Mt. Sinai re-creation. The second generation's Fall is seen in the sequence of Numbers 20:28 (the death of the High Priest cleanses the land), 21:1-3 (first victories against the Canaanites), 21:4ff. (the Fall; note the serpents).

separated from paganism by three factors: geography, occupation, and enmity. Persecuted by Egypt, they had reason to hate Egypt's gods. Even so, we are told that they worshipped them (Josh. 24:14). The threat of their mixing with the heathen was real, and the time for deliverance had come.

Redemption and Vengeance

The Hebrew term translated "to redeem" actually means "to act as kinsman, to redeem, to avenge." The participle form of this verb, which is brought over into English as *goel* ("GO-el"), becomes the noun, and thus means "kinsman redeemer-avenger." The duties of the goel were four. First, he was to redeem (buy back) any inalienable *property* sold by his kin (Lev. 25:25). This law applied to the property assigned to the family at the original division of the land of Canaan among the Israelites. Second, the goel was to redeem the *person* of his kin if he sold himself into slavery to a foreigner (Lev. 25:47ff.). Third, the goel was to act as a *proxy* for his deceased kin in receiving any restitution owed him (Num. 5:8). Fourth, the goel was to *avenge* the blood of his kin if he was murdered.

Redeemer and avenger are one and the same person. It follows that if the LORD is Israel's Redeemer, He is also their Avenger. In one important particular, the Divine Goel differs from His human copy (or analogue). The human goel redeems the person of his kin by paying a sum and buying him out of slavery. God, however, pays no one, since He is sovereign. God redeems by means of vengeance poured out upon the slave-holder. When God acts to redeem His people, we always see alongside of this an act of Divine vengeance directed against their oppressors. In redeeming Noah, God destroyed the wicked. In redeeming Israel, God destroyed Egypt. In redeeming the world through Jesus Christ, God poured out vengeance on Jerusalem, which had become His enemy and the enemy of His people. As Christ moved toward the cross, this act of vengeance was on His mind even as was the act of redemption He was to effect. He spoke of the destruction of Jerusalem just a couple of days before His death (Matt. 24, Mark

13, Luke 21). He spoke of it as He carried the cross (Luke 23:27-31). He spoke of it as He hanged on the cross (Ps. 69:20-28). The destruction of Jerusalem was the ascended Christ's initial work of wrath-vengeance. The progressive development of the Church in history sees progressive manifestations of God's wrath against His enemies, until the final day of judgment, the final manifestation of blessing and vengeance.

The definitive act of the Divine Goel in the Old Testament was the redemption of Israel by means of vengeance poured out on Egypt. Exodus 6:6 states, "I will also redeem you with an outstretched arm and with great judgments." Note that redemption is accompanied by great judgments. Psalm 106:10-11 points out that the mode of redemption was not the payment of a price but the destruction of the enslaving power.[13] God was Israel's kin, claiming to be their Father (Ex. 4:22). If Pharaoh would not let God's son go free, then God would kill Pharaoh's son.

Bloodshed is fundamental. God's vengeance is by bloodshed. So is redemption, except that in the case of redemption, it is Christ's blood that is shed as a Substitute. The Bible reveals that blood is in some sense the carrier of life (Gen. 9:4). Since one of the most common ways of slaying is by bloodshed, shed blood comes to be a synonym for death by murder. To say that blood must be avenged is to say that murder must be avenged. Blood poured out through murder cries out for vengeance (Gen. 4:10; Job 16:18; Is. 26:21; Ezk. 24:8). Since all men are wicked by birth, all men deserve to have their blood spilled under the avenging wrath of God. God graciously has, however, provided a Substitute, Jesus Christ, for His own people.

During the Old Testament, the shed blood of circumcision and of animal sacrifices represented this Substitute. In Exodus, the Angel of Death spared those who had marked their doors with blood, but struck down the firstborn of every other family (Ex.

---

13. "So He saved them from the hand of the one who hated them,
    And redeemed them from the hand of the enemy.
    And the waters covered their adversaries:
    Not one of them was left."

12:13). Similarly, when Moses was journeying toward Egypt, God
tried to kill his son because Moses had not yet circumcised him
(Ex. 4:22-26). God had just told Moses that all the firstborn sons
of the world deserved to die, but Moses still had not placed his son
"under the blood." Moses' wife circumcised the young man and
smeared the blood on his thigh, displaying it before God. Now the
lad was shielded by the blood of the Substitute, and God let the
lad alone.[14]

Vengeance is covenantal in nature. The rebellion of man was
the breaking of covenant life. Man came under the curse of the
covenant. The curse of the covenant is, specifically, to be ripped
into two halves and devoured by birds and other beasts (Gen.
15:10f., Jer. 34:19f.). All men are under the vengeance-curse of the
covenant, but Christ takes the place of His people. In this sense,
redemption, which is the foundation of our reentry into the covenant, itself is a covenantal act. In Exodus 11:7, we read that
"against any of the sons of Israel a dog shall not sharpen his
tongue." This Hebrew expression "sharpen his tongue" means in
English "lick his chops."[15] God's people will not be devoured by
the beast, but God's enemies will be (1 Kings 21:19-24; Matt.

---

14. This passage is discussed in detail in Appendix F.

15. This is what the Hebrew text literally says. The English translations are
most unhelpful. The New International Version, which is a sophisticated
paraphrase rather than a translation, says that no dog shall *bark*. The New
Berkeley Version says the same, as does the New American Standard Version.
The Hebrew term for bark (*navah*), seen in Is. 56:10, does not appear here. The
King James Version has "move his tongue," which is also a mistranslation. The
verb is *harats,* which the Brown, Driver, Briggs edition of Gesenius's *Hebrew Lexicon* translates as "cut, sharpen, decide." The NASV margin gives "sharpen his
tongue" as the literal translation of Ex. 11:7. The reference might be to the sound
of sharpening, analogous to growling, but such is not a clear analogy; also, the
Hebrew for "growl" is *hamah.* Far more likely is an analogy between the sharpening of a knife and a dog's licking his chops in preparation for a meal. The tongue,
then, is a sword or knife (cf. Rev. 1:16; 19:15, 21). The only other time this expression is used is in Joshua 10:21. Translators have universally taken it to refer to
men, so that the NASV, for instance, has "no one uttered a word [lit. sharpened
his tongue] against any of the sons of Israel." There is, however, no reference to
men here, and by analogy to the earlier occurrence of the phrase, we should understand it of dogs. That is to say, not one Israelite was killed in the battle.

24:28; Rev. 19:17-18). While Israel is being kept alive (Ex. 11:7) and celebrating Passover (Ex. 12), the Egyptians are perishing and being devoured at a feast for dogs (Ex. 11:4-7). This is parallel to the two feasts in Revelation 19:7-18 — the Marriage Supper of the Lamb and the Vultures' Feast.

In view of the importance and centrality of blood-vengeance to the plan of God, men must not be surprised when God's law requires capital punishment.

God and Pharaoh

The extended interchanges between Moses and Pharaoh are important to us for two reasons. First, they show the legal foundation for the exodus, and second, they show us one reason why the laws concerning slavery are placed first in the section we are investigating.

Daube points out that "the authors of the exodus story represented Pharaoh as flouting established social regulations, and God as making him comply with them, *malgré lui*, or suffer the sanctions of his breaches. They construed the exodus as an enforcement of legal claims. As one example of many we may quote God's demand to Pharaoh: 'Israel is my son. . . . Let my son go.' " Daube continues, "What we are at the moment concerned with is the confidence and stability which resulted from this anchoring in firm legal relations. As God had vindicated those relations in the exodus, one could be certain that he would vindicate them again, and again, unto the last. The kind of salvation portrayed in the exodus was not, by its nature, an isolated occurrence, giving rise to nebulous hopes for similar good luck in the future: It had its root in, and set the seal on, a permanent institution — hence it was something on which absolute reliance might be placed."[16] God's vindication of Israel during the exodus simultaneously vindicated the legal structure which was to govern social life in the land of Israel. It was reliable and stable because God is reliable and stable.

---

16. Daube, pp. 13f. I am greatly indebted to this book for the insights developed in this section.

God had prepared Moses to be His intermediary with
Pharaoh through eighty years of education and experience, first in
the court of Pharaoh, and then as son-in-law of Jethro, priest of
Midian (Ex. 2:21). As a Midianite, Jethro was a descendent of
Abraham (Gen. 25:2). Although not all the tribes of Midian retained the true faith (Gen. 25:4; Num. 22:4; 25:6), Jethro clearly
was a worshipper of the God of Abraham (Ex. 18:12). Jethro was a
priest somewhat like that of Melchizedek, that is to say, he was a
priest-king, firstborn of the ruling house (Heb. 7:1; Num. 3:12;
Heb. 1:6). Jethro was able to teach Moses about worship, and also
about how to rule (Ex. 18:13-26). Moses doubtless had many occasions to observe Jethro sitting in judgment, and to learn from it.[17]

The issues between God and Pharaoh were these: 1) Who is
God? 2) Are the Israelites properly Pharaoh's slaves? The LORD
went to war with the gods of Egypt to settle the first question. The
gods of Egypt were not able to protect Egypt from the nine
plagues, but it was in the death of Egypt's firstborn that the
LORD's victory was particularly won (Ex. 12:12; Num. 33:4). The
firstborn were the heirs of birthright, blessing, rule, and
priesthood — their death was the death of Egypt.

As regards the second issue between God and Pharaoh —
Were the Israelites properly Pharaoh's slaves? — we need to note
that *culture is an extension of religion,* and Egyptian culture was no
exception to this rule. Its statist organization shows it to have

---

17. It is unclear how the church and state functions were carried out before
Mt. Sinai among God's people. It seems that the patriarch of the clan (e.g.,
Abraham, or Jethro) served both as priest and as supreme judge. By the time of
the Exodus, there were thirteen tribal republics in Israel, each with elders and
princes, as we see from the book of Numbers. This matter receives further ex-
ploration in Chapter 3 of this study.

Also, it should be noted here that the priesthood of Jethro was not like that of
Melchizedek, in that it was inherited. The priestly *functions* of such men as Jethro
and Abraham were typical of the sacrifice of Jesus Christ, but their *persons* as
priests were not typical. In contrast to this, both Melchizedek and the Levitical
priesthood were types of the person of Christ. Perhaps another way of getting at
the distinction would be to say that Jethro was not a type of Christ, though the
sacrifices he offered were typical; while both Melchizedek and his sacrifices
typified Christ.

been an extension of blasphemous Babel, and its oppression of God's people showed it to have been Cainitic. At the top of the social pyramid, heir of Cain and Nimrod, was the Pharaoh, the incarnation of the sun god.[18] Although Israel was in cultural bondage to Egypt, this was *because* she was in *religious* bondage to Egypt (Josh. 24:14). In spite of the fact that God had separated Israel from Egypt geographically (Goshen) and occupationally (shepherding), they went after the gods of Egypt, and so God gave them into the hands of these gods. This same principle operated during the period of the Judges. God's actions and judgments in history are never arbitrary.

Rather than let Israel settle down in Egypt, God made it miserable for them, showing them what slavery to the Babelic state entails. His grace reached them and they repented, crying out to Him for deliverance. Because culture is an effect of religion, when God set about to free Israel, it would have done no good to free them from cultural bondage without breaking their religious bondage foundationally. Thus, it was not necessary at the outset for God to say to Pharaoh, "Let My people go free." All that was needed was a demand to "let us go on a three day journey into the wilderness, that we may sacrifice to the LORD our God" (Ex. 3:18). In our modern day of pretended religious neutrality and pluralism, this might appear to be deception: God intends to free Israel but He only asks that they be allowed to go on a religious retreat. That was not, however, the way it was understood then. Pharaoh knew that a man is a slave of whatever God or gods he worships, and that culture flows from religion. Thus, Pharaoh knew that this request carried with it a demand for political freedom. Pharaoh would have to recognize the distinctive purpose of the Old Covenant seed-throne people, and in so doing, would have had to permit them to return to the throne land of Canaan.

Pharaoh could not have acceded to this request without free-

---

18. Rushdoony, *The One and the Many,* pp. 40ff. This is also discussed at length, from a Christian viewpoint, in Gary North, *The Dominion Covenant: Exodus* (Tyler, TX: Institute for Christian Economics, 1984). The true pyramid, or ladder to heaven, is seen in Genesis 28:12, 17, and John 1:51.

ing Israel. If Pharaoh had allowed their three-day trip, he would have been recognizing the Lord as Israel's God and Master. He would have had to free them. If Pharaoh had himself converted to the Lord, he would have had to recognize the special status of Israel as a nation of priests of the Lord.

The fact that God demanded the release of Israel indicates that Israel was illegitimately held in bondage. According to the law, slaves from anti-God cultures, being slaves by nature, may be held indefinitely, but Christian slaves may only be held six years (Ex. 21:2). Pharaoh had broken this law. Moses' demand for Israelite freedom was grounded in this law, which was familiar to Pharaoh. Since Pharaoh did not recognize the Lord, he did not recognize that the Hebrews were true believers. In his eyes the Hebrews were the heathen, and so could be enslaved indefinitely.

Finally Pharaoh relented and said that the men might leave, but not their families (Ex. 10:7-11).[19] Pharaoh was invoking the principle recorded in Exodus 21:4, "If his master gives him a wife, and she bears him sons or daughters, the wife and her children shall belong to her master, and he shall go out alone." From Pharaoh's viewpoint, it was he who had provided the wives and children of the Hebrew men, so he had a legal claim to them. Again, however, Pharaoh was wrong, for Jacob had brought his women, children, livestock, and servants with him when he settled in Egypt, and so the Hebrews were under the law of Exodus 21:3, "If he comes alone, he shall go out alone; if he is the lord of a wife, then his wife shall go out with him." There were, doubtless, some

---

19. "And Pharaoh's servants said to him, 'How long will this man be a snare to us? Let the men go, that they may serve the LORD their God. Do you not realize that Egypt is destroyed?'

"So Moses and Aaron were brought back to Pharaoh, and he said to them, 'Go serve the LORD your God. Who are the ones that are going?'

"And Moses said, 'We shall go with our young and our old; with our sons and our daughters, with our flocks and our herds we will go, for we must hold a feast to the LORD.'

"Then he said to them, 'Thus may the LORD be with you, if ever I let you and your little ones go! Take heed, for evil is before your face. Not so! Go now, the men among you, and serve the LORD, for you desire it.' So they were driven from Pharaoh's presence."

non-Hebrew wives who had been "provided by Pharaoh," and Pharaoh might have had a legitimate claim to these. The law states, however, that a female slave goes free if the master reduces her lifestyle (Ex. 21:10-11),[20] and Pharaoh had certainly done that. Thus, Pharaoh had a legal claim neither on the Hebrews nor on their "mixed multitude" wives. On the contrary, Pharaoh was guilty of man-stealing, a capital offense (Ex. 21:16).[21]

God's law, familiar to the Pharaohs because of Joseph's influence and because it underlay the common law of the Ancient Near East, also orders that when a slave is set free, he is to be given going-away gifts (Dt. 15:12-16) to help him celebrate and to help him set up in business. God told the Hebrews to request (not "borrow") such presents from their neighbors (Ex. 3:22). Moses demanded such presents from Pharaoh (10:25). Those who give such presents are blessed by God (Dt. 15:18), and the Egyptians knew this. Thus, as the plagues grew more severe, they lavished gifts on the Hebrews (Ex. 11:2-3; 12:35-36).[22] When Pharaoh gave his presents, he specifically asked for this blessing (12:32).[23] Obviously, Pharaoh understood something about God's laws governing slavery.

If a man takes a slave wife in addition to his free, insured wife, there is always the danger that the slave wife and her son will rise up to inherit the family estate. Thus, to eliminate this threat, the free wife in great fear would be motivated to drive out the slave

---

20. " 'If he takes to himself another woman, he may not reduce her food, her clothing, or her conjugal rights. And if he will not do these three for her, then she shall go out for nothing, without payment of money.' "

21. " 'And he who steals a man, whether he sells him or he is found in his possession, shall surely be put to death.' " That Pharaoh died at the Red Sea is cogently argued by Donovan A. Courville, *The Exodus Problem and its Ramifications* (Loma Linda, CA: Challenge Books, 1971) I:36ff.

22. Another reason for the payment of this money is that it was the wedding money owed by a seducer to a girl if her father is unwilling for her to marry him. See the discussion in Chapter 8.

23. He did not receive any blessing, however. It was not legitimate for Pharaoh to ask a blessing, because he was not lawfully freeing slaves which he had lawfully acquired. He could not free them lawfully because he had never lawfully possessed them; thus, he was not entitled to the blessing.

wife, as Sarah did Hagar (Gen. 21:10). As the Israelites became ever more powerful, it began to look as if they would conquer and inherit all Egypt. After all, Goshen was exempt from the catastrophic plagues (numbers four through nine) visited on the rest of Egypt. God told the Hebrews that Pharaoh would drive them out "as a slave wife" (Ex. 11:1).[24] Here we see God's ironic humor, as He says to Pharaoh: "You have wrongly held My kin as *slaves.* Thus, you will set them free in great fear, as you would drive out a *slave* wife."

Specifically, Sarah feared that the firstborn son of Hagar would rise up and get Isaac's inheritance. Similarly, when their firstborn were slain, the Egyptians realized that the Israelites would surely acquire their inheritance, unless they were driven out.

Also, as a false god, Pharaoh was not a true and loving husband to Israel. Thus, Israel was free to divorce Pharaoh, as was the slave wife's privilege (Ex. 21:10f.). The Lord, their true Husband and Master, would never mistreat them. Pharaoh had taken their property, the land of Goshen, and had definitely reduced their lifestyle, in violation of the law for slave wives.

The exodus was not a political revolution but a religious deliverance, entailing cultural change, but rigorously grounded in the law of God and in the common law of the Near East, familiar to all parties.

The reader may be skeptical of the discussion above. What evidence is there that Pharaoh was operating under laws which were given to God's people? Our answer is that Pharaoh's arguments with Moses make no sense unless we presuppose that he knew these laws. Remember, the exodus took place 857 years after the Flood.[25] Shem, the Godly son of Noah, lived 502 years after the Flood.[26] Thus there was doubtless much Godly influence

---

24. "Now the LORD said to Moses, 'One more plague I will bring on Pharaoh and on Egypt; after that he will let you go from here. When he lets you go, he will surely drive you out from here *completely [as a slave wife].*' " This translation is defended in several recent studies. Cf. Daube, *Exodus Pattern,* p. 58.

25. Cf. Anstay, *Chronology.*

26. *Ibid.*

all over the ancient world until well into the history of the seed people, Israel. The mixing of God's law with local customary law is called "common law," and considering that at the outset, right after the Flood, God's law was the only law, it is reasonable to assume that at this point in history there was still a strong common law. The law codes of the ancient world are at many places quite similar to the laws recorded in the Pentateuch — again evidence of a common source (Noah, and behind him, God). The pagans, of course, increasingly perverted and lost God's law. In the case of Egypt, however, we must also reckon with their earlier conversion and the influence of Joseph, who ruled Egypt in all but name for 80 years.[27] Thus, there is every reason to believe that Pharaoh's concept of right and wrong, and therefore his legal beliefs, were still under the influence of God's law. This possibility is confirmed by the passage we have been looking at.[28]

---

27. *Ibid.*

28. This is not even to mention the teaching of Romans 2:14-15, "For when Gentiles who do not have law do perform by nature the things of the law, these, not having law, are a law to themselves, in that they show the work of the law written in their hearts, their conscience bearing witness, and their thoughts alternately accusing or else defending themselves."

3

THE BOOK OF THE COVENANT: ITS CONTEXT

In Exodus 24:7, we read that Moses "took the Book of the Covenant and read *it* in the hearing of the people." The context tells us that Moses "wrote down all the words of the LORD," so that the Book of the Covenant clearly includes the case law section from Exodus 21:1 through 23:19, the Ordinances. It is not clear whether, or how much more, of the book of Exodus is included. Some scholars have assumed that all of Exodus 19-24 is included in the Book of the Covenant, while others think it included only the Ordinances of 21:1-23:19. In the light of 24:3,[1] it seems that what Moses wrote down and read to the people included both the Ten Words (21:1; 34:1; Dt. 4:13; 10:4) and the Ordinances (case laws). God Himself was to later write the Ten Commandments (Ex. 24:12), but at this point, it was Moses who wrote them down (24:4). Thus, it seems most likely that the section written by Moses and read by him to the people consisted of Exodus 20-23, and so we take it that this is the Book of the Covenant.

It is now our purpose to explain why the book of the Covenant, this set of laws, occurs just where and when it does in the history of the covenant.

Redemption and Covenant

We have seen that God's way of redeeming His people is by means of vengeance, vengeance exacted against them in the Per-

---

1. "And Moses came and told the people all the words (Words) of the LORD, and all the ordinances; and all the people answered with one voice and said, 'All the words which the LORD has spoken we will do.' "

son of their Substitute, and vengeance exacted against their (and His) enemies. Once God has redeemed His people by taking the curse of the covenant upon Himself, He reestablishes the covenant relationship with them. The penalty for the breaking of the covenant has been paid, and the problem of the broken covenant has been fixed, and so the covenant is once more back in operation.

God made His covenant with Adam. When Adam sinned, the curse of the covenant (death) fell upon him, and upon all those in union with him (the whole human race). The covenant is reestablished through death and resurrection, so that the covenant in its new form (the New Covenant) is inextricably tied to the resurrection. Christ passes through death unto resurrection life, and as He does so He takes His people with Him. Christ was born "under the law" (Gal. 4:4), took the Old Adamic Covenant law and curse to Himself, and died under it. Christ embodied the law, so that Colossians 2:14 can say that He "cancelled out the certificate of debt consisting of decrees against us, which was hostile to us; and He has taken it out of the way, having nailed it to the cross." It was not the law which was nailed to the cross, but our Lord Jesus Christ.

When Jesus arose, the covenant rose with Him, for the covenant is in Him. The covenant is now the New (Resurrection) Covenant, and brings life instead of death.

Before the death and resurrection of Jesus Christ, however, the New Covenant had not been inaugurated, for it could not be. Instead, a provisional system was set up under the Old Adamic Covenant. In this system, the New Resurrection covenant would undergo a token death and resurrection in the form of animal sacrifices. In this way, the covenant would be in effect provisionally until the coming of Jesus Christ.

Think of an unconscious man, just rescued from nearly drowning. Someone is breathing into his mouth to keep him alive, but until his autonomic nervous system takes over, he does not have life in himself, so to speak. Throughout the Old Testament period, God continually maintained the covenant provisionally on the basis of the animal sacrifices, revivals, covenant renewals, and the like. Once Jesus came, however, the covenant was definitively established, once and for all, and God's people were not simply revitalized for a short time, but definitively resurrected from Spiritual death.

As yet, the New Covenant has definitively but not fully arrived, since we are not yet living in resurrection bodies, and this world has not been transfigured into the New Earth. Thus, we are living in the old Adamic world, but in the power of the New Resurrection Covenant. We still have the original Adamic tasks and responsibilities. We still need to set aside one day in seven for worship and rest, even though "in Christ" we are in a continual sabbath.[2]

All this helps us understand the covenant God made at Sinai. It was a provisional administration of the covenant, based on animal sacrifices, which was never intended to last for all time. Because the exodus is *the* preeminent redemptive event in the Old Testament, it is proper that the covenant be fully set forth and described right after this redemption. This is why so much of the covenant legislation in Exodus through Deuteronomy refers back to the exodus as its rationale and foundation. The covenant is only reestablished and republished on the basis of redemption, so the facts of redemption are adduced as arguments for keeping the covenant. To apply these laws to today's world, we should think of them as based not on the exodus, but based on the finished work of Jesus Christ.

This of course raises again the question we have taken up before, of whether we ought to regard these laws as our own. The

---

2. I have discussed this at greater length in a series of essays in "The Geneva Papers," starting with No. 1, published by Geneva Ministries, P.O. Box 8376, Tyler, TX 75711; available upon request for a contribution. The Bible presents us with a bipolarity of the "special" or particular, and the "general." This is a reflex of the one and three in God. There are general officers in the Church ("lay people"), and special office bearers. Concerning the sabbath, there is a general rest in Christ, and there is a special form of rest which is made manifest one day in seven. Rest is tied to the activity of faith, and there is a general faith-trust we are to have in Christ, and there is also a special act of faith which is connected to fellowshipping with His special presence at the Lord's Supper in special worship.

thing to keep in mind is that the Old Covenant laws describe and prescribe the tasks of man in the first creation, in the world of sin. We still live in the first creation, in the world of sin, and with the same tasks. For this reason, these laws, insofar as they bear on the Adamic task, are addressed to us. They will continue to be necessary for us until this creation is transfigured into the New Earth, and we acquire our resurrection bodies.

Israel got its power for living from the provisional grace of God, while we get our power from the definitive arrival of the Spirit on Pentecost. Israel got its rationale for faithfulness from the events of the exodus, while our foundation is in the work of Jesus Christ. Israel was to obey out of gratitude for their deliverance by God from Egypt, while we obey out of gratitude for our deliverance in Christ Jesus from the slave market of sin. The Adamic task, however, is common to both Israel and us.

To summarize, we can see that these laws continue to have relevance in the New Covenant era from at least two factors. First, the law has undergone a death and resurrection in Christ, so that it still has relevance in the New Creation of the Church. Second, since we are not yet fully in the New Creation, the very particulars of the law, insofar as they address the Old Creation situation, are directly relevant to us. Adam was to extend the Garden over the whole earth, following the four rivers to the four corners of the earth. So was Israel. So are we.

Adam was to create a God-honoring civilization, with worship of the true God at its heart. So was Israel. So are we.

Adam was to love righteousness, and guard Eden from the invasion of evil (Gen. 2:15, "keep" is "guard"). So was Israel. So are we.

Adam was to punish evil. So was Israel. So are we.

The law of God, as found in the Old Covenant books, describes the Adamic task, and prescribes how it is to be carried out. In no way has this aspect of the covenant changed. What has changed is the administration of the covenant, and its source of power. The basic standards have not changed.[3]

---

3. Of course, the applications do change with circumstances. See the discussion in Chapter 1.

The Law Before Sinai

Paul tells us that the law was in operation before Sinai, when he says "for until the law sin was in the world; but sin is not imputed when there is no law. Nevertheless death reigned from Adam to Moses" (Rom. 5:13, 14a). Before the law "came," the law was already in operation, for it was already dealing death to sinners. (Similarly, before the New Covenant "came," it was already in operation, for it was already granting resurrection life to repentent men.) At Sinai, the law was given a definitive publication, but it was already operating in the world, and was already known to men.[4]

Indeed, Paul says "just as through one man sin entered into the world, and death through sin, and so death spread to all men, because all sinned" (Rom. 5:12). In other words, the same law which came at Sinai was operating in the Garden. This is the connection between the Old (Adamic) Covenant and the Old (Sinaitic) Covenant.[5]

It is often thought that at Sinai God set up something new, a new administration of law, which had not been in force previously. We have seen from Paul that this was not the case, for the law was in operation in the Garden, and in the period between the Fall and Sinai. We can also turn to passages in Genesis and in Exodus before Sinai and see that people knew the law before it was written down by Moses.

First of all, we have demonstrated that the laws of slavery were known and functioned in the life of Jacob and in the interaction between Moses and Pharaoh. *Second,* the law of evidence concern-

---

4. In other words, in one sense the pre-Sinaitic period was one of "no law," for law had not yet "come." In another sense, however, the law clearly was in the world, because sin is not imputed apart from law, and sin was clearly being imputed, as the fact of death demonstrates. Before Sinai, the law had already but not yet come. This is parallel to the gospel, which had already but not yet come during the Old Covenant; and parallel to the consummation, which has already but not yet come in the New Covenant era.

5. On how I am using the terms 'Old Covenant' and 'New Covenant,' see Appendix A.

ing torn beasts (Ex. 22:13) is referred to by Jacob in Genesis 31:39. *Third,* Exodus 21:1 and 24:3 call these laws *mishpatim,* and Abraham is said to know the *mishpatim* in Genesis 18:19. Also, in Genesis 26:5, Abraham is said to have "kept My charge, My commandments, My statutes, and My laws." This is surely more than the Ten Commandments!

Fourth, Deuteronomy 22:28-29 does not order capital punishment in the case where a young man forcibly seduces a young girl, but commands him to marry her. This law was clearly being followed to the letter in Genesis 34, which concerns the relations between Shechem and Dinah. Because Simeon and Levi broke the not-yet-written law, Jacob condemned their actions (Gen. 49:5-7).[6]

Fifth, the laws of sacrifice were known, including the distinctions among various kinds of sacrifices (Ex. 20:24, which comes before Leviticus 1-7). *Sixth,* Noah knew the difference between clean and unclean animals (Gen. 7:2), yet the rules for these distinctions were not given in written form until Leviticus 11. *Seventh,* even though we do not read of God's commanding the people to have a tent of meeting until He ordered the building of the Tabernacle, from Exodus 33:7-11 it is clear that there already was one. It was the place of religious meeting and worship, and God talked with Moses there, before the Tabernacle was built.

Eighth and last, although other examples can be found, the law of the Levirate, requiring a brother to raise up seed for his childless dead brother (Dt. 25:5, 6), was clearly known and operative in the history of Tamar (Gen. 38).

Of course, unbelieving scholars use passages such as these to argue that somebody rewrote the "original myths" of Genesis to make them conform to the "later Mosaic legislation." The fact is,

---

6. Why did not Jacob have them put to death for blasphemy (misusing the covenant sign) and murder? Probably because he was not a magistrate, and as a father did not have the power to pass civil judgments. Jacob obviously feared reprisal from the near kinsmen of the Shechemites, who could properly act as avengers of blood. Perhaps we should see Jacob as functioning as a sanctuary for his sons, just as Abram had functioned as a sanctuary for Lot in Genesis 14.

rather, that God had been telling his people all along what He wanted them to do. The law was given many times before Sinai; but it was definitively written down by Moses, in connection with the preeminent redemptive event of the Old Covenant period (Dt. 4:2).[7]

Godly Civilization

We have been considering theological reasons why the law was published in written form at this time. The Bible also gives us a common sense reason: When you are establishing government for over two million people, you need *written* laws. This is the point, in part, of Exodus 18, which sets the stage for the writing of the law by Moses.

It is sometimes thought that Exodus 18 is out of chronological sequence, because in his summary of the history of the exodus, Moses seems to say that the appointment of judges came after the departure from Sinai (Dt. 1:6-18). According to Numbers 10:29-11:30, however, it was after Jethro had departed that God took of the Spirit that was upon Moses and distributed a portion of Him to 70 other elders, and it was on this occasion that Moses complained that he was unable to bear by himself the burden of all the people (Num. 11:11; Dt. 1:9). It is best, therefore, to regard Moses' rehearsal of these events as conflated; that is, the two events are put together. Why Moses did this is explained below.

Jethro was a descendent of Abraham, and a worshipper of the true God (Gen. 25:2; Ex. 2:16; 18:10-12). As priest-king of the faithful Midianites,[8] Jethro had been able to teach Moses much about Godly leadership. Moses had observed Jethro rendering decisions in matters of contest between persons, and was now imitating his style. In contrast to Jethro, however, Moses had over

---

7. " 'You shall not add to the word which I am commanding you, nor take away from it, that you may keep the commandments of the LORD your God which I command you' " (Dt. 4:2).

8. Some of the Midianites were apostate, and joined to the Moabites. See Numbers 22:4. Whether this was a separate clan among the Midianites, or whether Jethro was an exception to the nation as a whole, we cannot say.

two million people to deal with. People were lined up all day long
for judgments.

The wise Jethro right away saw that a corrective was needed,
and asked Moses what his time was taken up with. Moses explained to Jethro that he had two problems (Ex. 18:16): First, he
had to judge every case, and second, he needed to teach the people the laws and statutes of God. Taking the problems in reverse
order, Jethro told Moses to get the law from God and to teach it to
the people (v. 20). As regarded rendering judgments, Moses was
to divide the nation into groups of households, with judges over
groups of tens, of fifties, of hundreds, and of thousands (vv.
21-22). If a judgment in a specific case became too difficult, or if it
was appealed, it would be taken up through the ascending series
of courts, so that Moses would only have to hear the toughest
cases (v. 26). Examples of this procedure can be seen in Leviticus
24:10-23, Numbers 27:1-11, and 1 Kings 3:16-28.

In this way, Exodus 18 sets the stage for the giving of the law.
There needed to be a written book of law for use by the many
judges now present in Israel.

A few comments on these judges are in order. According to
Deuteronomy 1:15, Moses "took the heads of your tribes, wise and
experienced men, and gave them as heads over you, leaders of
thousands, and leaders of hundreds, leaders of fifties and leaders
of tens, and officers for your tribes." The "officers" were a kind of
scribe, whose principal duty seems to have been the recording of
court decisions and the maintenance of genealogies.[9] Notice,
however, that Israel already had elders or leaders in each tribe,

---

9. In Hebrew, *shoṭerim*. The New Covenant deacon, as an assistant to the
elder, is probably the New Testament equivalent. "The meaning of the root, by
analogy with its Semitic cognates, is 'write'; Assyr. *Sataru,* Arab. *satara.* In Exod.
5:6-19, the role of the *shoṭerim* (RSV 'foremen') was to keep tally of the building
supplies." P. C. Craigie, *The Book of Deuteronomy* (Grand Rapids: Eerdmans,
1976), p. 98. In military situations, the officer would be the equivalent of a
quartermaster. On their duties to record genealogies, see E. C. Wines, *The
Hebrew Republic* (The American Presbyterian Press, Box 46, Uxbridge, MA
01569 [1980], p. 102). The frequency with which the officers are said to be present
with the elders or judges indicates their role as court recorders.

and that Moses simply appointed these as judges. Elders are seen already functioning in Israel, in Exodus 3:16; 4:29; 12:21; 17:5; 18:12; and 19:7. While there might have been some judges who were not elders, and vice versa, for the most part the two terms doubtless refer to the same people, just as in the New Testament elder and bishop are the same. Throughout the Bible, both "elders" and "judges" are seen making the same kinds of rulings, and Deuteronomy 21:2, which speaks of "your elders and your judges" could as easily be rendered "your elders, even (or particularly) your judges."

In addition to elders, each tribe apparently already had a prince, or head, as seen in Numbers 1:4, 16. According to Numbers 7:2, these princes were "over the mustered men," a reference to Israel considered as a military power. Thus, the primary function of the princes does not seem to have been judicial in character, but administrative and military (and perhaps symbolic, representing the succession of the original twelve patriarchs).

Returning to the elders, or judges, then, we find in Numbers 11:16ff. that God appointed seventy elders to form a supreme council to assist in governing the people. These are not called judges at this point, so we might assume that they did not render judgments in court cases, but only helped Moses with administrative and legislative tasks. When Moses summarized the history, however, in Deuteronomy 1:9-18, he conflates Exodus 18 and Numbers 11 in such a way that we are forced to see the seventy elders as a supreme court, the top of the chain of courts. Anything they could not determine, Moses would then consult the Lord about (Num. 27:1-5).

From all this we can see that the Sinaitic Covenant does not represent some radical departure from the previous organization of Israel — from, say, a patriarchal to a national form. Rather, as Israel grew in numbers, the "national" form naturally developed. Abraham's household had included 318 fighting men, which meant that Abraham's entire household numbered conservatively around 3000 persons.[10] When the seventy "from the loins of Jacob" descended into Egypt (Ex. 1:5), they doubtless took a very large number of people with them. 1 Chronicles 7:20-24 records some Israelite activities in Canaan which took place during the sojourn in Goshen, showing that each tribal republic was actively pursuing its own endeavors during this period.

The major change instituted at Sinai was not in the area of civil government but in the area of the Church. We gather that the head of the house served as priest and teacher in his household, and that his right-hand man (and his successor) was the firstborn son. This is implied in the fact that the Levites were substituted for the firstborn of all Israel, to be teachers and priests (Num. 3:12; 8:16ff.). At Sinai the prophetic and priestly tasks were removed from the family and given to the Levites and priests. The older patriarchal arrangement was replaced by a system of local synagogues (Lev. 23:3) for prophetic (instructional) purposes, and a central sanctuary for priestly (sacrificial) purposes.[11]

After a century or so of slavery, God's people were now to form a "Christian" civilization. To do so, they needed courts of law, and a God-given, publicly available, code of law. The crises in Exodus 18 taught this to the people, and set the stage for the giving of the law.

A Renewed Creation-Covenant and Fall

Exodus 19:1 tells us that Israel arrived "on the third new moon" (literally) from the month they left Egypt. They had departed on the 15th day of the first month, so that *they arrived at Sinai at the beginning of the seventh week.* On the *second* day, Moses went up the mountain of God, and God told him that He was going to make covenant with Israel. Moses came down from the mountain and told the people, who rejoiced to have the Lord as their God (vv. 2-8a).

---

10. Folker Willesen, "The *Yalid* in Hebrew Society," *Studia Theologica* 12 (1958): p. 198 (footnote 11).

11. In terms of a theology of succession, the replacement of the firstborn son indicates that the old Adamic succession was corrupt, and could not produce satisfactory priest-kings. Christ, the Firstborn Son of God, would eventually replace the firstborn sons of fallen Adam. See the discussion of this in Chapter 8.

The *third* day, Moses told God what the people had said, and God told him that He would speak to Israel from the cloud of glory. Moses returned and told this to the people (vv. 8b-9).

The *fourth* day, Moses returned to hear what God had to say next, and God told him to tell the people to prepare themselves to receive the covenant on the third day, which would be the sixth day of the week. Adam was created on the sixth day of the creation week, and was established in covenant with God. Since, as we have seen, the Sinaitic covenant is a redemptive specification or republication of the Old Adamic Covenant (from one Biblical perspective, at least), it is telling that God "re-creates" humanity in covenant with Himself on this sixth day of the week.

The process of covenant renewal with man dead in sins and trespasses must involve resurrection. Death was symbolized under the Old Covenant by dirt, since the ground was cursed (Gen. 3:17), and since "of dust thou art, and to dust thou shalt return" (Gen. 3:19). Animals that crawled in the dirt, or whose flesh had any contact with dirt, or which ate dirt (including carrion, manure, and garbage — anything rotting and returning to dirt), symbolized the lifestyle of the serpent, who was cursed to crawl in the dirt and eat dirt (Gen. 3:14). To eat such an animal was to eat death, for dirt signified death. Also, any process whereby life flowed away from men or women, signified death, such as any issue of blood or seed from the private parts. Additionally, contact with the dead body of any man or unclean animal caused one to become ceremonially dead. The term for ceremonial death is "uncleanness," because to be dirty is to be covered with death.

To be cleansed, therefore, is to undergo a resurrection. This is the meaning of the cleansing rituals of Leviticus 11-15, and other places. The covenant can only be reestablished with resurrected men, so the people were to cleanse themselves before the third (sixth) day, when the covenant was to be made (Ex. 19:10-14). Indeed, they were to avoid marital relations (v. 15), lest there be any unintentional spillage of seed (Lev. 15:18).[12]

And so, God drew near on the third day (after God's announcement to Moses on the fourth day), which was the sixth day of the week, to renew covenant with men. It was not the New Covenant that God was renewing at Sinai, but the Old Adamic Covenant. It was the Old Covenant temporarily and provisionally reestablished in the sphere of temporary, provisional, ceremonial (New Covenant) resurrection. It was temporary; but just as the original Adamic Covenant had pointed forward to sabbath rest, so the renewed Adamic Covenant at Sinai pointed forward to the work of Christ and the New Future Sabbath Covenant to come.

It was the third day, and the third month (19:1, 16). For the significance of this we need to look at Numbers 19:11-12. The man who is unclean from contact with a corpse is to be cleansed on the third day and again on the seventh day. This *double resurrection pattern* is found all through the Scriptures. For instance, in John 5:21-29, Jesus distinguishes a first resurrection, when those dead in sin will hear the voice of Christ and live (v. 25); and a second resurrection, when those dead in the grave will come forth to a physical resurrection (v. 29). The *first resurrection* comes in the *middle of history* to enable men to fulfill the duties of the old creation. The *second resurrection* comes at the *end of history* to usher men into the new creation.

Jesus was raised on the third day, thereby inaugurating the New Covenant in the midst of the week of history. Christians live between the third and seventh days of history, Spiritually resurrected and in the New Covenant, but physically mortal and assigned to complete the tasks of the Old Adamic Covenant. The fact that the law was given at Sinai on the third day, and in the third month, was a provisional anticipation of the third-day resur-

---

12. " 'If a man lies with a woman *so that* there is a seminal emission, they shall both bathe in water and be unclean until evening.' " That is, until the evening sacrifice, so that their ceremonial death is removed by the death of the sacrifice. This command may also have been intended to highlight the consummation of the LORD's marriage to Israel (cf. Ezk. 16:8).

rection yet to come in Christ.[13]

The third-day resurrection was only provisional under the Old Covenant, so it had to be repeated year after year. Thus, every year, the third day after Passover, there was a waving of the first fruits before the throne of God (Lev. 23:5, 7, 10, 11). This was a prophecy of the resurrection of our Lord Jesus Christ, which came three days after Passover. Jesus' third-day resurrection, however, was not provisional but definitive, and never to be repeated.[14]

Thus, at Sinai, Israel was temporarily re-created on the sixth day of the week, and temporarily resurrected on the third day. (Chronologically it was the same day, but theologically there is a distinction.) A careful study of the chronology of Exodus will show that this third/sixth day came very close to 49 days after the waving of the sheaf; that is, very close to Pentecost (Lev. 23:15-16). It might have been on Pentecost, as many Jewish scholars argue. It is, however, so close that the careful Bible student cannot help but make the connection. Just as the Church received the definitive outpouring of the Spirit when the day of Pentecost was "fully come" (Acts 2:1), so the Old Covenant people of God received a provisional outpouring of the Spirit on the Sinaitic Pentecost (see, for instance, Numbers 11:17).

When God created Adam, he gave Him work to do. Adam was to dress or cultivate the garden, and to keep or guard it (Gen. 2:15). Now that God had recreated Adam at Sinai, He restored the terms of the covenant to him. The people were to guard themselves, their community, and the land from sin (Ex. 20:1-23:19); and they were to move into the new garden and cultivate it properly (23:20-33).

The covenant-making ceremony is described in Exodus

---

13. Some examples of third-day judgments and/or resurrections can be found in Gen. 22:4; 34:25; 42:18; Josh. 9:16; Jud. 20:30; 2 Ki. 20:5; Esth. 5:1; Hos. 6:2; Jonah 1:17.

14. Christ's resurrection came on the eighth day, not on the sixth. He did not revive the first creation, but inaugurated a New Creation. This ties to the notion of succession, mentioned above in footnote 11, and discussed further in Chapter 8.

24:1-8. After the people had ceremonially passed through death unto resurrection, they, in the persons of their elders, were privileged to sit at the Lord's Table and share a communion meal with Him (Ex. 24:9-11).[15] Then God told Moses to come up to Him, to receive instructions on building the Tabernacle, the house of prayer.

We cannot go into the details here, but just as the land of Canaan was a new garden of Eden to the re-created children of God, so the Tabernacle was a more concentrated form of a new garden of Eden, even including the Tree of Life (for the golden candlestick was tree-shaped, and signified the Holy Spirit, the Lord and Giver of life, Who stands before the throne of God).[16] Just as Adam was to start from the throne of God and cultivate the garden, and then move out to cultivate the land of Eden, and then out to the whole world; so Israel would start from the throne of God in their midst, proceed out to cultivate Canaan, and then hopefully spread the Word of Life to all the world.

Predictably, *the re-created Adam (Israel) did not delay to rebel against God once again.* While Moses was on the mountain, the people left the Lord and turned to the worship of the golden calf (Ex. 32), once again replacing God with an animal (Gen. 3:1-5).[17] As a result of this act of rebellion, together with several others, *God cursed the renewed Adams and cast them out of His presence, to wander and die in the wilderness* (Num. 14:20-25). Indeed, because they had been cast out of the kingdom of God, they did not practise circumcision while they were in the wilderness, because circumcision was the sign of entrance into the sanctuary, and they had forfeited the right to go in (Josh. 5:5-7).[18]

---

15. Sharing a communion meal is analogous to the consummation of a marriage; thus, the Lord's Supper is termed the "Marriage Supper of the Lamb" in the book of Revelation. See Appendix F.

16. On this see M. G. Kline, *Images of the Spirit* (Grand Rapids: Baker, 1980).

17. This is specifically likened to adultery in Exodus 34:12-17 (and note that v. 18 takes up a discussion of the proper covenant meals with God). See the discussion of this in Chapter 8.

18. Possibly they would not have practised it anyway, as long as they were outside of a land set apart by God for them (as Moses had not circumcised his sons while in the wilderness, away from Goshen). This is discussed more fully in Appendix F.

This is the context in which we find the Book of the Covenant. It is a republication of law relevant to the task of Adam and his children. It is addressed to a post-Fall situation, dealing for the most part with matters Adam would never have had to deal with, had he not rebelled against God. It is set in a provisional covenant made after a provisional redemption from Egypt. When Jesus Christ came, He came to "fulfill" the law, to establish it definitively, not provisionally (Matt. 5:17). Christians today still have the Adamic task to complete, and for this reason these laws are most relevant to us.

4

THE ORDINANCES: STRUCTURE
AND CHARACTERISTICS

The actual covenant God made with Israel consisted of two parts, the *Ten Words* and the *Ordinances or Judgments* (Ex. 24:3). We have argued that, although God wrote the Ten Commandments into stone later on (Ex. 24:12), Moses wrote them down for the covenant-making ceremony, so that the Book of the Covenant contains both the Ten Words and the Ordinances. It is not exactly clear what parts of Ex. 20-23 were included and which might not have been. The passage breaks down like this:

1. The Ten Commandments, Ex. 20:2-17.

2. The People's Response, Ex. 20:18-21. This was probably not included in the Book of the Covenant, though it might have been.

3. A Brief Warning against False Worship, Ex. 20:22-26. This section is neither Word nor Ordinance, but was probably part of the Book of the Covenant.

4. The Ordinances, Ex. 21:1-23:19 (or 23:33).

5. (Possibly) Warnings, Ex. 23:20-33. This section does not consist of actual laws, but again probably was part of the Book of the Covenant.[1]

This study is actually concerned with the Ordinances, and for our purposes we shall consider only Exodus 21-23, contenting ourselves with only a couple of remarks on Exodus 20:22-26:

---

1. Curses and blessings seem to be part of the normal covenant structure. See Meredith G. Kline, *The Structure of Biblical Authority* (Grand Rapids: Eerdmans, revised edition 1975).

22. Then the LORD said to Moses, "Thus you shall say to the sons of Israel, 'You yourselves have seen that I have spoken with you from heaven.

23. 'You shall not make other gods beside Me; gods of silver or gods of gold, you shall not make for yourselves.

24. 'You shall make an altar of earth for Me, and you shall sacrifice on it your burnt offerings and your peace offerings, your sheep and your oxen; in every place where I cause My name to be remembered, I will come to you and bless you.

25. 'And if you make an altar of stone for Me, you shall not build it of cut stones, for if you wield your tool on it, you will profane it.

26. 'And you shall not go up by steps to My altar, that your nakedness may not be exposed on it.' "

The inclusion of these prescriptions here can be understood by remembering the historical context. Moses was about to go up the mountain and receive detailed instructions regarding worship, sacrifice, and the Tabernacle. The preliminary instructions in 20:22-26 would suffice for the present. We know, for instance, from Joshua 24:14, that many of the people worshipped false gods along with the LORD while they were in Egypt. Doubtless other aspects of pure worship had also been corrupted. The Lord's remarks here were designed to correct these abuses.

The relevance of these rules can be seen from the fact that only a few days later, while Moses was on Sinai, the people broke all of them. In violation of v. 23, they made a false god of gold (32:2-4). In violation of v. 24, they offered burnt sacrifices and peace offerings in a place other than God had ordered, and did not remember His Name. In violation of v. 26, they exposed their own nakedness in the "play" they engaged in before their false god (32:6, compare Gen. 26:8 for the implied meaning of "play" here). Exposure of nakedness is generally connected with sexual sins (as in Lev. 18 and 20), and idolatry is connected with harlotry in Exodus 34:13-17. Participating in an idolatrous feast—eating the food of a false god—was sacramentally equivalent to Eve's eating the forbidden fruit given her by Satan, again a form of Spiritual adultery (2 Cor. 11:1-3).² In both cases, expulsion from God's presence followed.

We have already discussed the relationship between the Ten Commandments and the case laws in Chapter 1. As we shall shortly see, the Ordinances can be grouped in sections around certain of the Ten Words.

The Arrangement of the Ordinances

Liberal scholars often assume that the collection of ordinances grew up over a period of time, and that there is little logical arrangement in the ordering of them. Others hold that the laws follow one another in terms of key phrases, analogies, or associations — "free association," if you will. The mention of God in a given law causes the writer to think of some other law pertaining to God, and that law causes him to think of something else, and so forth. Supposedly, such an ordering would help with memorizing the ordinances.³

There is good reason to believe, however, that the ordinances are attached to the Ten Commandments, and that they can be grouped around them. The outline that follows may initially seem a bit forced at a few points, but the overall sectioning and its relevance to the Ten Words is convincing enough to cause me to try to group all the laws into sections, and to proceed on that basis throughout this study.⁴

---

2. Adam and Eve were naked and not ashamed (Gen. 2:25), until they sinned (3:7). Insofar as their sin amounted to Spiritual fornication, the exposure of their now-defiled nakedness called forth the proper and fiery jealousy of God (3:10,11). To protect Adam and Eve from Himself, God gave them clothing (3:21). Thus, exposure of man's defiled nakedness to God angers Him, and He requires that man be covered (Ex. 20:26; 28:42f.). In Ezekiel 16, God's covenant with Israel at Sinai is seen as a marriage covenant, in which God clothed His defiled and naked bride. The sin of Israel (whoredom-idolatry) is seen as the exposure of nakedness.

3. Umberto Cassuto, *A Commentary on the Book of Exodus,* trans. by Israel Abrahams (Jerusalem: The Magnes Press, 1967), p. 264; and Shalom M. Paul, *Studies in the Book of the Covenant in the Light of Cuneiform and Biblical Law.* Supplements to *Vetus Testamentum* XVIII (Leiden: E. J. Brill, 1970), pp. 106ff.

4. Just before this book went to the typesetter, I obtained a copy of Walter C. Kaiser, Jr., *Toward Old Testament Ethics* (Grand Rapids: Zondervan, 1983). Kaiser

I. *Laws Concerning Slavery (21:2-11)*

   A. Five laws concerning the freeing of male slaves (21:2-6)
   B. Five laws concerning the freeing of female slaves (21:7-11)

These laws are positioned first because of the deliverance of Israel from slavery in Egypt, and to correspond to the first sentence of the Decalogue: "I am the LORD, your God, who brought you out of the land of Egypt, out of the house of slavery." They relate to the fourth commandment, rest from bondage, for these laws focus on *release* of slaves (vv. 2, 3, 4, 5, 6, 7, 8, 11).

II. *Laws Concerning Violence (21:12-36)*

   A. Assault to death (21:12-14)
   B. Willful equivalents of assault to death (21:15-17)
   C. Assault to wound (21:18-27)[5]
   D. Violence: animal property to man (21:28-32)
   E. Violence: dangerous inanimate property (21:33-34)[6]
   F. Violence: animal property to animal (21:35-36)

Each of these laws seems clearly to be associated with the sixth commandment, "Thou shalt not kill." (I discuss below a possible

admits "there is no easy outline for dividing up the topics and sections of the covenant code" (p. 97). His own suggestion does not attempt to tie the sections to the Ten Words, though he does follow Kaufman's outline of Deuteronomy (see Appendix B in this book). Kaiser's outline of the Book of the Covenant breaks it down into cases involving slaves (21:2-11), homicides (21:12-17), bodily injuries (21:18-32), property damages (21:33-22:15), society (22:16-31), justice and neighborliness (23:1-9), and laws on sacred seasons (23:10-19). I shall call attention in the footnotes below to my reasons for not following the same division as he sets out.

5. Kaiser separates this into a new section on injuries, continuing through verse 32. I believe it still comes under the sixth commandment, and is but a subsection of the laws regulating violence. Kaiser, *idem.*

6. Kaiser begins his section on cases involving property damages here. There is clearly some shading from the sixth to the eighth commandment at this point. Grammatically, however, 21:33 and 35 begin, as does verse 28, with *vki,* "and if." In contrast, 22:1 (in Hebrew, 21:37) simply begins with *ki,* "if," and I take it that this begins a new section. Similarly, 21:12 does not begin with "and," indicating the start of a new section. All the cases within the section begin with "and." Kaiser, *idem.*

correlation with the fifth commandment for verses 12-17.) The word for "kill" in this commandment is not the word for murder, but has more to do with offering violence. Thus, Jesus expounds the law in terms of verbal violence and unrighteous anger (Matt. 5:21f.). Moreover, as we shall see in Chapter 6, these laws are arranged in a descending order of severity in terms of punishments.

III. *Laws Concerning Property and Stewardship (22:1-15)*
   A. Theft (22:1-4)
   B. Pollution (22:5-6)
   C. Safekeeping (22:7-13)
   D. Borrowing and Rent (22:14-15)

It is not clear why we skip to the eighth commandment here, before going to the seventh. Most likely it is because the laws against violence are organized in such a way as to lead into laws against theft. This demonstrates the overlap between these two root norms. (See Appendix B on the overlap between the seventh and eighth commandments in Deuteronomy.)

IV. *Laws Concerning Marriage and Faithfulness (22:16-31)*[7]
   A. Seduction (22:16-17)
   B. Spiritual adultery (22:18-20)
   C. Mistreatment of God's bride (22:21-27)
   D. Respect for God as Divine Husband (22:28-31)

This might seem just a bit arbitrary, but the language of marriage is found throughout the passage, and it seems to fit better than any other category (see Chapter 8). The widow and fatherless have God as their Husband and Father (v. 22). If they cry out to Him, He will destroy the family of their oppressor (v.

---

7. Verse 16 does not begin with "and," indicating a new section. The concatenation of "and" is not, however, maintained in this section, or in the remainder of the covenant code. Kaiser, *idem.*, calls this section "cases involving society." I can agree with that, but I think that it is precisely society as the bride of YHWH that is addressed, so that the seventh commandment is the overarching principle.

24). It is the presumption of vv. 25-27 that God, the Husband, has given the cloak to the poor man (as Boaz spread his cloak over Ruth, Ruth 3:9). The final section uses marital language in v. 31, where the phrase "holy men *to Me*" occurs (cf. Ezk. 16:8, "Mine" "to Me"; Lev. 20:26, also a marital passage; etc.).

V. *Laws Concerning Witness-Bearing (23:1-9)*
  A. False Witness (23:1-3)
  B. Personal Adversaries (23:4,5)
  C. Courtroom Justice (23:6-8)
  D. The Sojourner (23:9)

Each of these laws concerns the ninth commandment. The command not to bear false witness is a command to be impartial in dealing with people. Thus, not only do we find laws against false witness both in court and in the general round of life, but we also find laws enjoining impartiality in the treatment of people who are our personal adversaries (for instance, helping the donkey of a personal enemy, 23:5).

VI. *Laws Regulating Time and Rest (23:10-19)*
  A. Sabbath years and days (23:10-13)
  B. Annual festivals (23:14-19)

These laws pertain to the fourth commandment, which has to do with the time of rest, festivity, and worship.

VII. *Epilogue: Exhortations to Obey God and Conquer Canaan (23:20-33)*
This section corresponds to the curses and blessings so often added to the law codes in Scripture (Lev. 26; Dt. 28). Here what is set before the people is the blessing that will come from obeying God and following His Angel. This corresponds to the first commandment: God brought them *out* and they were to worship him only. Now He is bringing them *in*, and they are to worship Him only.

*   *   *   *   *

Why no section dealing with either the fifth or the tenth commandment? John M. Frame has suggested that the fifth commandment forms a bridge between those commandments which pertain primarily to God and those which pertain primarily to man. The first commandment enjoins worship and the fear of God; the fifth enjoins reverence for human beings.[8] The tenth commandment primarily seems to summarize and intensify (internalize) the others.

I can suggest one other possible reason. The history of Israel in the wilderness is a history of continual rebellion against authority, and of the staged magnification of human authority in the eyes of the people. Each time rebels were dealt with by God, Moses and Aaron grew in the eyes of the people. Being slaves, the Israelites were good democrats. They would not submit to authority, either God's or that of His appointed servants. God pastorally took them through a series of experiences which taught them respect for authority. The revelation of the meaning of the fifth commandment, then, took 40 years. At the end of this period, it was possible for Moses to summarize that commandment in Deuteronomy 16:18-18:22. It probably would not have been understood before that time. Thus, we can conceive of at least a pastoral reason for dealing with the subject of human authority in a more indirect fashion.[9]

Possibly, however, Exodus 21:12-17 should be seen as dealing with the fifth commandment rather than with the sixth. We instinctively group these with the sixth because the first case deals with murder. Of the five cases, however, two deal with relations of inferiors to superiors (striking and cursing parents), one deals with relations of superiors to inferiors (kidnapping a powerless person), and two deal with relations between equals (murder or accidental manslaughter). The fifth commandment adds "that thy

---

8. Unpublished class syllabus, "Doctrine of the Christian Life" (February, 1984), p. 193.

9. Churches which try to maintain discipline in the present American context will find the same problems Moses faced in the wilderness. The book of Numbers can form a model for the Church today.

days may be long upon the land which the LORD thy God giveth thee," and the reference to the city of refuge provision in this section, together with the four mandated death penalties, can easily be connected with living long upon the land.

My decision to keep these five cases grouped with the sixth commandment is, thus, open to challenge. Verse 18 begins with the word "and," which indicates continuity, and not the opening of a new section.[10] And I suppose, on balance, it seems to me that the equity of the passage is more directed toward the sixth than toward the fifth commandment. There does seem to be some overlap in category here, which we should expect, since each law ultimately implies the rest. (See the discussion of multiple equity in Chapter 1.)

This shading or overlap of legal loci is seen in Ex. 21:28-36, which begin to move from laws about violence to laws about property. Also, 22:16-17 treat the seduced daughter as property, in some sense, and thus overlap the eighth commandment with the seventh. And 22:21-27 can be seen as having to do with fairness, and thus overlap the seventh commandment with the ninth. I have attempted to locate the actual boundaries based on grammatical considerations, as footnoted above, together with conceptual considerations.

Characteristics of the Case Laws

One of the problems we make for ourselves when we read the Bible is that we impose modern ideas onto it. In our world, we distinguish among various kinds or categories of law: Church law, judicial law, civil law, criminal law, moral law, corporate law, etc. We err if we assume that the Bible was written with our modern categories in mind.

The creeds of the Reformation, building on medieval tradition, state that there are three kinds of laws in Scripture: moral, judicial, ceremonial. As we have seen, these distinctions do not stand up to theological scrutiny — all of God's law is moral,

---

10. See footnotes 6 and 7 above.

although circumstances have changed and thus the way we observe some of the laws has correspondingly changed. We must now also see that there is no exegetical basis for this three-fold categorization.

In the *first* place, there is no place in Scripture where "judicial" laws are set apart. Scripture nowhere indicates that there is any such thing as "judicial" laws, nor is there any "judicial" section in the legal corpus of Exodus-Deuteronomy. Rather, the various "kinds" of laws are all mixed up together. The Presbyterian creed, the *Westminster Confession of Faith,* in chapter 19, section 4, refers us to Ex. 21:1-22:29 as the "judicial law," but although many of the laws recorded in that passage do have penal sanctions attached to them, not all of them do (for instance, 22:24, 28, 29).

In the *second* place, even where there are penalties included in the laws, *the text does not direct the civil magistrate to enforce these penalties.* Of course, we know from other places in Scripture that it is only the magistrate who is allowed to wield the sword of iron for the suppression of evildoers, and thus we know that where there are penalties included in the law, it is the civil ruler who is to enforce them. In the legal sections themselves, however, it is not the magistrate who is addressed; rather, it is the people as a whole.

The proper way to view it is this: God gives His law, which applies to all of life in every sphere, and included in that law are rules which show how the law is to be applied in the several spheres. There are no judicial laws as such, which can be isolated and listed. For instance, what shall we do with Deuteronomy 19:14, "You shall not move your neighbor's boundary mark, which the ancestors have set, in your inheritance which you shall inherit in the land that the LORD your God gives you to possess"? Is this a judicial law? Or is it a ceremonial law? Or a moral law? Well, first, it is obvious that there is a *moral* side: Moving the boundary mark would be a form of theft, a violation of the (clearly moral) Eighth Commandment.

Second, however, it is also clear that there is a *"ceremonial"* side, for the law speaks particularly with reference to the divisions of the land of Canaan which were made when the Hebrews initially entered the land. These plots of land were inalienable; they were never to be sold in perpetuity and were to be returned to the original owners in the Year of Jubilee. This peculiar arrangement has not been repeated in modern countries because it cannot be. This arrangement presupposes a conquest of an entire land and the dispossession of its original inhabitants, and then a parcelling out of the land. This was done in ancient Israel in order to set them apart as a nation of priests, mediators for all the other nations of the world. Strangers might convert to the faith, but might never own land within the borders of the throne-land.[11] So, there is a "ceremonial" side to this law.

Third, however, there obviously must be a *judicial* side as well, for surely a man would be allowed to sue in court against his neighbor if his neighbor were to move the boundary mark. Therefore, what shall we say? Is this law to be pigeonholed into the moral category or into the ceremonial category or into the judicial category?

We have seen that there is no "judicial section" in the law, and that it is illegitimate to pigeonhole the laws neatly into a "judicial category." (For a further discussion of this, see Appendix E.) What are some other characteristics of Biblical law, which will shed light on this phenomenon?

Third, in contrast to the laws of the ancient pagan nations, *Biblical law comes from God.* This seems obvious, but it is important to see that Israel's neighbors did not write their laws in the way God wrote Israel's. Cassuto summarizes his discussion of this point by noting that "the sources of the law were on the one hand usage — *consuetudo* — and on the other, the king's will. In all the aforementioned codes we observe that the law does not emanate from the will of the gods."[12] In other words, the law codes of the

---

11. The Jubilary provision also maintained the notion of succession among the people, and heightened their sense of the integrity and inviolability of private ownership (stewardship) of property. It was also a picture of the salvation of the world, when the Satan-held earth would revert to its proper original owners (the Bride of God).

12. Cassuto, p. 260

other nations were secular and judicial, i.e., state-centered. Israel's laws were God-centered, and always, thus, primarily religious laws.

Fourth, in Israelite law, *directly religious matters are mixed in with social matters.* Cassuto notes that "none of the aforementioned codes contains any law pertaining to the rituals of worship or to other religious matters; and their content is wholly secular. For religious subjects, specific separate manuals were composed."[13] Paul agrees: "Man's civil, moral and religious obligations all ultimately stem from God, and hence are interwoven within a single corpus of divinely given law. These three realms, which in extra-biblical societies would be incorporated respectively in law collections, wisdom literature, and priestly handbooks, are here combined into one body of prescriptions."[14]

Fifth, and very important, *Hebrew law is public and addressed to all.* Increasingly in our modern world, law has become a complicated, esoteric matter which can be understood only by lawyers. This is a trend away from Hebrew-Christian law, which is simple and public. In the ancient world, both cultic and judicial laws were often hidden from the people,[15] but in Israel the law was to be read to everyone, every seven years (Dt. 31:10-13). Moreover, since the law is addressed to everybody, not just to rulers and priests (indeed, Israel was a "nation of priests"), "everyone is held personally responsible for the observance of the law. This leads, in turn, to the concept of individual and joint responsibility. No longer is it the sole concern of the leader of the community (e.g., the king in Mesopotamia) to maintain justice and to protect the rights of his community. This responsibility is now shared by every member of the society. . . ."[16]

Because God's law is publicly addressed to everyone, it has a strongly pedagogical (teaching) function. Thus, *sixth,* Israelite law differs from heathen law in that *it has motivations included in it.*

---

13. *Idem.*
14. Paul, p. 37.
15. *Ibid.,* p. 38.
16. *Idem.*

Berend Gemser has called attention to the motive clauses in the law; that is, the arguments attached to various laws. For instance, Exodus 22:26f., "If you ever take your neighbor's cloak as a pledge, you are to return it to him before the sun sets, for that is his only covering; it is his cloak for his skin. *What else shall he sleep in?* And it shall come about that *when he cries out to Me, I will hear, for I am gracious.*" Two motives are incorporated into this law: an exhortation to mercy ("I am gracious. What else shall he sleep in?"), and a threat of Divine vengeance ("when he cries out to Me, I will hear"). If these passages of Scripture are "pure law," why are these persuasive arguments included? Gemser notes that "the motive clause is clearly and definitely a peculiarity of Israel's or Old Testament law."[17] They are not found in any other law codes of the ancient Near East. Again we see that Old Testament law was never intended to be simply a national state constitution or legal system. Rather, it gives the foundation for such a legal system.

Seventh, the *content of the law given in the Pentateuch is incomplete if it is intended as a full-scale legal code.* As Cassuto points out, the Torah is very sparse in its treatment of most subjects, as compared with the law books of the ancient Near East. "Although the codes of the Eastern kings are also incomplete and do not include every branch of law, yet, when they deal with a given subject, they enter into all its detail. . . ."[18] Biblical law, however, selects certain key cases, and by showing how Divine wisdom deals with these cases, gives us insight into how to deal with other similar cases. The Bible gives legal instruction, not a legal code as such.

Eighth, if the case laws are designed as a judicial code, then they are *incomplete as to form.* As Cassuto again remarks, "Another important distinction between state legislation and the Torah laws is to be seen in the fact that the form of the latter is not always that of a complete statute. They do not always state the penalty to be

---

17. Berend Gemser, "The Importance of the Motive Clause in Old Testament Law," in *Adhuc Locuitur: Collected Essays of Dr. B. Gemser.* Ed. by A. van Selms and A. S. van der Woude. Pretoria Oriental Studies VII (Leiden: E.J. Brill, 1968), p. 99. Cf. also Paul, *Studies,* p. 39.

18. Cassuto, *Exodus,* pp. 262f.

imposed on the transgressor; sometimes only an absolute command or prohibition is enjoined as an expression of the absolute will of the Lord."[19] Under the principle of case law, some judicial penalties are spelled out in the Bible, but not necessarily all. In some cases, only the moral prohibition is given, and we are left to discern for ourselves what an appropriate civil penalty would be, if any. On the other hand, in Deuteronomy 25:1-3, we find the provision that the court may determine to punish a man with a public beating, though no more than forty stripes might be administered; yet, there is no crime mentioned in the law for which a beating is the prescribed penalty. Apparently the court had liberty of discretion to apply a beating in some cases, perhaps if a man were a second or third time offender in a case of theft, or if a man were found guilty of assaulting his wife (wife-beating).[20]

In summary, we must agree with Cassuto when he writes that the case laws, insofar as they have a judicial application, are "ethical instructions in judicial matters."[21] Precisely. These are *moral* laws, in which God has graciously taken pains to show his people what the proper civil or criminal penalty should be for those who break them. *God has reserved judgment to Himself, and thus it is He and He alone Who can prescribe the penalties for sin.* When we realize this, we realize that in the nature of the case, *God's penalties cannot change from age to age, unless God changes.*[22]

We may make two mistakes in reading the laws in the Pentateuch. First, we may mistakenly think these laws are given as a complete civil legal code for the Godly state. As we have seen, this is impossible. Thus, the Reformation creeds are misleading when they assert that there is such a thing as "the judicial laws of Moses." There is no such thing. Since there is no such thing, it

---

19. *Ibid.,* p. 263.

20. This latter would be a specification of the principle "eye for eye, wound for wound" (Ex. 21:23ff.).

21. *Ibid.,* p. 262.

22. Again, let me reiterate that the law, including its penal aspect, does not essentially change. Applications can change, when circumstances differ. The point is that adultery today is no different from adultery in the ancient world, and the penalty God set forth for it then is still our standard today.

cannot have been designed "only for Israel," and it cannot have "expired."[23] Second, we may mistakenly think that these laws have no reference for modern society. This is also wrong, for *as long as men live in society, there will be need for social laws which reflect God's Trinitarian social life; and as long as men commit crimes, there will be need for penalties.* Are we wiser than God, that we can improve on His penalties? Or have we become God, that we can determine the judgments on sin?

In closing, let me cite some remarks by P. J. Verdam, Professor of Roman Law and Private International Law at the Free University of Amsterdam. ". . . Mosaic law, unlike modern law systems, must not be seen as a law which pertains in the first place to the state. . . . This state element is not a prominent feature of Mosaic law. Mosaic law . . . is first of all of a religious nature. Not the state organization, but the covenant governs the law. Not the nationality, but the line of generations marks one as a subject."[24]

---

23. Of course, the laws were framed for the Israelite situation, as we said in Chapter 1 of this study. Our situation may differ in many ways, so we have to examine the basic principles of the law. Still, wisdom comes to the man who grasps what the law meant to Israelite society of old, and that wisdom will enable such a man to apply God's law to society today.

24. P. J. Verdam, *Mosaic Law in Practice and Study Throughout the Ages* (Kampen: Kok, 1959), p. 5.

SLAVERY (EXODUS 21:2-11)

The laws concerning slavery come first in the Ordinances. There are two general reasons for this. First, since Israel had just been delivered from bondage in Egypt, it was fitting that their law code should begin with laws regulating slavery. As we have seen (Chapter 2), these laws were pertinent to the legality of the exodus itself, for Pharaoh had violated these very laws.

Second, the dramatic action of the book of Exodus as a whole is from bondage to sabbath rest. The sabbath pattern is set out right away in the Ordinances (21:2), and the Ordinances close with sabbath legislation (23:10-19). God had told Moses that the proof of His Word would be that Israel would worship Him on Mount Sinai (3:12), which was a three-day (sabbath) journey (3:18). Once Israel arrived, God gave them His law, and instructed them in the time and place for worship. The instructions for the design of the Tabernacle culminate in sabbath rules (31:12-17), and the procedure for building the Tabernacle commences with sabbath rules (35:1-3).[1] The book closes with the definitive establishment of Old Covenant worship on the very first day of the new year. Thus, the book moves from the rigors of bondage to the sinful world order, to the glorious privilege of rest in the very throne room of God.

There are two sections in the slavery legislation, concerning male and female slaves respectively.

---

1. See James B. Jordan, *Sabbath Breaking and the Death Penalty: An Alternate View* (Tyler, TX: Geneva Ministries, forthcoming).

Male Slaves

2. When you buy a Hebrew slave, six years he shall serve, and in the seventh he may go free, for nothing.[2]

3a. If by himself he comes in, by himself he may go out.

3b. If he is lord of a wife, then his wife shall go out with him.

4. If his master gives to him a wife and she bears him sons or daughters, the wife and her children belong to her master, and he may go out by himself.

5-6. But if the slave says plainly, "I love my master, my wife, and my children; I will not go out free;" (6.) Then his master shall bring him to The God (or, the judges); and he shall bring him to the door or to the doorpost and his master shall bore through his ear with an awl, and he shall serve him for life.

The Bible draws a distinction between Hebrew slaves and slaves who had not previously been members of the covenant.[3] The Hebrew slave may only be retained for six years, and then is to be set free, with gifts (Dt. 15:12-15). The slave purchased from heathendom, although immediately circumcised (Ex. 12:44; Lev. 22:11; Gen. 17:12, 13), was not released in the sixth year (Lev. 25:44-46), but the law did guarantee him the right to save money and buy his freedom (Lev. 25:49, 26).

While Exodus 21 does not say so, Deuteronomy 15 makes clear that the only condition apart from crime in which a Hebrew man might legitimately be reduced to slavery is in connection with debt. Since all debts were cancelled at the beginning of the seventh year, that was also when debt-slaves were released. So, the seventh year in Exodus 21:2 is not necessarily the seventh from the beginning of enslavement, but is the sabbath year.

The man takes with him what he brought to the condition of

---

2. This is my own translation. I am indebted to J. Wash Watts, *A Survey of Syntax in the Hebrew Old Testament* (Grand Rapids: Eerdmans, 1964) for certain features of the translation. When a verse contains more than one case law, I have separated the verse into segments, as verse 3 at this point.

3. A much fuller treatment of the subject of slavery in the Bible is found in James B. Jordan, *Slavery and Liberation in the Bible* (forthcoming). This chapter frequently condenses information contained at greater length, and with fuller argumentation, in that book.

slavery. If the master gives him a wife, the wife and her children remain with the master, for they are his property. The husband, of course, is free to earn money and purchase freedom for his wife and children; and even if the wife remains the property of the master, the husband would have the right to visit her as her lawful husband. (For an analogous situation, see Judges 15:1.)

This may seem a bit cruel, but it is actually for the best. *The purpose of slavery,* as we shall see, *is to train irresponsible men into productive covenant members.* It is for the wife's protection that she not be sent out with an apparently irresponsible man, who might soon be back in serious debt. She has the joys of marriage, and also the protection of the master. If her husband has genuinely profited from his period of slave-apprenticeship, he will be able to save up money, and soon purchase her freedom. This is fair to all, since the master recovers the money he paid for the woman he provided the slave.

Suppose the slave decides to remain in bondage? If so, he must say so plainly, and before the judges of Church and state at the Tabernacle. This is what it means for the master to bring him to God, for the judges at the Tabernacle-Palace are God's officers, and as mature men are called "gods" as far as their office is concerned (see Ps. 82:1, 6; Ex. 22:8, 9).[4] This is for the protection of the slave, so that he is not forcibly reduced to a permanent condition of servitude.

In a sense, the slave is rejecting freedom by staying with his master, but the text does not mention this. Rather, we are told that the slave decides to stay because he loves his master, is loyal to him. In other words, *the slave has found true freedom in the service of this kindly master.* There is no indication anywhere in Scripture that the piercing of the ear is a sign of humiliation, or a token that this slave is somehow like a woman and needs a lord. As we shall see, the circumcision of the ear is a sign of adoption.

Since the slave is joining his master's household permanently,

---

4. See Jordan, *Trees and Thorns,* (forthcoming,) for a larger discussion of what the Bible means by calling magistrates "gods."

it is at the doorpost of the master's dwelling that his ear is bored (compare Dt. 15:17). This means that the slave's ear is open to receive the word of the master and to obey him. This is the circumcision of the ear spoken of in Jeremiah 6:10 and Acts 7:51. To understand this fully, we have to make a short excursion into the Biblical doctrine of circumcision.

The Circumcision of the Ear

In the Bible, circumcision means at least three interrelated things. First, it is *a sign of death and resurrection,* for it implies castration. A man who has been castrated cannot have children, for his organ of generation is permanently dead. Circumcision symbolically castrates a man, but leaves his reproductive ability still alive.[5] Thus, circumcision is a sign of new life through death, *a sign of rebirth.* Abram's first son, Ishmael, was conceived before Abram was circumcised, and was a son of the flesh (Gen. 16); but Isaac was conceived immediately after Abraham was circumcised, and this was a son of the Spirit (Gen. 17).[6] Interestingly, those who refuse circumcision are to be "cut off" (Gen. 17:14), and while literal castration is not in view, cutting off a person from the cove-

---

5. We can compare this with baptism, which symbolically drowns a man by returning him to the original waters of the earth, the watery grave, but does not actually drown him. It is the enemies of God who are drowned at the Flood and at the Red Sea.

The "drowning" (death) of Jesus Christ, and his resurrection, are sacramentally *applied* to Christians by the sprinkling of water baptism. Christians are not saved by their own deaths and resurrections, but by the application of Christ's death and resurrection to them. This application causes Christians to undergo resurrection also, but the salvation lies not in the experience of Christians, but in the application of the experience of Christ to them. Similarly, Abram's rebirth was not due to a power in his own circumcision, but because in his circumcision, the death of Christ was being signified to him.

6. For a parallel situation, see Genesis 30:22, in context. Joseph is the son born on the other side of miracle, who replaces and then redeems the firstborn sons. Chronologically speaking, some of the other sons were younger than Joseph, for Joseph was six years younger than Reuben, but Leah stopped bearing after Judah, which was probably about the time Joseph was born. The chronological parameters are clear from 29:30 and 30:25. Theologically speaking, all but Joseph and Benjamin were firstborn.

nant was the same as cutting him off from the Seed-Savior who was to come into the world for salvation. Thus, the very word for circumcise can also be used for "cut off" (Ps. 90:6; 118:10-12). Particularly graphic is Psalm 58:7, which uses the word "circumcise" to refer to arrows which have the heads cut off the ends — the parallel to castration is obvious.

Second, circumcision means *the removal of shameful clothing,* and implies that the man who is naked before God is truly clothed. We go back to Genesis 3:7 to find that Adam and Eve, in sin, felt a sense of shame, and this sense of shame was localized in their "private parts" (note that expression). They made aprons of leaves, but God removed them, and re-clothed them Himself. The foreskin is a kind of apron, and its removal is a removal of shame, according to Joshua 5:9. Men must uncover their nakedness before God, confessing their sin and shame, before they can be clothed in righteousness (compare Zechariah 3:3, 4).

Third, circumcision means *the removal of a block or hindrance.* The man who cannot speak well has uncircumcised lips (Ex. 6:12, 30), and this hindrance needs to be removed. When Abram and Sarai find they cannot have children, it is as if they were both uncircumcised. Once Abraham has been circumcised, and the hindrance of the flesh (the foreskin) removed, they can have children. Once Abraham is circumcised, he is able to circumcise Sarah, so to speak, for the woman also has a strip of flesh that hinders procreation.[7] Women are not physically "circumcised" in the Bible, for this would destroy the symbolism of the tokens of virginity (Dt. 22:13-21).[8] The circumcision of the male child serves as a

---

7. Obviously, Sarai and Abram had been married for a long time, but Sarah and Abraham can be seen to consummate their marriage anew after the circumcision and name-change of Genesis 17.

8. Well, not circumcised in the private parts. There is a rite which may be seen as an analogue to circumcision in Deuteronomy 21:10-14. The woman who is being "converted" into the Israelite nation is to cut off her nails and shave her head, as well as change her clothes (on this, cf. Gen. 35:2). The hair-glory of heathendom is stripped, and a new glory is grown within the covenant (cf. 1 Cor. 11:15). This fulfills all three meanings of circumcision: the change of clothing, the transition from death to life in the covenant, and the removal of hindrance to marriage and procreation (since the Israelite was not to marry a foreigner).

substitute for the woman, by pointing to the circumcision of the promised seed, Jesus Christ, the "bridegroom" whose blood provides the tokens of virginity that an unfaithful wife (Israel, the Church) needs as legal evidence of her ethical purity. The circumcised baby is called a "bloody bridegroom" (Ex. 4:26).[9] The cutting off of the husband's flesh is extended or applied to the woman's flesh also, when the circumcised man goes into his wife on the wedding night.

Now, these three meanings of circumcision also apply to the *ear,* and to the *hands* and *feet.*[10] Sinners cannot serve God, so their ears, hands, and feet are, metaphorically, *chopped off* or *stabbed through.* By putting the blood of the sacrifice on the ear, thumb, and big toe of the priests (Lev. 8:23f.) and of the cleansed (resurrected) Israelite (Lev. 14:14), God ceremonially applied death and resurrection to them. The enemies of God, however, are permanently destroyed in hands and feet (Jud. 1:6, 7). The hands and feet of the cleansed Israelite are not only (1) resurrected, but are also (2) re-clothed in the oil of the Spirit (Lev. 14:28), and (3) freed from sin's hindrances.

The Bible speaks more specifically concerning the ear. The ears of sinful men are ethically stopped up (Is. 48:8), so they have to be opened (Is. 42:20), and God then speaks His Word into the ear of His servants (Dt. 5:1; 31:28, 30; and many other passages). Opening the ear is literally "uncovering" the ear, using the same word for uncovering nakedness ("show," "reveal," lit., "denude": 1 Sam. 20:2, 12, 13; 22:8, 17; "uncover": Ruth 3:4). The man whose ear has been opened not only hears God's Word, he also obeys it (Is. 50:5; Job 33:16; 36:10, 15). The man whose ear is opened, or

---

9. See Appendix F.

10. The three meanings of circumcision correspond to the three aspects of salvation: (1) death-resurrection correlates to judgment and justification; (2) nakedness-clothing correlates to dominion and adoption-glorification; and (3) removal of hindrance correlates to obedience and sanctification. (Note: I am not correlating these three *meanings* of circumcision in any way to the circumcisions of ears, hands, and feet.) On the relationship of resurrection to the area of justification, see R. B. Gaffin, Jr., *The Centrality of the Resurrection* (Grand Rapids: Baker, 1978).

uncovered, is the true servant (slave) of God (2 Sam. 7:27; 1 Chron. 17:25).

Jeremiah 6:10 and Acts 7:51 speak of those false slaves whose ears are uncircumcised, so that they neither listen to the voice of the Lord, nor obey Him. They are dead, not resurrected. They are clothed in leaves, not in Christ. They are in the flesh (hindrance of sin), not free in the Spirit. Because they did not repent, their ears were chopped off. We see this in all four Gospels, when Peter cuts off the ear of the *slave* of the high priest (Matt. 26:51; Mark 14:47; Luke 22:51; John 18:10).[11] In the *garden* of Gethsemane, the slave's nakedness is exposed. Jesus replaces the ear, giving Israel one last chance to repent before destroying them in 70 A.D. God prefers obedience (the bored ear) to sacrifice (Psalm 40:6).[12]

On the cross, our Lord Jesus Christ was circumcised. (1) He underwent death, cut off and having no personal seed (Is. 53:8). (2) His nakedness was exposed. (3) In His death, our sinful flesh (hindrance) was cut off. His hands and feet were pierced through (Ps. 22:16). As a result of His taking our sin upon Himself, His ears were stopped up, so that He did not hear the comforting voices of His Father and of the Holy Spirit (Matt. 27:46).

We are now in a position to understand why the slave has his ear bored at the master's doorpost. First, *it takes him through death unto resurrection, so that he is born again as a son of the house.* This is the meaning of the term "homeborn slave." *A homeborn slave is not a man born into slavery as an infant, but a man reborn through the circumcision of the ear.* The doorway of the house is a place associated with birth

---

11. The high priest represented the LORD to Israel, so that his slave signified Israel.

12. Psalm 40:6 states, "Sacrifice and grain offering You have not desired; My ears You have dug open." This is paraphrased in Hebrews 10:5, "Sacrifice and offering You have not desired, but a body You have prepared for Me." Thus, the author of Hebrews equates Christ's incarnation with His taking on the form of a slave (Phil. 2:7). Christ was not a homeborn slave by adoption, but Son is His own right. He took on the form of those who would be adopted as slave-sons. The reader might keep in mind three categories: Christ the True Son, Christians who are slave-sons, and the non-Christians who are slaves pure and simple.

(Gen. 18:10; 1 Sam. 1:9; Jud. 11:31).[13] This adopted son is clearly distinguished from other slaves in Genesis 17:12-27 and Leviticus 22:11. If there were no physical sons, the homeborn adopted slave could inherit the household (Gen. 15:2, 3).

Second, since circumcision is a clothing ceremony, we must see the homeborn slave as *invested with a certain privilege and authority.* This again is related to *adoption* in Scripture, for it is as a son that a man is clothed.[14] Third, the removal of the fleshly hindrance means the homeborn slave's ear is open *to hear and obey the word of the master.*

Finally, a few words about the boring of the ear at the *doorpost.* The Passover blood was placed on the doorposts (Ex. 12:7, 22, 23), and Israel was to remain in their houses all night (12:22). Exiting through the bloody doorway, the place of birth, was a token of new birth or resurrection for Israel. Similarly, when God tried to kill her son, Zipporah understood that blood needed to be placed on the "doorposts" of the "house" of the firstborn,[15] for the redemption of the firstborn was the redemption of the whole household, and the destruction of the household was the consequence of not circumcising and dedicating the firstborn, as God

---

13. In Judges 11:31, Jephthah is offering to sacrifice whoever is firstborn from his house after the battle. Coming out of the doors can be seen as a birth. The threshold is also a place of death, where birth is undone: "And as she was entering the threshold of the house, the child died" (1 Ki. 14:17). See also Judges 19:27. The importance of the door as a place of transition from death to life is highlighted by Jesus' claim to be The Door (John 10:1-9).

14. Investiture with the robe of the father is always a sign of privilege in Scripture (Gen. 37:3). Jesus, in John 15:14, 15, indicates that the slave-sons of the Kingdom are in a far higher status than the mere-slaves outside, for they can be called "the King's friends." The King confides everything, His entire Word, to the members of His entourage who are designated "friends." See 1 Ki. 4:5; 2 Sam. 15:27; 16:16; Gen. 41:40-44; Esth. 8:2, 15; 2 Chron. 20:7; Is. 41:8; James 2:23. The extent to which the King consults his slave-son-friend is seen in Genesis 18:23ff.

15. The comparison of the human body to a house is quite common in Scripture. See, for instance, Eccl. 12:3, 4; 1 Cor. 6:19; John 2:21. Legs are explicitly compared to pillars or doorposts in Canticles 5:15. The context of Exodus 4:24-26, the threat against the firstborn (vv. 22-23), makes clear the connection with Passover. The angel of death was the would-be killer in Exodus 4, but when he saw the blood on the doorpost, He passed by (Ex. 12:13, 23). See Appendix F.

had just finished telling Moses (Ex. 4:22, 23). Thus, Zipporah cut off her son's foreskin and touched it to her son's legs, thereby putting blood on the "doorposts of his house," and the angel of death stopped trying to kill him.

Here again we see why the Ordinances start off with this law of the adoption of the homeborn slave, for it helps explain what was going on at the exodus. The blood of foreskin-circumcision smeared on the legs is functionally equivalent to the blood of the Passover smeared on the doorposts, and these are equivalent to the blood of ear-circumcision smeared on the doorposts. *Thus, the Passover can be seen to signify Israel's moving from being chattel slaves to becoming adopted sons of God's household.* To move out of the dead womb-houses of Egypt was equivalent to moving into God's house.[16]

Practically speaking, then, the slave was to move out of slavery in the sabbath year. He could either be born again as a full citizen in Israel, having had several years of apprenticeship as an indentured servant, or he could join the household of his master as an adopted son. Either way, slavery was designed to produce a responsible citizen.

When we take the Gospel to unbelievers, we address them as chattel slaves, who live in the Master's house and eat the crumbs that fall from the Lord's Table (which is sometimes called "common grace"). We invite them to go to the doorway and let themselves be adopted as homeborn slave-sons. We show them the blood of the circumcision of Jesus Christ's ear on the door, and inform them that if they trust this blood, they may become King's

---

16. Coming out of sin is always equivalent to coming in to the Kingdom. There is no neutral place. The wilderness wanderings, thus, were an anomaly in the process of redemption. Just as the Red Sea parted when Israel left Egypt, so the Jordan parted when they entered Canaan. As soon as they entered, they were circumcised, to "roll away the reproach (shame) of Egypt" (Josh. 5:9). Supposedly, the first Passover had removed the shame of Egypt. Here again is a connection between circumcision and Passover: They are to be seen as one event, theologically. The hill of foreskins (Josh. 5:3), becomes a bloody marker at the doorway into Canaan, the promised land and house of God's people. Immediately after this circumcision, Passover was celebrated (Josh. 5:10ff.).

Friends, and may sit at the Lord's Table as full members of the household, and heirs. We let them know that as long as they are alive they live in the Lord's house, and partake of certain benefits of the death of the Son; but that if they refuse the offer to become adopted slave-sons, they will eventually be cast out and lose all benefits.

Female Slaves

A separate set of laws governs the female slave:

7. When a man sells his daughter as a slave, she shall not go out as male slaves do.

8. If she is not pleasing in the sight of her master, who has designated her to himself [or, who has not designated her], then he shall cause her to be redeemed; to a foreign people he shall have no right to sell her, since he has dealt faithlessly with her.

9. If he should designate her for his son, he should deal with her as with a daughter.

10. If he should take to himself another wife, her food [flesh], her clothing [covering], and her marital rights [response] he should not diminish.

11. And if he does not do these three things for her, then she shall go out for nothing, without payment of money.

There seems to be a contradiction between this passage and Deuteronomy 15:12, which says "If your kinsman, a Hebrew man or woman, is sold to you, then he shall serve you six years, but in the seventh year you shall set him free." Here the woman is let go in the sabbath year. The contradiction, however, is easily resolved. If the woman is purchased in order to become a wife, she is not set free, because marriage is permanent. If, however, the woman is purchased for labor alone, to be a lady's servant for example, she is to be returned to her family's house in the sabbath year.

As regards the daughter sold to be a wife, the following may be observed. Ordinarily, a husband provided his wife with "bride money" which was a form of insurance for her. Robert North explains: "The purchase of the bride was generally made by the father of the youth. The lady retained the payment, at least in some cases, in the form of coins strung upon her body as ornaments, so that if at any time she was divorced, she would not be wholly unprovided; moreover, the cupidity of her spouse would deter him from rashly giving up control of such tangible assets."[17] In the case of the daughter sold into slavery, this bride money went to the father of the girl instead of to her. Thus, she was a wife without property or insurance, and therefore not a free woman. Exodus 21:7-11 speaks of such a girl as the wife of the master or of one of his sons, but vv. 2-6 indicate that the girl might be purchased to become the wife or one of the master's slaves. This would be part of the contract at the time of sale. Mendelsohn points out that documents from Nuzi reveal that the status of the man whom the girl married was written into the contract when she was sold.[18] Because the uninsured slave-wife was exposed to greater liabilities than her free counterpart, special provisions are included in the law to protect her.

Verse 8 can be read either of two ways, depending on how one interprets a Hebrew particle. In one reading, the master had designated her for himself, but once the girl became nubile, he changed his mind. The alternate reading gives that she was not pleasing to the master, and he designated her for nobody. Either way, the girl is not to be married after all. The master is not permitted to sell her outside the covenant family, though possibly he might sell her to another household. Her own family, however, has the first right of redemption in this case. In the second case, the master contracted not for a wife but for a daughter-in-law. The girl must be treated as a daughter (v. 9), which makes this an *adoption* contract. A third case, understood from Exodus 21:4f., is for the girl to be purchased in order to be given as wife for a slave.

There are three things that the husband-master of the slave-wife must do for her. *First,* he is not to diminish her "flesh." This

---

17. Robert North, *Sociology of the Biblical Jubilee.* Analecta Biblica Investigationes Scientificiae in Res Biblicas 4 (Rome: Pontifical Biblical Institute, 1954), p. 151. See Chapter 8 for further discussion of this matter. I don't agree that the bride was "purchased" in this transaction.

18. Isaac Mendelsohn, *Slavery in the Ancient Near East* (New York: Oxford, 1949), pp. 10ff.

word is used for meat in Psalm 78:20, 27 and Micah 3:2, 3, and seems to refer to good food. When the people tired of manna, they wanted tastier food, called "flesh" in Psalm 78:20, 27. Thus, the master is not only to provide her with food, but with food as good as what the other members of his household eat.

Second, he is not to diminish her "covering." This means not only clothing in general, but the protective covering of a heavy cloak. (The same word appears in Exodus 22:27, with this meaning.) Metaphorically, the husband must grant her protection, as well as warmth and clothing.

Third, he is not to diminish her "response." Traditionally, this term has been seen as referring to sexual relations. The only other place where the term "answer" seems to have a sexual meaning is Malachi 2:12, "*As* for the man who does this [fornicates with a foreign woman], may the LORD cut off from the tents of Jacob *everyone* who arouses and responds. . . ." In the context of Malachi, what is in mind is the action of Phinehas in skewering a fornicating couple in Numbers 25:8. The man was involved with a foreign woman, and they were killed in the tents of Jacob. The covenant of peace with Phinehas (Num. 25:11-13) is referred to in Malachi 2:15.[19]

The occasion for the master's mistreatment of his slave-wife is his marriage to a second woman. Clearly, however, mistreatment of the woman for any reason would be grounds for divorce. And clearly this is a divorce, the grounds being maltreatment. Those who insist that the wife should remain with her husband, even if he beats her and otherwise abuses her, are completely out of line with Scripture at this point.

If a slave wife can get a divorce for maltreatment, how about a free wife? This is a hard question to answer. A free wife in Israel had certain privileges, particularly access to considerable monetary property (the bride money). Having this property gave her a

---

19. The verb for "arouse" can be seen to have some degree of sexual overtone in Canticles 2:7; 3:5; 4:16; 5:2; 8:4. The phrase "arousing and responding" can easily be seen as a discreet reference to the pleasures of sexuality. For alternative views of Exodus 21:10, see Jordan, *Slavery and Liberation* (forthcoming).

position of power with her husband. Indeed, free women in patriarchal times had their own tents and servants. The wife in Canticles had her own quarters. Thus, perhaps a free woman could not sue for divorce on the grounds of maltreatment. On the other hand, maltreatment probably could not even arise in the case of a free woman.

To apply this law today we need to ask whether the modern American wife is more like the Israelite free wife (with lots of independent power and property), or more like the slave wife. Without intending any insult, I think the modern wife is more like the slave wife, having relatively little independent power. The proof of this, for me, is the fact that men so frequently beat their wives in this society, and get by with it. Thus, extending the equity of this law, by ethical analogy, I believe that women today should be permitted to sue for divorce on the grounds of serious maltreatment.

Slavery in the Bible [20]

As a creature of God, man was created to be bound to God as his Master. In rebellion against God, man will have anything but God to be his master; yet man will have a master, for man is by nature a subject, a slave of something or other. Generally speaking, when men reject God as Master, they wind up with other men as their masters. Tyrants ancient and tyrants modern always find the masses more than willing to become their slaves, provided they are given meager bread and occasional circuses. (It helps, too, for the tyrant-elite to couch its regime in the acceptable language of democracy and human rights.)

Slavery in the Bible is a product of sin, like divorce, disinheritance, and the death penalty. Like these, slavery can be administered properly as a restraint on sin, or can itself be an occasion of sin. We may, then, distinguish among Biblical household slavery, pagan household slavery, and pagan statist slavery.

Since God approves of the institution of household slavery for fallen men, it clearly is in some ways a blessing. *First* of all, it is a blessing in that *it restrains the natural laziness and anti-dominical tenden-*

---

20. See footnote 3 above.

cies of sinful men. Ideally, the wicked are forced by the righteous to work whether they want to or not; indeed, this is set forth as a future blessing for God's people in Isaiah 14:2 and 61:5.

Second, it is a blessing in that *it trains men to work, and it does so in the best possible environment, that of the family or household.* In that the slave is attached to the household, is not paid for his labor, and is beaten for disobedience, the slave is really an adult child, and is receiving in his adult years the same kind of formative education that children receive. The Bible contemplates that there will come an end of this pedagogy, at least for the faithful converted slave, after which he takes his place as a late-blooming but now mature citizen.

Third, it is a blessing in that *it places sinners and unbelievers in the best possible environment for evangelization: the Christian home.*

Thus, household slavery is a *healing* institution. Man's relationship to God has been distorted by the rebellion of man. Household slavery restores order by forcing the unbeliever under the rule of God, in the persons of the Godly; and places him in the way of the gospel. Man's relationship to the cosmos has been perverted by sin. Household slavery restores sinners to a right relation to the cosmos, by forcing them to work, and by directing their labors in a proper, "Jerusalem" direction. Man's relationship to his fellowman has been warped by man's fall. Household slavery restores order by breaking down statism, and by placing natural subjects under their proper rulers. Slavery, then, is a byproduct of the rebellion of man, but in the proper form and administered by covenantally faithful people, it is a means for restraining and even rolling back the effects of the Fall and of the curse, by "common grace" discipline and by "special grace" evangelization.

In these respects it is like the institutions of divorce and disinheritance. Had there been no rebellion of man, there would have been no occasion for divorce or for disinheritance. Because of the hardness of man's heart, however, there come times when a spouse or child is so far gone into sin and rebellion that the only remedy is that he or she be excised, cut off from the household.

This is for the good of the Christian, for the health of the home, and for the health of society. Sadly, the institutions of divorce and disinheritance, especially the former, can be evilly used, and the same thing is true of the beneficently-designed institution of household slavery.

While the purpose of Biblical slavery is the healing of life, *the purpose of heathen slavery is, in part, sado-masochistic*; for the unbeliever hates God, and hates the image of God (men). His heart of violence has not been turned to peace by the operation of the Spirit of God. His need to be cleared of guilt has not been met in Christ Jesus, so he sets up scapegoats to punish. Thus, brutality ever accompanies slavery in heathen settings.

Characteristically, the heathen reduce men to slavery through the kidnapping of outsiders, a capital crime in Scripture (Ex. 21:16). In the Bible, persons may enter slavery as a result of debt, or to make restitution for theft (Ex. 22:3); or, if heathens, they may be purchased from traders or acquired through war (Lev. 25:42, 44, 45; Num. 31:26-47; Dt. 21:10-14). From the standpoint of the Bible, if a man is already a slave, it is better for him to be purchased by a believer and put into a Christian home than for him to remain a slave in heathendom; thus, Christians may purchase slaves, though they may not engage in kidnapping.[21]

Slavery was not designed to be paradise, however. (Note: We are not speaking of the homeborn adopted slave-son, but of the mere slave.) Slaves may be beaten to extract their labor, for unlike free men, they have no economic incentive to work, and those who are not believers cannot be appealed to by evangelical motives or ecclesiastical discipline. What remains is the rod, and Solomon recommended strictness (Prov. 29:19, 21; cf. 13:24). Common sense dictates that the proper part of the human body to

---

21. Such foreign slaves, though circumcised, did not go free in the sabbath years, as Leviticus 25:46 makes clear. The whole drive of the law, however, is the production of free men, either adopted homeborn servants or fully free. Thus, the tendency in a Godly society is for a slaveholder to be pressured to raise up his slaves into responsible citizens, and permit them to earn and save extra money, and purchase freedom.

which the rod is to be applied is the buttocks, which is well padded. Some masters might exceed this common-sense restriction, and if they do any irreparable damage to the slave, he is to go free on that account. Exodus 21:26, 27 specify the loss of eye or tooth, but any permanent damage would be equivalent.

If the slave is beaten to death, the master is to be "punished" (Ex. 21:20).[22] The punishment is spelled out in Leviticus 24:17, 22 as death. Murder is murder. If, however, the slave lingers for a day or two before dying, the law assumes that the master did not intend to kill him, and the loss of the financial benefit of the slave is regarded as sufficient punishment (Ex. 21:21).

A notorious ox which gores a free person to death brings death to its owner (Ex. 21:29), though a pecuniary compensation is possible in this case (vv. 30f.). In the case of the slain slave, however, the owner of the ox is not executed, but merely gives 30 shekels to the slave's owner.

To be a slave was to run something of a *risk:* the risk of being beaten to death, of losing an eye or a tooth, of being exposed to goring oxen. Are these laws unjust? Obviously not, being God's laws. To understand this situation it is only necessary to keep in mind that *slavery is a remedy for sin, and the goal of slavery is its own self-elimination.* If slavery were a socialistic dream paradise, many people would be attracted to it as an escape from responsible living. The condition of slavery is made sufficiently hard that men will be discouraged from entering it, and encouraged to seek to earn their freedom.

Practical Observations

Slavery is still very much with us in the last years of the 20th century. The most notable example is communism, which has enslaved vast portions of the world. In the United States, large groups of people have approached the national government in re-

---

22. Shalom Paul points out that this stipulation is absolutely unique in the Ancient Near East legal material. This is also true of the Exodus 21:26f. protection of the slave against permanent bodily injury. Cf. Shalom Paul. *Studies in the Book of the Covenant* (Leiden: Brill, 1970), pp. 69, 78.

cent years, begging to be made wards of the state, demanding bread and circuses; and this is the case all over Western Europe as well. Furthermore, traffic in human flesh continues to characterize the Moslem world.

The slave trade existed all over Africa long before the coming of white traders, and the cruelties of the European slave trade were not necessarily worse than conditions for enslaved people in Africa at the time. The advantages for those slaves who survived the voyage to the United States were considerable, both materially and spiritually. Though there were indeed cruel masters in the South, a Christian civilization served to restrain most excesses, and Christian leaders worked to institute better laws in this regard. The failure of the South, however, to be consistently Christian at this point resulted in the destruction of Southern civilization. Southern theologians were frequently more interested in detailed and excessively rigorous observance of the weekly sabbath than in the weightier matters of the law: mercy and justice and faithfulness (Matt. 23:23). There was no provision whereby slaves might earn their freedom, nor were the Biblical laws governing slavery respected. Theologians strained at sabbatical gnats and swallowed a sabbatical camel. Because deliverance from bondage into sabbath freedom is so central to Biblical theology, the hypocrisy of the Southern churches at this point could not help but call down the wrath of God.[23]

Because of this background, the term 'slave' can hardly be used in any positive way in American literature. The beneficial provisions of Biblical household slavery might be reintroduced into society, but some other term such as 'indentured servitude' will doubtless have to be used for it. Indentured servitude as a

23. The finest defense of Old South slavery is Robert L. Dabney, *A Defense of Virginia* (1867, reprinted by Sprinkle Publications, Harrisonburg, VA). Dabney argues that the Bible allows slavery, but also argues that we are no longer bound to observe the Mosaic laws regarding slavery. This convenient position, a smorgasbord approach to Scripture, aptly illustrates the contradictory nature of the evangelical theology of recent years. The history of slavery in America illustrates the point that a casual approach to the biblical regulations surrounding household slavery leads to much abuse and suffering.

means to pay debts is manifestly preferable to debtor's prison on the one hand and irresponsible declarations of bankruptcy on the other. Enslavement for theft, to make restitution, is manifestly preferable to the execution or imprisonment of thieves. Such persons could be sold to local businesses or large corporations ("households"), for set terms, to be trained and supervised and rehabilitated. Sadly, the only suggestions along these lines at present is "workfare," which is a form of slavery to the state (forcing people to labor in order to get statist welfare), and slavery to the state is a far cry from indentured servitude in a household business.[24]

Finally, while the cruel slave trade is not found in the Western world today, Christians in North Africa might consider the value of purchasing slaves as a means of evangelization, as under the Old Covenant.

---

24. The reader should keep in mind that household slavery does not imply a small family setting. Abraham had 318 homeborn adopted sons who were trained for war (Gen. 14:14). There is no telling how many regular slaves he had. His household doubtless numbered in the thousands. Thus, indentured servitude to a large business easily corresponds to Biblical household slavery. Once a man had paid off his debt, he might choose to remain with the company as an employee, a situation analogous to adoption.

6

VIOLENCE (EXODUS 21:12-36)

The laws against violence are concerned with the sixth commandment, "Thou shalt not kill." The word for kill means *slay* — not murder, and not kill. It is used only with reference to human beings, but is used both for premeditated murder and for accidental manslaughter (see for instance throughout Numbers 35). There are no real accidents in God's world, so that killing a man through negligence or carelessness is still a violation of the sixth commandment, although not so serious a violation as murder. The man who accidentally slays his friend was "punished" by being shut up in the city of refuge, possibly for years (Num. 35:25). Laws regulating violence, then, particularly belong under the sixth commandment. Before turning to a consideration of the laws themselves, it would be well for us to have before us some general considerations regarding violence.

The Nature of Violence

1. *The Murder of God.* Sinful man hates God and would like to kill Him. Thus, all violence is directed against God, unless it comes from God through His magistrates or in the fires of hell. Man hates God and wants to destroy everything that reminds him of God. God is life, and so man hates life and loves death.[1] First of all, sinful men hate Christians, since they most closely resemble God. This is why they killed Christ and the prophets. Second,

---

1. Proverbs 8:35-36, "For whoever finds Me finds life, and shall obtain favor from the LORD. But he who sins against Me wrongs his own life. All those who hate Me love death."

each sinful man hates himself, since he is made in the image of God. Third, sinful men hate each other, since all are made in God's image. Fourth, sinful men hate the creation, since the creation reflects the glory of God. Thus, violence and killing are innate to sinful man.

2. *Sinful men want to play god.* They want to impose and legislate their fantasies onto the world. When the creation and other people resist his totalitarian design, the sinner resorts to violence to get his way. The sinner wants absolute dominion (sovereignty) over everything. To the extent that God crosses his plans, he is frustrated. The saint learns to relax in God's providences, but the rebel reacts against them.

The first stage of dominion is language (Gen. 1:5; 2:19). The wider a man's vocabulary and the more precise his language, the greater his dominion and the less his frustration.[2] Where men lack the words to express their thoughts, frustration turns them to the first level of violence: swearing. The levels of violence are:

1. Verbal violence
   a. Swearing
   b. Blasphemy
2. Physical violence
   a. Fighting
   b. Killing

3. *Vengeance.* Vengeance is basic to a world in sin. Sin must be dealt with; wrongs must be avenged. God alone is Avenger, though He carefully delegates this work in some measure to the magistrate (Rom. 12:19; 13:4).[3] Blood vengeance is the same thing as sacrifice. If a man will not own his sin and take Christ as his Sacrifice, he will make someone else the scapegoat and sacrifice him, as Cain did Abel (Gen. 4:3-8). Thus, sinful men will always exercise violence against those they choose to blame for their misfortunes.

Since the state is grounded in vengeance, a neutral state is im-

---

2. Frustration can have other causes, of course.
3. See Chapter 2 of this study.

possible. Either the state will exercise the wrath of God against sin, or it will exercise the wrath of man against God and his people. The notion of a neutral society is dangerous and perverse. The idea of neutrality is simply a Satanic cloak for anti-Christianity.

4. *Sado-masochism*. Guilt is basic to sinful man. If a man will not have Christ as his atonement, he will either try to pay for his guilt himself (masochism) or he will try to make someone else pay for it (sadism). Since a guilty man wants everyone to share his guilt, and is deeply offended if people claim to be innocent, his masochism and sadism go together like two sides of one coin.[4]

5. *Dominion*. Man was created to exercise dominion, and the urge to rule and take dominion is present in every man to some degree. Sinful man, however, being innately irresponsible, does not want to work for dominion. Instead he tries to get dominion through violence: war (conquest) and enslavement (man-stealing).

6. *Revolution*. God rules through authority structures. Hatred of authority stems from hatred of God. Thus, sinful man has a natural tendency to resent and exercise violence against authority, whether the authorities are good, bad, or relatively indifferent. Sometimes this violence takes the form of a contentious and litigious abuse of legal privileges, but the violence involved is easily discerned behind the false front of lawfulness.

Note that the sinner is caught in an irreconcilable tension. On the one hand, he is a slave who wants to be irresponsible and cast all responsibility onto a master, usually the state. On the other hand, he is a rebel who hates all authority. This love-hate relationship to authority is obvious in the way modern men relate to the state. They constantly complain about the government, and resent taxation; yet they want the state to care for them from womb to tomb.

7. Only the *preaching of the gospel* can cure violence. The Christian state is to restrain violence, but only regeneration can transform the violent heart of a man. The pagan state is itself gen-

---

4. See Rousas J. Rushdoony, *Politics of Guilt and Pity* (Tyler, TX: Thoburn Press, [1970] 1978).

erally an instrument of violence; but the Christian takes comfort in Zechariah 1:18-21, which says that the work-dominion of the righteous will gradually and eventually replace and overthrow the violence-dominion of the wicked.

The Ordinances of Exodus 21:12-36 are designed to restrain and minimize violence. There are four basic sections:

1. Five cases concerning capital offenses in the area of violence (vv. 12-17).

2. Five cases concerning violence which do not result in death (vv. 18-27).

3. Five cases concerning violence done to men by animals (vv. 28-32).

4. Three cases concerning violence done to animals (vv. 33-36).

These three cases form a bridge into the section of laws concerning property.

Capital Offenses

12. Whoever strikes a man so that he dies, shall most certainly be put to death.[5]

13. Unless he did not lie in wait, but The (One True) God let him fall into his hand; then I shall appoint for you a place to which he may flee.

14. But if a man willfully attacks another to kill him treacherously, from My altar you shall take him that he may die.

15. And whoever strikes his father or his mother shall most certainly be put to death.

16. And whoever steals a man, and sells him or is found in possession of him, shall most certainly be put to death.

17. And whoever curses (repudiates) his father or his mother shall most certainly be put to death.

---

5. The verb is duplicated, as in Genesis 2:17, "in the day you eat of it, you shall most certainly die"; or, literally, "dying, you shall die." This duplication of the verb, called "pleonasm" in Hebrew grammar, forms the testimony of two witnesses (Heb. 6:13-18), and indicates strong emphasis. The emphasis means that the death penalty cannot be set aside by any payment of money.

I. *Premeditated Murder*

According to verses 12 and 14, the man who murders his fellow deliberately shall most surely be put to death. This is elaborated in Numbers 35:16-21 to cover every kind of case that might come up, whether the murder weapon is an iron object, a stone, a wooden object, or the shove of a hand. In Numbers 35:31, we are told "you shall not take ransom for the life of a murderer who is guilty of death, but he shall most certainly be put to death."

Shalom Paul tells us that "this absolute ban on composition[6] for homicide is without parallel in all Near Eastern law. Since homicide is considered to be contrary to the divine order (cf. Gen. 9:6), it cannot be atoned for by a pecuniary or property settlement; the murderer must be put to death."[7]

II. *Accidental Manslaughter*

A special provision was set up for the man who accidentally killed his fellow. "Such an institution, which ensures the safety of one guilty of manslaughter, is without parallel in the entire ancient Near East."[8] The negligent manslayer could run to a *city of refuge* to escape the avenger of blood. The details of this are set out in Deuteronomy 19:1-13 and Numbers 35:10-34.

The avenger of blood was the nearest of kin of the dead man.[9] It was his appointed task to remove the killer from the land, but only under the control of God's law as administered by the civil authorities. A trial was to be held, and if the manslayer was found guilty of murder, the nearest of kin was privileged to execute God's judgment by casting the first stone. In the modern world he might pull the switch on the electric chair. From the perspective of the Bible, it is a *privilege* to execute God's judgments in the earth.

---

6. Composition is a monetary settlement to avoid punishment.
7. Shalom Paul, *Studies in the Book of the Covenant* (Leiden: Brill, 1970), p. 61.
8. *Ibid.,* p. 63
9. The Hebrew word *goel* refers to the kinsman-redeemer and to the kinsman-avenger. See Chapter 2.

Satan wants Christians to feel bad and guilty about this, so that they will be weak and helpless, but Psalm 58:10 tells us that "the righteous will rejoice when he sees the vengeance; he will wash his feet in the blood of the wicked."

This was the attitude of Jesus Christ, as Isaiah 63:1-6 indicates:

> 1. Who is this who comes from Edom, with garments of crimson colors from Bozrah, this One who is majestic in His apparel, marching in the greatness of His strength? "It is I who speak in righteousness, mighty to save."
>
> 2. Why is Your apparel red, and Your garments like the one who treads in the wine press?
>
> 3. "I have trodden the wine trough alone, and from the peoples there was no man with Me. I also trod them in My anger, and trampled them in My anger, and trampled them in My wrath; and their juice is sprinkled on My garments, and I defiled all My raiment.
>
> 4. "For the day of vengeance was in My heart, and My year of redemption has come.
>
> 5. "And I looked, and there was no one to help, and I was astonished and there was no one to uphold; so My own arm brought salvation to Me; and My wrath upheld Me.
>
> 6. "And I trod down the peoples in My anger, and made them drunk in My wrath, and I brought down their juice to the earth."

According to Numbers 35:24, 25, when the manslayer arrived at the new city of refuge a trial was held by the "congregation," doubtless in the persons of their representatives, the elders. If the man were found guilty of murder, he was taken even from the very altar of God (1 Kings 2:28ff., Rev. 6:9-10, 9:13-14), and turned over to his hometown elders (Dt. 19:12) for execution at the hands of the avenger of blood.

If the man were found innocent of murder, he had to remain in the city of refuge until the death of the high priest, which might take years. Of course, his family would move in with him; this is not some kind of prison. It is, however, something of a punishment; after all, it would result in economic losses, for the man would no longer be able to farm his land, and would have to take up a new life as a tradesman or craftsman in the city. The purpose of this legislation might seem, thus, to be to punish carelessness and negligence.

The Bible gives us a somewhat different reason for this temporary incarceration, however. *Blood, even blood spilled accidentally, pollutes the land* (Num. 35:32-34). The land cries out for vengeance because of the blood spilled on it, according to Genesis 4:10-11. Thus, if the guilty manslayer leaves the city of refuge, even though the killing was an accident, the land cries out for his death, "for blood pollutes the land, and no expiation can be made for the land for the blood that is shed on it, *except by the blood of him who shed it.*" The death of the high priest, however, serves as a substitute for the death of the accidental manslayer, so that he may return to the land.[10] Until the death of the high priest, however, the land keeps crying out for the death of this man, even if he was guilty of nothing at all.

Let us take a case. Suppose a child runs out in front of your car, and your brakes fail due to negligence, and the child is killed. You have been involved in causing blood to be shed on the land, and now the land cries out for your death as an atonement. *The avenger of blood is the agent of the land. He acts on behalf of the land to execute vengeance for the land.* In this particular case, he is the father of the boy you accidentally killed. It is his duty to kill you, even though he knows you are not guilty of murder, and even though he may not be angry at you at all.[11] He has an appointed task, and that task is to satisfy the land, which cries for your blood.

The only way you can escape is to get out of the defiled land, and into the special place God has set aside, the city of refuge. After you arrive in the city, the avenger shows up at the gates and

---

10. Thus the death of Aaron enabled Israel to leave the wilderness and to begin the conquest of Canaan (Num. 20:22 - 21:3).

11. I may be stretching things a bit to say it is his duty, but the language of Numbers 35:19, 21, 27, and especially 33 seem to indicate that the man *must* be put to death if he does not stay in the city, and it is the task of the avenger to kill him.

demands that you be turned over to him, to satisfy the land. The
Levites and elders in the city hold a hearing, and find that you are
not guilty of premeditated murder. They give you the right to stay
in the city until the death of the high priest. If, however, you set
foot outside the city, the land will cry for your blood and the
avenger will be duty-bound to track you down and kill you. Thus,
all space outside the walls of the city becomes a threat to you. You
are cut off from the land God gave to your ancestors, and like
Cain you are cut off from the fruit of the land.

Then, one day the news comes that the high priest has died.
His death atones for the blood accidentally spilled on the land.
You are free to go. The boy's father meets you at the gate, and you
go home together. He no longer has the task of killing you, for
God has killed a substitute, the high priest.

Some commentators think that the avenger of blood was an
agent of the family, and was engaged in a blood-feud with the
man who killed his kin. They see the Bible as permitting this kind
of feuding, but only within carefully restricted bounds. This is not
correct, however. The avenger of blood is not a man carrying out
personal revenge on behalf of the family. Rather, he is an agent of
God, enlisted to be an agent for the land.[12] God nowhere gives the

------

12. The connection between humanity and earth is made in Gen. 2:7 and
3:19. God commanded men to take dominion over land and to have seed, Gen.
1:28. Land and family are tied together under the Old Covenant, and when
Israel entered Canaan, the land was divided into family plots, which were inalienable (Lev. 25). The goel was the redeemer of the family land, and the
avenger of family and land. In fact, it seems that the goel's duty of redeeming the
enslaved kinsman is always with a view to setting him back on his land. Thus,
the goel acts *for* the family, but always with a view to giving them good land. His
specific task is to make sure the land is available and undefiled, and in that sense
he is really an agent for the land.

Notice that when God destroyed Egypt, He acted as Avenger of blood, by
turning the Nile to blood, thus defiling all Egypt. This was a symbolic manifestation of the previous bloodying of the Nile which occurred when Israelite babies
were thrown into it (Ex. 1:22). The bloodied land cried out for God to destroy
each family in it, by destroying the firstborn of each household. Each household
which was under the blood of the Passover, under the blood of the death of the
high priest Jesus Christ (symbolized by the blood of the lamb), was a miniature
city of refuge. The death of this high priest enabled them to leave these sanc-

family the right to take its own vengeance. Rather, it is because the land was tied to the family that the next of kin was commandeered to act as avenger of blood. Someone not related to the dead man might not take his job so seriously. Of course, a man might want to see his slain brother avenged, and provided his wrath was a holy wrath, there is nothing wrong with this. Such, however, is not the essence of the institution of avenger of blood. The avenger of blood acts on behalf of God, not on behalf of the family.

When Jesus Christ died, He died as the great High Priest. His death permanently, once and for all, atoned for blood spilled on the ground. We may say that shed blood still defiles the ground, but that the way the remedy for this is to be applied has been altered. Man is still made of earth, and still tied to the earth. There is in some sense an organic relationship between humanity and the world. When a society allows murder and other crimes to go unchecked, the very soil wars against it. There will be peculiarly bad weather, earthquakes, crop failures, and the like. The remedy is repentance. Society must come within the sanctuary of the faith, expressed in loyalty to Christ's true Church. It is in the Church where the shed blood of the True High Priest is *applied* to His people, in the faithful administration and reception of the sacramental body and blood.

In the Old Covenant, the land was perpetually defiled, and

---

tuaries in the morning of the exodus. The inhabitants of these cities of refuge were the firstborn sons, spared by the Angel of Death. Later, when the firstborn were replaced by the Levites (Numbers 3), they become the inhabitants of the cities of refuge, which were all Levitical cities (Num. 35:6). Thus, the cities of refuge were created by the Passover.

It might occur to the reader that, since the goel was avenger of his family land, then the proper avenger of blood in any given case is the man on whose property the killing occurred. The Bible indicates, however, that the death does not defile only the plot on which it occurred, but defiles the entire land. Thus, a killing on unclaimed property would still have to be avenged. 2 Samuel 14:4-11 indicates that the avenger was next of kin of the dead man, rather than the owner of the property on which the killing took place.

The death of Jesus Christ redeemed His kin, and gave them good unpolluted land: the whole earth.

only provisionally cleansed by a variety of cleansing actions, the most prominent being the annual cleansing on the Day of Atonement (Lev. 16). Apart from this, the holy land of Canaan would revert to a defiled status. Within this annual provisional cleansing, there was the possibility of local, occasional defilements, such as what we have been describing (and cf. Dt. 21:1ff.). In the New Covenant, the land is perpetually cleansed. It is only the occasional defilement which must be dealt with. The ceremony of dealing with it is not the sacrifice of slaying an animal, or the death of a Church leader, but the ceremony of the Church's declaring a man forgiven and permitting him to partake of the Holy Eucharist, which applies the finished sacrifice to him. Such a ceremony would be an important part of a Christian society.

The only permanently defiled place in God's universe any more is hell, and in hell the great Avenger of Blood pours out eternal wrath against those who refused to flee to Jesus Christ, our City of Refuge (Heb. 6:18), the Heavenly Jerusalem.

This law is sometimes applied to argue that we need laws against negligence in Christian civilization today. This is only so indirectly. As we shall see, Exodus 21:28-36 prescribes rules for compensation in the case of negligence. In this law, however, the man who flees to the city of refuge is not told to pay any amount to the widow. We definitely do need laws against negligence, but they cannot be grounded solely in Exodus 21:13.

Although legislation against negligence cannot be grounded here, certainly this law reinforces such legislation. We find here a general doctrine of carefulness with human life. As John Frame has put it, "The slayer is impressed with the need to be *careful* with human life, to avoid even the *possibility* of its unjust destruction. The punishment fits the crime. As he has been careless, so now he must be very, very careful with his own life. . . . Similarly, Jesus in Matthew 5:21-26 places a high priority on the sanctity of life. He tells us to guard against even the *causes* of murder (anger — only a *potential* cause). He gives a higher priority to reconciliation than to worship."[13]

---

13. Unpublished Class Syllabus, "Doctrine of the Christian Life" (Westminster Theological Seminary, February, 1984), p. 204.

Secondly, this law is sometimes assumed to regulate or prevent clan feuding. This is based on the false notion that the avenger of blood is nothing more than a family agent. The Bible eliminates clan feuding by insisting that cases of alleged murder be tried before a court of the congregation. The family may not take revenge in Scripture, and clan vengeance is a manifestation of pagan *familism*, which absolutizes the family at the expense of the proper role of Church and state.

The bipolarity of sanctuary and avenger historically gave rise to the Christian doctrine of Church and state. The church buildings were sanctuaries or asylums to which people might flee for refuge. If the Church officers determined that a man was guilty, or would at least receive a fair trial, they would turn him over to the state. If he were being hounded by a mob, they could protect him until he might be helped by civil authorities. In the later Middle Ages, this practice tended to be abused, and the Reformation, in that it was usually linked to nationalism in the early days, suffered the Church to lose its social role as sanctuary. During the Middle Ages, neither king nor mob dared invade the sanctuary of the Church. Part of the reformation needed in our day is a return to this system.[14]

III. *Striking Parents*

The death penalty is mandatory for a son who strikes his father or his mother. The word for "strike" or "smite" here, and throughout the passage, means "to attack with great force." A man who slapped his mother or father, for instance, would not necessarily have committed a capital crime. It would have to be something close to attempted murder: beating his father up, hitting him hard with an implement, trying to kill him, and the like.

Ordinarily, assault is not punished by death, as we shall see (Ex. 21:18-19). In the case of parents, however, the Bible makes

---

14. I have dealt with this at greater length in a forthcoming monograph, *Avenger and Sanctuary: The Biblical Conception of Church-State Relations* (Geneva Ministries, forthcoming).

special provision. According to Shalom Paul, this also is unique to the Bible: "Only in Biblical legislation does the parents' authority receive a divine sanction (cf. Ex. 20:12), and this helps to explain the severity of the punishment in Exodus."[15] Mesopotamian cultures were statist, and treason against the state was a capital offense, but not treason against the family. We might add that the Bible is not family-*centered* (familistic), but does grant a high value to the family and to parental authority when compared with statist cultures.

As Appendix B indicates, the Bible puts submission to any earthly authority under the fifth commandment. Thus, by extension, the death penalty for attempted murder can be applied to a man who attacks Church elders, civil magistrates, or policemen (cf. Dt. 17:12); and to a slave who attacks his master. As we shall see below, the Bible never condones violence, and always enjoins arbitration.

IV. *Kidnapping and Slave Trading*

The other law codes of the Ancient Near East also punished kidnapping with death, but only if the stolen person were an aristocrat.[16] The Bible punishes all man-stealing with a mandatory death penalty. In Deuteronomy 24:7, the kidnapping of covenant members is particularly forbidden, but in Exodus 21:16, all man-stealing is prohibited. It might be maintained that if we read v. 16 in context of v. 2, it is only Hebrews who are protected and avenged by this law. The text simply says "man," however, and there is no indication in the immediate context (vv. 12, 14) that "man" is restricted to covenant members.

The death penalty is appropriate because kidnapping is an assault on the very person of the image of God, and as such is a radical manifestation of man's desire to murder God. Like rape, it is a deep violation of personhood and manifests a deep-rooted contempt for God and his image.

-----

15. Paul, p. 64.

16. *Ibid.,* p. 65. Those who were not full members of the city were always regarded as outsiders or barbarians, and were not given full protection under law.

The prohibition of kidnapping speaks to a number of issues, such as the proper penalty for ransom-kidnapping, the impressment of seamen, and perhaps even the military draft. Naturally, it also speaks to the slave trade. Note, however, that slave traders are not sentenced to death here, but only kidnappers. This may seem strange, but as we pointed out in Chapter 5, heathen cultures regularly practise slavery, and the sale of such slaves to Israelites was a means of evangelizing them. The Hebrews were free to purchase slaves from traders (Lev. 25:44).

The Bible is not revolutionary. As the world becomes Christian, chattel slavery will disappear for two reasons: First, slaves will become converted, and earn their freedom. Biblical law protects their right to do this. Second, no new people will enter slavery as a result of kidnapping and slave raiding. Thus, the laws of Scripture are designed to eliminate slavery without destroying the existing fabric of society.

V. *Repudiating Parents*

God requires death for the son who "curses" his father or his mother. There are two words for "curse" in Hebrew. One has as its basic meaning "to separate from or banish," and is used for the curse in Genesis 3:14. The second, which is used in Exodus 21:17, basically means "to make light of, or repudiate." As Umberto Cassuto has pointed out, this verb "to make light of" is the opposite of the verb which means "to make heavy, honor, or glorify."[17] For the Hebrew, to glorify or honor someone was to treat them as weighty, just as American slang in the 1970s and 1980s uses the word "heavy" to refer to important or impressive matters.

The fifth commandment orders sons and daughters to honor

---

17. Umberto Cassuto, *Exodus* (Jerusalem: Magnes Press, 1967), p. 271. Cassuto calls attention to 1 Samuel 2:30 and 2 Samuel 6:22 as examples where "to make light of or curse" is set in opposition to "to glorify or honor." An extended discussion of the conception of cursing in Scripture, relevant to Exodus 21:17, is Herbert C. Brichto, *The Problem of "Curse" in the Hebrew Bible,* Journal of Biblical Literature Monograph, Series XIII (Philadelphia: Society of Biblical Literature, 1963). The verb "to make light of" (*qalal*) is discussed on pp. 134ff.

their parents, and the verb used is the verb "to make heavy, to glorify." Thus, to make light of, to despise, is the opposite. An example of this is clearly set out in Deuteronomy 21:18-21: "If a man has a stubborn and rebellious son who will not obey his father or his mother, and when they chastise him he will not even listen to them, then the father and mother shall take hold of him and bring him out to the elders of his city at the gate of his place. And they shall say to the elders of his city, 'This son of ours is stubborn and rebellious; he will not obey us; he is a glutton and a drunkard.' Then all the men of his city shall stone him to death; so you shall remove the evil from your midst, and all Israel shall hear of it and fear."

Notice that it is an *older child* who is in view, not a little boy; he is old enough to be a drunkard. Second, notice that the sin is a settled disposition to rebel, not a one time act of disobedience. Third, notice that the young man has given public witness to his rebellious heart; the parents can remind the judges that they all know he is a drunkard and a glutton. Note, fourth, that the parents do not have the power to deal with this rebel on their own; they have to bring evidence and testimony to the judges. This shows us how the law was carried out, and what is involved in making light of one's parents, ridiculing them, and repudiating them.

In 1 Timothy 5:3, 17, to "honor" someone means to give them money, to care for them financially.[18] In line with this understanding, Jesus applies the death penalty for dishonoring parents directly to those who refuse to care for them in their old age. Mark 7:9-13, "He was also saying to them, 'You nicely set aside the commandment of God in order to keep your tradition. For Moses said, "Honor your father and your mother," and "He who reviles father or mother, let him die the death."[19] But you say, "If a man

---

18. Obviously, to honor someone entails more than just money, but in a practical, down to earth, legal sense, giving money is a strong evidence of honor. Proof that money is partially in view in 1 Timothy 5:3, 17 is in vv. 16 and 18.

19. "Die the death" is a Greek rendering of the Hebrew doubling spoken of in footnote 5 above. Jesus very definitely establishes the death penalty for this offense.

says to father or mother, anything of mine you might have been helped by is 'corban' (that is to say, an offering [to God])," you no longer permit him to do anything for father or mother; invalidating the word of God by your tradition which you have handed down; and you do many such things like that.' " Notice that Jesus sets Exodus 21:17 right next to the fifth commandment in binding force. Notice also that "cursing" father and mother is definitely said to include verbally reviling them.[20] Principally, however, this passage shows us that *in the practical legal sense, refusing to care for parents in their old age is a capital offense.*

Practically, then, "repudiating" parents could mean a settled, publicly manifest disposition to reject Godly household rules. It could mean a refusal to care for them in their old age. It could mean reviling and cursing them. For the death penalty to be applied, however, there would have to be evidence that would stand up in court. The small boy who wants to appear tough to the fellows may call his parents "the old man" and the "old lady." He is not guilty of a capital crime, though he is in sin nonetheless. The teenager who is upset with household rules may get mad and yell at his parents, "You don't love me; you've never loved me. I hate you." He has not committed a crime worthy of death either, though he has sinned in the passion of frustration. Those who hate the law of God, and that includes many in the so-called evangelical churches today, like to twist the Old Testament Scriptures to make it appear that small children are commanded to be put to death for minor offenses. That is not, however, what is in view.

A few comments may be helpful. When a son marries, he sets up a new household, according to Genesis 2:24. If parents come to live with their married children, they must adjust to the rules of their son's or son-in-law's house. Honoring parents does not mean permitting them to destroy one's home. If grandparents undermine the discipline of the children, or if the mother-in-law constantly badgers and harasses her daughter-in-law, something will

---

20. Some translations give "speak evil" for "revile." The Greek word indicates something stronger than the English "speak evil," which could mean "say bad things about."

have to give. Parents do not have an absolute claim to honor. Their claim is only good if they live righteously according to God's law. Lazy parents who leech from their young married children, who refuse to go to church with them, and who undermine their homes, should be shown the door, if the elders agree. They have forfeited the right to honor by their actions. We must ever honor God first, and parents second.[21] Only in this way can we truly honor parents.

At the same time, this is not to say that we should not put up with senility in aged parents. It is simply to say that not all parents have an equal claim to honor. The law is deliberately phrased in a somewhat vague manner. The poor son will not be able to honor parents in the same way as the wealthy man. Bitter, nasty, pagan parents do not have the right to the same kind of privileges as saintly, Godly parents do. Any case that comes before the judges, therefore, will have to be assessed in terms of its situation. The mother who claims that her son has "pushed me off into an old folks' home" will not necessarily get to see him die if he can prove that she was intolerable to live with, and that in order properly to cleave to his wife he had to put his mother at a distance.

There is no sound reason for rejecting this law. God wrote it for His commonwealth, and man can hardly hope to improve on it. Jesus repeated it, as we have seen, and applied it to the people of His day. Unless we believe we are smarter than God, we should do well to take it seriously.

One closing remark on the order of these last three laws. At first glance, it looks as if the two laws against attacking parents should be together, instead of having the law against kidnapping sandwiched between. The logic of the overall passage, however, is to move from the greater to the lesser, in three interlaced ways:

1. Criminals and victims (people to people; animals to people;

---

21. "If any man come to me, and hate not his father, and mother, and wife, and children, and brethren, and sisters, yea, and his own life also, he cannot be my disciple" (Luke 14:26). Our covenant with Christ must take precedent over all human covenants, if there is a conflict.

animals to animals).

2. Degrees of punishment (death penalties first, lesser penalties later).

3. Degrees of apparent violence (striking to kill, striking to wound). The third category explains the order of the three laws in Exodus 21:15-17. Kidnapping is a physical assault, so it comes after striking parents; while repudiating parents is a more general kind of assault, so it comes after kidnapping.

Assault

18-19. And when men quarrel and one strikes the other with a stone or with his fist, and he does not die but is laid up in his bed, (19.) then if he rises up again and walks abroad with his staff, he that struck him shall be clear; he shall only give the loss of his time, and shall have him thoroughly healed.

20-21. When a man strikes his slave, male or female, with a rod, and he [or she] dies under his hand, he shall be punished; (21.) But if he [or she] survives a day or two, he shall not be punished, for he is his money.

22. And when men strive together, and they hit a pregnant woman so that her children [offspring] go out, and there is no harm, he most certainly shall be fined according as the husband of the woman shall lay on him, and he shall give as the judges determine.

23-25. And where there is harm, then you shall give life for life, eye for eye, tooth for tooth, hand for hand, foot for foot, burn for burn, wound for wound, stripe for stripe.

26-27. And when a man strikes an eye of his male slave or an eye of his female slave and destroys it, he shall let him [or her] go free for his [or her] eye. (27.) And if a tooth of his male slave or a tooth of his female slave he knocks out, he shall let him [or her] go free for his [or her] tooth.

There are two basic cases here. The first concerns what happens if two men fight, and one or both is wounded but does not die. Then a variant of the law is given pertaining to slaves. The second concerns harm to a third party, the punishment for inflicting harm, and again a variant concerning slaves.

I. *Fighting or Dueling*

The Bible does not permit the use of force to resolve disputes, except where force is lawfully exercised by God's ordained officer, the civil magistrate. To put it another way, the Bible requires men to submit to arbitration, and categorically prohibits them from taking their own personal vengeance (Rom. 12:17-13:7).

The verb used here for "quarrel," *ribh,* has to do mainly with verbal and legal disputes, though it can also refer to physical struggling (Dt. 33:7; Jud. 11:25). The basic picture is of two men who have a dispute. The dispute escalates from the stage of verbal violence to the stage of physical violence. The individual who initiates the escalation to physical violence, injuring his opponent, is the guilty party.

The case here is, as always, exemplary and not exhaustive. Perhaps the escalation to fierce physical violence was relatively gradual, and both men are to blame. Perhaps each injured the other. In such a case each is guilty. Alternatively, perhaps when the first party attacked the second, there was no one to intervene, and the second party was forced to harm the first party in self defense. This would also have to be taken into account. Bystanders could testify as to whether or not the injury was inflicted in self defense.

If death results from the fight, the crime is murder. There is no excuse for a "crime of passion," or any similar rationalizations. If death does not result from the fight, then each man must pay for the medical attention required to dress the wounds of the other, and each man must pay for the other's loss of time on the job. Payment for loss of time probably means that the man's employer should be paid for his loss of help during the recuperative period, and probably that the wounded man should as well be provided the pay he was accustomed to receiving, as if he were still working.[22] The law here is sufficiently vague to cover several possible

---

22. Possibly the phrase "pay for his loss of time" could be rendered "but he shall provide someone in his place," meaning that the employer was to be compensated. The evidence for this is not terribly convincing. See F. Charles Fensham, "Exodus XXI:18-19 in the Light of Hittite Law 10," *Vetus Testamentum* 10 (1960): 333-335.

cases. *First,* clearly dueling is excluded. Dueling is part of the system of honor and pride of paganism, and has no place whatsoever in Christian culture. It is pure barbarism. Dueling to death is murder.[23] Also, in the light of these provisions, the infliction of injury as a means of entertaining a crowd, as in gladiatorial combats or modern prizefighting, must be seen as perverted. God does not give men strength so that they can use it to beat each other up, defacing the very image of God. Historically, Christianity has always worked to reform or eliminate such practices.

Second, in a case of pure assault, the judges would likely rule that the guilty party was responsible to pay medical expenses, pay the man his salary while recuperating, and provide compensation to his employer for the loss of the wounded man's labor.

Third, in a case of street fighting, each man would have to pay the other's medical expenses, and compensation to each other's employers. The judges might rule that each forfeits his salary.

Another application: Children ought not to be allowed to fight either. Children should be taught to bring to their parents any matter of grievance, and the parents should arbitrate. Unfortunately, we live in a barbarous age, and many of us live in neighborhoods in which there are vicious children whose parents will not correct them. Training one's child in self defense in such situations is not wrong, but the child should realize that self defense is always a last resort. (The right of self defense is grounded in the provision of Exodus 22:2.) Any time one child attacks another, the matter should be brought to the attention of both sets of parents, and the offending child dealt with.

A final word on dueling. Under pagan influence, Western civilization has sometimes adopted a notion of "fair fighting." *There is no such thing as a fair fight.* The notion of a fair fight is Satanic and barbarous. If a child or a man finds himself in a situation where an appeal to arbitration is not possible, he should fight with all he

---

23. On dueling, see Robert L. Dabney, *Lectures in Systematic Theology* (Grand Rapids: Zondervan, [1878] 1972), pp. 404-406; and a shorter discussion in Charles Hodge, *Systematic Theology* (various editions, originally published in 1872), III:368.

has. If the neighborhood bully catches your child on the way home from school, and your child cannot escape by fleeing, your child should poke a hole in him with a sharp pencil, or kick him in the groin. If the bully's parents will not restrain him, call the police.

If you or your child has been trained in self defense, of course, you may be able to dispatch your assailant with a minimum of force. Always realize, though, that the man who attacks you, or your wife, has forfeited all his rights to "fair" treatment. Women should be prepared to gouge out the eyes of any man who attacks them.

In summary, the Bible teaches us to avoid all fighting, and to suppress it. Only in the case of a direct threat to one's person or property, when an appeal to arbitration is not possible, is fighting permissible (Ex. 22:2). The woman attacked in the city is expected to fight back and cry out (Dt. 22:24).

Finally, this law implies that flight is an alternative preferable to fighting. If two men strive, and there are no witnesses, it would be impossible to prove self defense if one man harmed another. If a man attacks me, and I harm or kill him in self defense, I may be charged with murder, for there are no witnesses. My best recourse, then, is flight, if it is at all possible. This may not square with modern notions of honor, but Christians are concerned first with God's law and honor, not with their own.

This law concerns fighting and its consequences. If a man dies, the killer is treated as a murderer. What is not in view here is attempted murder, a situation where it is clear that one party was trying to kill the other, but was stopped from it. Biblical law treats an attempted crime the same as if the crime had actually been committed. This is discussed in my monograph, *Sabbath Breaking and the Death Penalty* (Geneva Ministries, forthcoming).

II. *Slave Beating*

We have discussed this law in Chapter 5. The placement of the law here is to modify the previous law. Obviously, the master will have his slave healed, if he lives. Also, the law makes it clear that murder is murder, even in the case of the slave, for the slave also is the image of God (Gen. 9:5, 6). The only other situation is one in which the slave is severely beaten, but does not die immediately. In such a case, the law assumes that the master did not intend murder. The master does have the right to beat the slave, even severely. If the slave dies, the master has lost the value of his labor, and that is considered punishment enough.

III. *Bystanders*

There are two general interpretations of verse 22. The first is that two men are fighting,[24] and a pregnant woman happens to come too close and is accidentally harmed. The second is that two men are fighting and the wife of one of them intervenes, and her husband's opponent deliberately strikes at his enemy's unborn child by kicking or hitting the stomach of the pregnant woman.

It is difficult to determine which interpretation is correct. The verb for "hit" is different from the verb used for "strike" throughout the passage elsewhere.[25] While the two words are largely synonymous, it may be that a different word is used to indicate that a non-deliberate, accidental striking is involved. Indeed, the word "hit" can be used for accidental striking, as in striking one's foot against a stone. At the same time, whenever it is used in an accidental sense, it is used with a preposition ("hit against," "strike upon"); wherever it is used with a direct object ("hit someone or something"), a deliberate act is in view (unless this verse is the sole exception.)[26] On the other hand, the verb is plural: "and *they* hit"; we do not read, "and one of them hits." This tends to work against the notion that one man is deliberately attacking the woman or fetus — the plural seems to indicate that the woman is hit somehow as a result or byproduct of both men's fighting; that is, they may both be to blame. It is only the man who actually struck the woman, however, who is guilty before the court, as the singular

---

24. "The Niphal form of [the verb] emphasizes blows were traded back and forth." Kaiser, *Toward Old Testament Ethics*, p. 102.

25. "Strike" is *nakhah*, "hit" is *nagaph*. The only other place in the entire law where *nagaph* is used is Ex. 21:35, and there the ox is definitely attacking another ox.

26. The champion of this position is David Daube, *Studies in Biblical Law* (Cambridge: University Press, 1947), pp. 107f., 148, fn. 12.

verbs in v. 22b indicate.

We have to say that there is a certain vagueness in this law, which enables it to cover several similar but slightly different situations. The particular case indicates that a bystander has been hit, but "there is no harm." We are not told explicitly whether the harm is to the woman or to her child, or to both, but there can be no question that the harm could be either to the woman or to her child, since both are referred to immediately prior to the phrase. Moreover, the Bible always considers the child in the womb to be fully alive, a person in the fullest sense, so that if the child came out dead or damaged, that would constitute "harm" to the child. The situation as described in v. 22 is that the woman is late in pregnancy, and as a result of the blow is caused to deliver the child prematurely, but neither the child nor the mother is harmed by the blow.

In this case, the husband of the woman is permitted to sue his wife's assailant in court. The judges oversee the suit to make sure that the payment required is not excessive.

Verse 23 goes on to say that if there is harm either to mother or to child, then the assailant must pay a more severe penalty. "Life for life" means that if either the mother or the child is killed, the assailant must also be put to death. The position of this law, after the mandatory death penalties of vv. 12-20, but before the provision for composition in vv. 29-30, indicates that compensation is not permissible in this case.

If we assume that the woman is a mere bystander, and is only accidentally struck, then the penalty is strict indeed. Two men preparing to fight in the street would have to keep in mind that if they accidentally hurt a bystander, they will have to pay, even with the death penalty. This constitutes a very strong incentive to resort to arbitration rather than to violence.

If we assume that the woman has been deliberately struck, then the death penalty is simply a specification of the death penalty for murder. One man has sought to strike at his enemy by killing his enemy's unborn child. This, of course, is deliberate murder.

Certain applications follow from this case. *First,* if we take the approach that the killing or maiming is accidental, then this law indicates that a man is responsible for his actions when he deliberately places himself in a situation where he loses control of himself. The drunk driver, by analogy, is guilty of murder if he runs over someone, because he is responsible for getting drunk and driving under those conditions. There is no excuse for street fighting (except immediate self defense, and flight is preferable), and there is no excuse for drunk driving; anyone harmed as a result is considered to have been deliberately harmed.

Second, in either situation, the unborn child is considered a person, and is avenged. The Biblical penalty for abortion is mandatory death. The "physician" responsible for performing the abortion is a murderer and should be put to death. Since at least two people are always involved in it, *abortion is conspiracy to commit murder,* and the "mother," the "physician," the anesthetist, the nurses, and the father or boy friend or husband who pay for it, all are involved in the conspiracy, and all should be put to death for conspiracy to commit murder. Until the anti-abortion movement in America is willing to return to God's law and advocate the death penalty for abortion, God will not bless the movement. God does not bless those who despise His law, just because pictures of salted infants make them sick.[27]

In summary, it is difficult to determine whether this case law deals with an accidental or a deliberate assault. The vagueness of the wording indicates that we should allow it to speak to either situation.

IV. *Retaliation and Recompense (The Law of Equivalence)*

The placement of the so-called *lex talionis* (law of retaliation) here indicates that the section on murders and assaults is at an end. This is the summary of all the previous laws in this section

---

27. It is interesting, though, that the injection of a salt solution into the uterus, which burns the unborn child to death, is very similar to the eternal punishment described by God as a permanent salted sacrifice that burns forever: "salted with fire" and "salted with salt" (Mk. 9:49). The punishment for abortionists meets the crime.

(Ex. 21:12ff.), and so has reference not only to the case set out in v. 22, but to all preceding cases of assault.

The major question is whether compensation is permitted in this law, whether "eye for eye" means that the eye of the offender must be gouged out, or whether he might pay a sum of money and redeem his eye. Some modern scholars tend to believe that a literal, physical enforcement is in view in this law, because it is "early" and "primitive." This is an evolutionary argument, and is incompatible with the Christian faith that God Himself gave these laws.

More to the point is the fact that it is not until vv. 29-30 that commensurate compensation is mentioned, in the case of a notorious bull's goring someone to death. Also, to the English reader, Leviticus 24:19-20 certainly seems to demand a literal enforcement: "And if a man gives a blemish to his neighbor, just as he has done, so it shall be done to him: fracture for fracture, eye for eye, tooth for tooth; just as he has given a blemish to a man, so it shall be given to him." The strongest case for taking the law literally is put by W. F. Albright: "This principle may seem and is often said to be extraordinarily primitive. But it is actually not in the least primitive. Whereas the beginnings of *lex talionis* are found before Israel, the principle was now extended by analogy until it dominated all punishment of injuries or homicides. In ordinary Ancient Oriental jurisprudence, men who belonged to the higher social categories or who were wealthy simply paid fines, otherwise escaping punishment. . . . So the *lex talionis* [is] . . . the principle of equal justice for all!"[28]

At the same time, Numbers 35:31 specifies that no ransom is to be taken for a murder, implying that commensurate compensation might be possible in other cases of lesser harm. It is also noteworthy that the verb "to give" is used in Exodus 21:23. In the surrounding verses, "to give" always is used in connection with money (vv. 19, 22, 30, 32), and in the sense of compensation (v. 30). This con-

---

28. W. F. Albright, *History, Archaeology, and Christian Humanism* (New York, 1964), p. 74, as cited in Paul, *op. cit.,* p. 77. A case of literal infliction is seen in Judges 1:6, 7.

trasts with the verb "to make whole," which is used everywhere else in the Ordinances for paying back, and always in Scripture means to restore in kind, or in money exactly equivalent.[29]

Perhaps equally important is a point made by D. Daube concerning criminal law (the principle of punishment) and civil law (the principle of commensurate compensation): "The difference between the primitive [earlier] stage and the present lies chiefly in this, that the two, criminal law and civil law, were not always so strictly distinguished as they are nowadays. Any given case was considered from both the criminal law standpoint and the civil law standpoint at the same time, or better, from one standpoint that embraced everything."[30] Daube points out that the preposition (*taḥath*) meaning "in the place of" is used both in cases of retaliation and in cases of compensation and restitution. In v. 23 we read "life in the place of life," and we know that no compensation was permitted. This is criminal law, according to modern classifications. In 22:1, we read, "he shall pay five oxen in the place of an ox," clearly a case of compensation or restitution. This is civil law according to modern classifications.[31]

What this means is that vv. 23-25 are not a lex talionis, a law of retaliation, but something more fundamental. Literal retaliation is, thus, not required by the formula, but compensation or composition can equally fit its requirements. The formula, then, applies not only to the laws preceding it, but also to those following it, in that it applies to theft as well as to assault.

Why, then, is it included at this point? In part, as we have noted earlier, because this is the conclusion of the section on assaults on men by men. In part, also, because of the need to make clear that the *principle of equivalence* applies also to third parties, involuntarily drawn into a clash. There are no mitigating circumstances involved when two fighting men harm a bystander;

29. "Give" is *nathan;* "make whole" is *shalam.* A full discussion is found in Daube, *Biblical Law,* pp. 133ff. *Shalam* is used for precise restorations; *nathan* for compositions, amounts set by the court as a result of lawsuits.

30. Daube, p. 103.

31. *Ibid.,* p. 104.

the punishment in such a case is the same as in any other.

Thus, since this *law of equivalence* applies both to the preceding and the following verses, the fact that compensation is not explicitly set out until vv. 29-30 does not rule out compensation in the case of wounds and blemishes. Also, while Leviticus 24:19-20 emphasizes equivalence of punishment, there is no compelling reason to assume that physical blemishing is the only way the law could have been obeyed.

Albright's point seems sound at first glance: Paying back in physical terms in all cases puts the rich and the poor on equal footing. But does it? Suppose a singer got angry at a pianist and stabbed him through the hand. Is it equivalent punishment to stab the singer through the hand? Hardly. The equivalent punishment would be to damage the singer's vocal chords, if the wound to the pianist's hand were such as to prevent his playing recitals permanently. Thus, to be fair, "hand for hand" would have to be modified conceptually to "means of livelihood for means of livelihood."

This might be seen as substantiated by Deuteronomy 25:11-12, "If men, a man and his countryman, are struggling together, and the wife of one comes near to deliver her husband from the hand of the one who is striking him, and puts out her hand and seizes his private parts, then you shall cut off her palm; your eye shall not pity." Cutting off the palm seems to mean not chopping off the hand at the wrist, but splitting the hand through the middle fingers, so as to incapacitate the hand. Since the woman has no private parts to be crushed, "eye for eye" means that her hand is to be ruined instead. Notice, by the way, that this law seems to be the obverse of Exodus 21:22. There the woman and child are protected from the (possibly) deliberate attack by the husband's enemy. Here the man is protected from a deliberate attack by his opponent's wife. All forms of assault are punished in Scripture.

It is noteworthy, however, that an almost exact correspondence of physical mutilation is prescribed in Deuteronomy 25:11-12. The genitals were not cut off, so the hand is not. The genitals are incapacitated; so is the hand, so that it can never grasp again. All the same, equivalent compensation is not ruled out.

The idea that monetary compensation would favor the rich is a logical error. The same standard of punishment — commensurate compensation — would apply to all; thus there is no favoring of any class in society. Both rich and poor resent having their money taken away. The fact that the poor assailant might have to endure slavery in order to pay his fine, which the rich would not, is a reflection of their previous socio-economic condition. *A man's socio-economic background or condition is irrelevant in considerations of justice, which views all men equally.* If we do not favor the rich, neither may we favor the poor. It is a logical error to assume, then, that such a system of justice would favor one group or another. The perceived advantage of the wealthy is due to his previous circumstances, not to the system of justice.

All the same, there is no reason to believe that society maintained then, or should maintain now, a schedule of monetary equivalences for bodily parts, so that a hand is worth so much, and an eye so much, etc. The payment is "as the judges determine," and it is quite likely that the rich man would be made to pay a larger amount than would a poor man. I argue in Appendix G that the attack of a rich man upon a poor one requires four-fold restitution as punishment.

This raises the question of whether a man might demand a physical equivalence in lieu of monetary payment. In light of the fact that physical equivalence was justly effected in Judges 1:6, 7, we cannot say that there is anything wrong with it. Doubtless a blinded man might demand that his assailant be blinded, and reject a monetary composition; though ordinarily his friends would probably prevail on him to take the money.[32]

Thus, in the actual case described in Exodus 21:22-25, a man might take a monetary composition if his infant son's foot was damaged. The monetary composition would doubtless be far greater than the fine for inconvenience assessed in the case where

---

32. An elaborate discussion of the ins and outs of this law is found in Gary North, *The Dominion Covenant: Exodus* (Tyler, TX: Institute for Christian Economics, 1985).

there was no physical harm at all (v. 22).

The sequence of equivalences breaks down into three parts. First, as we have seen, no composition is possible in the case of a man's taking the life of another. "Life for life," then, stands apart.

Next comes an equivalence in permanent bodily damage: "eye for eye, tooth for tooth, hand for hand, foot for foot."[33] Permanent damage to any of these would require equivalence.

Suppose, however, that the hand were wounded, but recovered. The third section deals with wounds that heal, according to the kind of wound: "burn for burn, wound for wound, stripe for stripe." While it is not altogether clear precisely what each of these Hebrew words entails, the overall meaning is clear. A man who horsewhipped another might be horsewhipped himself, or have to pay equivalence. A man who burned down another's house or field might have to suffer the same, or pay a heavy compensation.

The placement of the law of equivalence here also implies that a man who damages another's wife or child is *himself* to be punished; equivalence does not mean his wife or child is to be punished. We shall take this up at length when we get to verse 31.

Unlike the other laws, the law of equivalences is phrased "you shall give," not "he shall give." This indicates that *the principle is broad and fundamental,* and simply invoked at this point. It also implies the involvement of the community, in the persons of the judges. The particular cases read "if a man does such and such, then he shall give such and such." Here, however, the phrasing indicates the application of a general rule: "If a man does such and such, then you shall use the rule: eye for eye, etc." In other words, the case of the bystander is no different from any other case of assault. The same general rule applies to it as to every other case of assault.

---

33. Daube points out that Lev. 24:20, "fracture for fracture," most likely refers back to Lev. 21:19, the only other place "fracture" is used in Leviticus. There the priest is said to be disqualified if he has a fractured foot or a fractured hand. Thus, "fracture for fracture" in Leviticus is likely equivalent to "hand for hand, foot for foot" in Exodus. Daube, *op. cit.*, p. 113.

V. *Equivalence for Slaves*

The master has the right to beat his slave, but not to injure him. As we have seen, if he kills his slave outright, he must himself be put to death for murder. If he beats him, and he dies a few days later, the master goes unpunished; or rather, the loss of the value of the slave is his punishment. Here, now, is the intermediate case: The master beats the slave severely, permanently damaging him, and the slave recovers. In such a case, equivalence does not require an equal beating for the master, for such would be absurd; rather, the slave is freed in recompense. The master is made to pay composition, a fine consisting of the value of the slave, in letting the slave go free.

The two cases, concerning eye and tooth, start off the series which is found in the immediately preceding verses. We may assume that permanent damage to hand or to foot would also carry with it freedom for the slave. In the cases of bruises or stripes, however, the master has the right to inflict such on a recalcitrant slave. "Burn for burn" is something of a conceptual problem, but doubtless does not refer primarily to the burning of a person's skin, but of a man's house or land. Since slaves would ordinarily not own property, it would not pertain to them, though it would where they did.

The kinds of protections for slaves we find in these laws are unique to Scripture in the Ancient Near East.

The Goring Ox

Laws concerning dangerous property, which can cause harm to human life, are encapsulated here. The hardest case is given, that of an animal's killing a human being. The principles involved in cases of non-fatal assault have to be mixed with these laws to determine just penalties in cases of an animal which only harms a human being. The five cases are found in Exodus 21:28-32.

> 28. And when an ox gores a man or a woman, then the ox most certainly shall be stoned to death, and its flesh shall not be eaten, and the owner of the ox is clear.

29. And if the ox has been apt to gore in the past [literally, "from the third day"], and its owner has been warned and has not kept it in, and it kills a man or a woman, the ox shall be stoned and its owner may be put to death.[34]

30. If a ransom [propitiatory covering] is laid on him, then he shall give for the ransom [buying back, deliverance] of his life whatever is laid upon him.

31. If it gores a son or gores a daughter, according to this same rule shall he be dealt with.

32. If the ox gores a male slave or a female slave, thirty shekels of silver shall be given to his master, and the ox shall be stoned.

I. *The Rebellious Beast*

All unclean animals *resemble the serpent* in three ways. They eat "dirt" (rotting carrion, manure, garbage). They move in contact with "dirt" (crawling on their bellies, fleshy pads of their feet in touch with the ground, no scales to keep their skin from contact with their watery environment). They revolt against human dominion, killing men or other beasts. Under the symbolism of the Old Covenant, such Satanic beasts represent the Satanic nations (Lev. 20:22-26), for animals are "images" of men.[35] To eat Satanic animals, under the Old Covenant, was to "eat" the Satanic lifestyle, to "eat" death and rebellion.[36]

The ox is a clean animal. The heifer and the pre-pubescent bullock have sweet temperaments, and can be sacrificed for human sin, for their gentle, non-violent dispositions reflect the character of Jesus Christ. When the bullock enters puberty, however, his temperament changes for the worse. He becomes ornery, testy, and sometimes downright vicious. Many a man has lost his life to a goring bull. *The change from bullock to bull can be seen as analogous to the fall of man*, at least potentially. If the ox rises up and gores a man, he becomes unclean, fallen.

---

34. He must be put to death unless he pays the ransom; so, he may be put to death, or he may not be.

35. Cf. Prov. 6:6; 26:11; 30:15, 19, 24-31; Dan. 5:21; Ex. 13:2, 13.

36. On this subject in general, see James B. Jordan, *Food and Faith* (forthcoming).

Man was created to have dominion over the animals. When animals rise up against man, they are guilty of rebellion, insurrection against the very image of God Himself: "And surely I will require your lifeblood; from every beast I will require it. And from man, from every man's brother I will require the life of man. Whoever sheds man's blood, by man his blood shall be shed, for in the image of God He made man" (Gen. 9:5, 6). Shalom Paul has pointed out, referring to work done by J. J. Finkelstein, "The ox's goring a human being to death is an 'insurrection against the established order' since 'man was ordained to rule over earthly life.' It is thus equated with other insurrections against religious order such as the cursing of YHWH, the rebellion against one's parents, idolatry, etc."[37]

The *unnaturalness* of an animal's killing a man is only highlighted in the case of a clean, domesticated beast like the ox. Such an ox, by its actions, becomes unclean, so that its flesh may not be eaten.

The owner of the ox is not assumed to be at fault, since the ox is a clean animal, and this animal had no history of violence. The owner suffers the loss of the work of the animal, of its meat, and probably of its hide as well, since stoning doubtless did not do the hide any good.

The fact that the animal is stoned indicates that the purpose of the law is not simply to rid the earth of a dangerous beast. Stoning in the Bible is the normal means of capital punishment for men. Its application to the animal here shows that animals are to be held accountable to some degree for their actions. It is also a visual sign of what happens when a clean covenant man rebels against authority and kills men. Stoning is usually understood to represent the judgment of God, since the Christ is "the rock" and the "stone" which threatens to fall upon men and destroy them (Matt. 21:44).[38] In line with this, the community of believers is

---

37. Paul, *op. cit.,* p. 79

38. Treating animals like people to this degree seems strange to modern men. Modern science *assumes* that animals are simply machines, programmed by genetics, functioning solely in terms of something called "instinct." Some say the

often likened to stones, used for building God's Spiritual Temple,
and so forth. In stoning, each member of the community hurls a
rock representing himself and his affirmation of God's judgment.
The principle of stoning, then, affirms that the judgment is God's;
the application of stoning affirms the community's assent and participation in that judgment.

What if the ox gores, but does not kill? Again, if the animal
had no history of violence, the owner would not be responsible. If,
however, the ox ever gored again, then the owner would be
responsible next time.

II. *The Incorrigible Beast*

The ox with a history of goring is in the category of a violent or
unclean beast. If he gores a man or a woman to death, the owner
is liable, even to the death penalty. He should have kept the
animal under closer supervision. This will, by extension, be true
of any violent animal.

What if the ox gores, but does not kill? In that case, the law of
v. 19 would apply. The owner would have to pay the medical expenses of the injured man, and his loss of time.

How shall we apply these laws? I should like to suggest that
our laws should distinguish between ordinarily vicious animals
("unclean") and ordinarily tame or domestic animals. Certain
kinds of dogs, in certain social settings, can be considered potentially vicious. The local laws (specifications of God's law) might
read in such cases that the owner is responsible for any harm done
by the animal, regardless of the personal history of the animal.
People who keep wildcats or other dangerous animals as pets
would be under this same law. On the other hand, small dogs and

---

same for human beings, though most want to maintain that people are capable of
"personal" action. This way of cutting the pie is not grounded in anything other
than prejudice and opinion. In Scripture, all creation images the Creator, but
man is the special and particular image of God. To a greater or lesser degree
animals image God by having some intelligence, emotion, and will, and animals
are directly accountable for their actions. Since man is responsible to shepherd
the whole creation, however, the owner of an animal is also accountable for the
actions of the beast.

cats and rabbits could be covered by another law which states that
the owner is not liable if the animal has no personal history of
violence.

This Biblical law implies that leash laws are entirely proper.
Towns with leash laws have stated a presumption that animals are
a nuisance. In such places, if a dog gets loose and tears up a flower
bed, the owner should be held accountable; and if the dog kills a
child, the owner should be liable to death.

III. *Ransom*

Because the man is not directly responsible for causing the
death of his ox's victim, he is given the possibility of ransoming his
life. The text does not indicate that he has the *right* to ransom himself; indeed, the phrase "if a ransom is laid upon him" indicates
that it is up to the family of the slain man whether they want the
owner killed or not. Nor are we told, as in v. 22, that "he shall pay
as the judges shall determine." Possibly that is understood in the
later verse, but more likely the man is obliged to pay a ransom
consisting of whatever the slain man's family cares to demand.
While this might not seem "fair," it surely is a strong incentive to
keep one's ox or one's nasty dog penned up! Moreover, it makes
sense, since the alternative is death, and thus no amount of
money would be too great for a man to spare his own life. So, the
man who does not keep his vicious animal restrained faces the
possibility of death or total impoverishment and self-sale into
slavery.

IV. *Appropriate Punishment*

Under pagan law, if a man killed your son, the proper punishment would be for the state to kill, not the man himself, but his
son.[39] While Israel remained in Canaan, before being isolated
from evil influence in Goshen (see Chapter 2), Reuben had come

---

39. For instance, "According to the Code of Hammurabi, if a builder works
badly and the house collapses and kills its owner, the builder is to be put to death:
but if the owner's son is killed, it is the builder's son who is to be put to death."
Daube, *op. cit.,* p. 16.

under the influence of this pagan conception of justice: "Then Reuben spoke to his father, saying, 'You may put my two sons to death if I do not bring him [your son] back to you . . .' " (Gen. 42:37). The Bible abominates this cruel legislation. "Fathers shall not be put to death for sons, nor shall sons be put to death for fathers; everyone shall be put to death for his own sin" (Dt. 24:16).

The same thing is taught here. If the ox gores a son or daughter, the owner is either liable or not liable, according to the same rules already considered. "According to this rule shall *he* be dealt with." It does not say anything about putting the owner's son or daughter to death, as the pagan codes would have said at this point.

The concept found here and in Deuteronomy 24:16 is extremely important for the Christian view of the state and of the family. There are occasions in Scripture when whole groups of people are guilty of complicity in the crime committed by the father and thus all die;[40] but where there is no *complicity*, there is no guilt, and punishment is inappropriate. While the family is very important in Christian civilization, it is not so absolute a structure that the state cannot deal with one member of it alone. The family does not die just because the head has committed a crime, nor does the head have the right to transfer guilt to some other family member. Children are not owned by their fathers, so that the loss of my child must be paid for by the loss of yours; rather, children are persons in their own right, and if you kill mine, it is you who must die.

---

40. For instance, Achan's whole family perished with him, because they doubtless knew of his crime and helped him conceal it (Joshua 7). When Korah, Dathan, and Abiram rebelled against God, the family of Korah distanced themselves from Korah, and did not die with him (Numbers 26:10, 11). When David numbered the people, he sinfully did not collect the atonement money, so that the blood of war was not covered, and the Angel of Death attacked the people; yet the people were involved in the sin, for they had not paid the required money (2 Sam. 24; cf. Ex. 30:11-16). For an extensive treatment of 2 Sam. 21:1-14, see Greg L. Bahnsen, "Law and Atonement in the Execution of Saul's Seven Sons," *Journal of Christian Reconstruction* II:2 (Winter 1975):101-109. Bahnsen points out that 2 Sam. 21:1 states that Saul's house was involved in the crime, not just Saul himself.

This might seem to cause a theological problem with the exodus itself. Did not God threaten to kill Pharaoh's son if Pharaoh did not let God's son go (Ex. 4:23)? In reply we may point out two things. First, not all matters of justice have been committed into the hands of men. God brings punishment upon whole nations because of the sins of the fathers, and little children suffer. God has not delegated this right to human government. Human government deals with individual judgment, but God alone takes care of the judgment of whole cultures. Second, God's judgment against children is based on the fact that they have the sin of Adam, and deserve to die. God's judgment of Egypt at the exodus was not simply designed to illustrate principles of human legal justice, but to display His wrath against sin (Ex. 9:16). All children deserve to die; it is of the mercy of God that He spares most.

V. *The Price of a Slave*

If a notorious ox, or other vicious animal, kills another man's slave, the owner of the animal is not liable to death, but simply pays for the slave. A study of Leviticus 27:1-7 shows that persons were valued, depending on strength (sex and age) at between three and fifty shekels of silver. Thirty, then, is a good average; and in the case of the slave killed by the ox, thirty shekels of silver was mandatory.

This really puts the slave in the same category as the animal in v. 36. If a notorious ox kills another ox, the owner simply has to make it good. But, that is part of the risk of slavery; you might be gored by an ox. It is best to avoid slavery if you can.

The *comparison of the slave to the animal* is interesting. It is the reverse of the comparison of animals to men. The slave is subject to other men in a way analogous to the subjection animals are supposed to have. As we have seen (Chapter 5), the Bible wants the slave to save his money and buy his freedom, or become adopted into the master's household as a son-servant.

As we have seen, our Lord Jesus Christ was born into the world as a homeborn slave-son, for His incarnation was His ear's circumcision. On the cross, he was made sin for us, and thus came under condemnation of death. He became an abject slave, that we might be elevated into the status of adopted slave-sons. He was killed by the wild beasts, the lions of paganism, and the apostate unclean goring bulls of Israel: "Many bulls have surrounded Me; strong ones from Bashan have encircled me. They open wide their mouth at me, as a ravening and a roaring lion. . . . Save Me from the lion's mouth; and from the horns of the wild oxen Thou dost answer Me" (Ps. 22:12, 13, 21). Thus, the price given for Christ's death was the price of the gored slave, thirty pieces of silver (Matt. 26:15). At His resurrection, however, our Lord overcame the bulls and trampled on the silver for which He was sold: "Rebuke the beasts of the reeds, the herd of bulls with the calves of the peoples, trampling under foot the pieces of silver; He has scattered the people who delight in war" (Ps. 68:30). Thus, Judas found no joy in his silver, and it was used to buy a burying field for dead strangers, pagans destroyed by the wrath of God (Matt. 27:2-10).

Hazardous Property

The last three laws in this section (Ex. 21:12-36) form a bridge into the laws concerning property. We have placed the actual division at 22:1, for there the conception of theft is set out initially, while in these verses we are still in the realm of violence and harm. The three hazardous property cases are in 21:33-36.

33-34. And when a man leaves open a pit [or well, or cistern], or when a man digs a pit and does not cover it, and an ox or an ass falls there; (34) the owner of the pit shall make [the situation] whole: He shall give money to its owner, and the dead beast shall be his.

35. And when one man's ox hurts another man's ox so that it dies, then they shall sell the live ox and divide the price of it, and also they shall divide the dead beast.

36. Or if it is known that the ox has been apt to gore in the past [literally, "from yesterday and the third day"], and its owner has not kept it in, then he shall most certainly make [the situation] whole, ox for ox, and the dead beast shall be his.

I. *The Open Pit*

The word for "pit" can also mean well, cistern, or any other cavity dug into the earth. Such were not to be left uncovered. If a man leaves his well or pit open, and an animal falls into it, he is liable. Double restitution is not owed, as in the case of theft (Ex. 22:4), but simple compensation. He is to make the situation whole or right by paying for the animal, and the carcass (valuable for the hide, but not for the meat since it died by itself, Dt. 14:21) becomes his.

By extension, if a human being fell into the well and died, the owner would be liable to the death penalty, as in the case of the notorious ox (21:29). Since deliberate murder was not his intention, the man would be allowed to ransom his life if the family of the dead person were amenable.

In the Bible, a man's home is his castle, and family property is most important, but not absolutely so. All property is ultimately God's, and men hold it in stewardship from Him. He has chosen to allot the land by families, rather than to communes or to states, but His law still governs the family property. Thus, the man who says he is not liable for hazards on his property is assuming too much. He is playing God, assuming that his right and power over his property are absolute.

Not so. If you have a balcony, you had better put a rail on it, or you are liable if someone falls off (Dt. 22:8). If you have a pile of broken glass, make sure children cannot get to it. If you have a swimming pool, make sure access is limited. If you have an old refrigerator in your yard, make sure the door is broken so that children cannot shut themselves in it.

Liability is not absolute either, however. Any social system must define the limits of liability, but there is always to be some liability. If your swimming pool is fenced and you have a sign up saying that your permission is required before anyone may enter the pool, chances are you have fulfilled the law in your county or township, and you are no longer liable.[41]

II. *Ox Gores Ox*

As in verse 28, the owner is not liable if his ox has not been notorious in the past. If the ox gores another ox, the value of each is divided between the two owners, the dead ox for its hide, and the live ox for full value.

If, however, the ox was notorious, then the owner is liable. He has to pay the full value of the dead animal to its owner, but gets to keep the hide for himself.

Now, suppose the law in your town reads that dogs are to be penned or leashed. Your dog escapes and kills the neighbor's prize winning cat. What is to be done? Well, in this case, your dog is assumed to be notorious because the law said to keep it restrained. You, therefore, owe the neighbor for the full value of the cat, whatever your neighbor might have gotten on the open market if he had sold the cat alive.

Suppose, however, that there is no ordinance requiring dogs to be penned or leashed. In that case, your dog is not assumed to be notorious unless it has a personal history of viciousness. In that case, however, you do not get off scot free, because you lose your dog. The dog must be sold, if it can be, and the money divided with the neighbor whose cat was killed. Thus, you still have some incentive to act responsibly, even if your dog or ox is not notorious.

---

41. To say that liability for hazardous property must be limited to some degree is not to grant approval to the modern limited liability corporation. The merits of limiting liability must be considered on a case by case basis. See Rushdoony, *Institutes of Biblical Law*, pp. 664ff., for a critique of the limited liability corporation. For another viewpoint, see Gary North, *I.C.E. Position Paper #1* "Why Churches Should not Incorporate." (Institute for Christian Economics, P.O. Box 8000, Tyler, TX 75711.)

7

PROPERTY (EXODUS 22:1-15)

The laws in this section have to do with the protection of property. In contrast to the laws of the nations around Israel, theft is never punished by death in Scripture, as Nehama Leibowitz points out: "The Hammurabi code imposes penalties on theft that vary with the status of the victim, depending on whether the ox was stolen from the king, temple, a man of middle station, a slave, etc. The sliding scale of penalties ranged from death at one end to tenfold at the other with thirtyfold in the middle for good measure. If the thief could not pay the penalty it was death. Several scholars have pointed out that one of the crucial differences between the Torah and the Babylonian codex is the fact that the former makes no distinction between rich and poor, king or priest. It goes without saying that the death penalty is only invoked for the kidnapper."[1]

On the other hand, the Biblical view of property ties it directly to man's fundamental calling under the Old Covenant to take dominion over the earth. As T. Robert Ingram has pointed out, "the mysterious power of ownership of property" is exactly "what dominion is. The power to own anything is peculiar to man; to own anything is to have . . . control over it. . . . There is no such thing as a distinction between 'private' and 'public' property since no one but an individual or a corporate body of individuals can own anything. It is a human power; it is the crown of man's cre-

---

1. Nehama Leibowitz, *Studies in Shemot* (Jerusalem: The World Zionist Organization, 1976), p. 361f. Cf. also Shalom Paul, *Studies in the Book of the Covenant*, p. 86.

ated glory; it is the image of God who is Christ under whose feet
are all things in heaven and on earth."[2]

The Importance of Property

Man was created to exercise dominion. In Genesis 1 we see
God naming the day, the night, the heavens, the earth, and the
sea (vv. 5, 8, 10). After that, God does not name anything. In
Genesis 2, God teaches man to name things (v. 19f.). Not only
does the man name the animals, but the husband names the
woman, giving her both her generic name (2:23) and her personal
name (3:20). The woman names the children (4:1), unless the
father overrules (35:18).

Language is the first stage of dominion. If we do not have a
word for a certain thing, we cannot readily come to grips with it.
Moreover, language is powerful, and knowing someone's name
gives us power over him to some extent. All public relations
courses stress the importance of using a person's name frequently
when talking with him. Salesmen know this. People respond to
their names. Using someone's name gives us influence over him to
some degree. This is why God cannot be named—we cannot
define Him exhaustively, and we cannot have dominion over Him
(Ex. 3:13f., Judges 13:17f.).[3] Magical conjuring is based on the

---

2. T. Robert Ingram, *What's Wrong with Human Rights?* (Houston: St. Thomas
Press, 1978), p. 26. The last sentence is a bit rhetorical, in my opinion. I should
prefer to say that the ownership of property is the first part of the image of God in
man, but that the crown of that image is the exercise of judicial authority. See my
Trees and Thorns, forthcoming. Also, Ingram is not clear on the distinction between "public" and "corporate" property, though we might assume that in corporate property, some group of persons is collectively and distributively accountable; while generally no *person* is held accountable for what happens on public
property.

3. God reveals various names for Himself to us, linked with various covenant
promises, and to that extent he gives us a certain kind of "power" over Him. To
the extent that He has given promises, we can claim those promises and thus
rightly expect God to act in certain ways. The name YHWH or Jesus is God's
covenant name, and sums up His promises. There is, however, a fundamental
difference between the kind of dominion man exercises in naming the animals on
the one hand (which names he invents), and on the other hand man's claiming
God's promises on the basis of His names (which names He gives).

notion that using the spirit's name gives the magician power over him.

Finally, language is the first stage of creativity. God created via the Word. All cultures and societies are shaped by verbal concepts. This is why proclamation of the Gospel is the foundation stone of Christian society. Scientific advance usually comes about when a new understanding or new verbal distinction arises. The Reformation was based on a verbalized distinction between justification and sanctification; Rome had confused the two.

If language is the first stage and prerequisite of dominion, property is the second. Adam was given the garden to beautify and protect (Gen. 2:15). He was to name it, get power over it, and creatively remold it. The eighth commandment protects private property, as do other provisions in the law of God (cf. esp. Lev. 25:13; and see 1 Ki. 21). Every man is to have his own garden. His marriage and his garden (work) are the major axes around which the ellipse of his temporal life is drawn. In pagan aristocratic societies, few men have gardens, and many men are slaves. Moreover, such aristocrats often exercise only minimal dominion, preferring to war or entertain themselves.

Under the influence of Christian concepts of familistic property, the free market has acted to break up such large aristocratic holdings. The industrious poor eventually buy out the lazy rich, and anyone with thrift can eventually obtain his own garden. Dominion is multiplied.

There are two basic sections in the Ordinances concerning property. These two sections can each be further divided:

A. Seven cases concerning the unauthorized invasion of another's property:

    1. Five cases concerning the punishment of a thief who breaks into his neighbor's property (vv. 1-4).

    2. Two cases concerning pollution (vv. 5-6).

B. Eight cases concerning the abuse of the authorized use of another's property:

    3. Five cases concerning bailment or safekeeping (vv. 7-13).

4. Three cases concerning borrowing and rent (vv. 14-15).

As in the Ordinances concerning violence, these laws are generally arranged in order from the most offensive crimes to the least.

Theft

1. When a man steals an ox or a sheep and butchers it or sells it, five oxen must he pay [make whole] for the ox, and four members of the flock for the sheep.

2. If the thief is discovered while he is breaking in, and he is struck, and he dies, there is no bloodguiltiness for him.

3a. If the sun has risen upon him, there is bloodguiltiness for him;

3b. He must make the situation whole; if he has nothing, then he shall be sold for his theft.

4. If the stolen beast is indeed found alive in his possession, whether ox or ass or sheep, he must repay [make whole] double.

I. *Restitution.*

"Making whole" (*shalam*), as we noted in Chapter 6, is used for precise restorations, not for amounts set by the court as a result of lawsuits. Whether four actual sheep had to be given to replace the one butchered, or whether the monetary value of four sheep would satisfy the requirement, is not at issue. In all these cases, the penalty is fixed by law, not arrived at by adjudication.

Restitution is not made to the state, but to the man robbed. The state is not wronged in any of this, and the wrong done to God is satisfied by sacrifice.

Restitution involves both compensation and retribution. The man robbed is compensated for his loss, and then the thief is punished by having to pay double or more. He must forfeit exactly what he sought to gain. There are three degrees of restitution in scripture.

Voluntary Restitution. If a thief comes to his senses and voluntarily seeks to make restitution, he is to add a fifth part to what he stole when he returns it (Lev. 5:14-16; 6:1-5; 22:14; Num. 5:5-8). Thus, if a man steals a sheep, he has an incentive to return it before he is caught; the penalty is less.

Ordinary Penal Restitution. Double restitution is the normal rule. A stolen animal found alive is returned, plus another (or its value, Ex. 22:4). Inanimate stolen property is paid back double, whether the stolen piece is destroyed or not (Ex. 22:7).

Special Penal Restitution. There are three cases of multiple restitution set out in Scripture. First of all, if a man steals an ox, signifying a revolutionary attack upon authority which entails the destruction of property, he must pay five-fold. Second, if a man steals a sheep, signifying the use of power to oppress and rob the poor, he must pay four-fold.[4]

Third, if a man steals *food,* the punishment is seven-fold restitution (Prov. 6:30f.). This is a law of Solomon the king, so it is a valid case law. The poor are taken care of under God's law by the tithe (Dt. 14:28f.), by gleaning laws (Lev. 19:9f.; Ruth 2), by the sabbath year elimination of debt (Dt. 15:1-6), by prohibition of interest on charity loans (Lev. 25:35ff.), and by other provisions (Lev. 25:39ff.). Thus, the poor man who steals is actively despising *grace,* not simply breaking the law. He actively spits in the face of God and His provisions. He is too *proud* to take a handout, even from God Himself! Note, however, that these laws go together. Christians should hardly be working to reinstate seven-fold restitution without also working to reinstate the other poor laws as well![5]

Restitution is clearly seen in the New Testament in the history of Zacchaeus (Lk. 19:8-9); Jesus said that salvation had come to his house when he declared his intention to make restitution. Also, in Philemon, Paul declares that he will make restitution for anything Onesimus has stolen.

---

4. See Appendix G for a full development of this thesis.

5. Conceivably the expression "seven-fold" simply means that the poor man, like all men, must make *full* restitution, since the number seven frequently signifies fullness in Scripture (cf. Gen. 4:24; Ps. 12:6; Ps. 79:12). For the reasons given, I think this the less likely understanding of the text.

There can be no question but that the laws of the Bible here are much superior to the penalties for theft today. If the thief is penalized at all, the payment goes to the state. The man robbed gets nothing, but has to pay taxes year after year to put the thief up in prison (there are no prisons in Scripture).

If the thief cannot make the required restitution, he is sold into slavery to raise the necessary money. The provisions of the sabbath year and Jubilee, which freed Hebrew slaves, would not apply to the thief, for obvious reasons: This would be arbitrary justice, and would give the thief an incentive to steal as the years of release approached. Such a man forfeits his right to the consideration given other Hebrews who wind up in slavery. Jesus says that the man sold to pay for his theft will not come out of the prisonhouse of slavery until he has paid it all (Matt. 5:26; and cf. Matt. 18:23ff.). The slave contract for the thief would be for as many years as were needed to pay his debt.

II. *Self defense*

Sandwiched in among these laws of restitution is the provision that if a thief is caught breaking in at night, the owner of the house is not guilty if he kills him. He does not know the intent of the thief, so he rightly suspects the worst, and kills him to protect himself and his family. On the other hand, if he comes home during the day and finds a thief, he may not kill him. In a small community, he will recognize the man, and can set the authorities on him. Obviously, if the thief tried to kill the man, the owner would have the right to defend himself.

Cassuto has noted that "the Bible presents the case in usual circumstances."[6] What about our circumstances? Are we bound to stand by and let a thief steal from us if we come home and find him in our house? I think not, for two reasons. First, the law is written in terms of the thief's "breaking in." We take this as indicating a breaking into a house, but in the context of this verse it is a breaking into a yard which is in view. The immediate context

---

6. Cassuto, *Exodus*, p. 283.

deals with a thief who steals animals. This is a slow process. A man has to drive the animal away. If we see him during the day, we can raise an alarm, and neighbors will help us track him down. At night, however, we cannot see — no street lights in ancient Israel, and none in rural areas today. We don't know the thief's intention. Maybe he is invading our yard with a view to killing us. Thus, we may go into the yard and kill him. Thus, the law is not directly addressing the situation of a man's breaking into the house, the sleeping area, of a family.

Secondly, the concepts "day" and "night" in Scripture have an extensive metaphorical meaning. In Genesis 1:5, God called the light day, and the darkness night. Light and darkness are frequently used in Scripture to describe Spiritual or social conditions. Moreover, this passage does not actually use the terms day/night or light/darkness, but says "if the sun is risen upon him." The rising of the sun sheds light upon the situation. Moreover, the rising of the sun is a token of power (Jud. 5:31; Gen. 32:31; Ps. 19:4-6). Thus, we may understand the verse as meaning that the owner is able to identify the thief (the sunrise of understanding), or is able to overpower him without killing him (the sunrise of strength). I suggest that the meaning of the law is this: If you don't recognize him, and cannot deal with him in any other way, you may kill him; but if you know who he is, or have the strength to deal with him, you may not kill him. This will vary from situation to situation, and local ordinances specify what a shopkeeper or houseowner may do to a person who breaks in. It is up to the elders of any given local community to determine under what circumstances the sun may be said to have risen upon a situation.

Pollution

5. When a man causes a field or vineyard to be grazed over, or he lets loose his beast and it grazes in the field of another, from the best in his field or vineyard he must make it whole.

6. When fire breaks out and catches in thorns, and shocks of grain, or standing grain, or the field is consumed, the one causing the burning must most certainly make the situation whole.

There is a slight problem in the interpretation of these verses, since the verb for "graze" in Hebrew is the same as the verb for "burn" (*ba'ar*). The first clause of v. 5 might read, "when a man causes a field or vineyard to be burned up." Whether we take it that way or not, the difference in the two cases is that the first case is an act of deliberate sabotage or trespass, and the second is accidental. The punishment in both cases is simple compensation, not double restitution, but in the first case the compensation must come from the very best of the aggressor's produce.[7] Thus, there is some additional penalty involved in the case of deliberate sabotage or theft.

In our modern age, it is frequently more difficult to assess damages in cases of pollution. Gary North explains:

"The problem is especially acute when there are multiple and basically unidentifiable polluters — very often those who simultaneously suffer from the pollution. A man starts an automobile engine. He becomes a polluter of the air (exhaust, noise). His contribution to overall levels of exhaust pollution is infinitesimal — unmeasurable from thirty feet away. Yet three million cars in a valley like Los Angeles and Orange counties create pollution that is all too measurable. If the total pollution is to be reduced, then all the polluters must be restrained. In principle, the pollution control device is no different from the exhaust muffler, although the latter is more readily understood. Both raise the price of the car, reduce its engine's efficiency, and increase gasoline consumption. Both protect innocent bystanders: less noise, less bad air. Furthermore, neither can be paid for by the automobile manufacturers, for they are not the polluters. Drivers are. Drivers wish to convert private costs (lower performance, the cost of the device) into social costs (noise and air pollution). Only they can pay for the device; the companies must pass along the added costs to them. Pollution control devices, biblically, are like

---

7. J. J. Rabinowitz, "Exodus XXII:4 and the Septuagint Version Thereof," *Vetus Testamentum* 9 (1959):40-46, thoroughly establishes that the compensation in v. 5 consists of the produce of the best of the aggressor's land, not the land itself.

spark retarding devices: They protect other people's property. Where there are multiple polluters, only the civil government can effectively restrain all polluters, for all are bound equally under civil law.

"In the case of a single violator, or potential violators, there are two reasons justifying the coercive intervention of the civil government. *First,* to use the biblical example of fire, a man who permits a fire to get out of control may see an entire town burned to the ground. There is no way, economically, that he can make full restitution. In fact, it would be almost impossibly expensive to assess the value of the destroyed property. Therefore, in high-risk situations, the civil government can legitimately establish minimum fire prevention standards. (Analogously, the civil government can also establish medical quarantines to protect public health.) *Second,* and far less relevant, there may be cases of polluters who are identifiable, but who injure many neighbors in a minor, though measurable, way. The costs of assembling all the injured parties — search costs, lawyer fees, delays in court hearings, injury assessments — into one or more legitimate complaining units may be too high for each member of the group to bear. Class-action suits are one means of seeking restitution. Another is the establishment of fines for polluters, including graduated fines as the levels of pollution increase. Least desirable, probably, is the outright abolition of the pollution-producing activity, although the costs of pollution abatement may in effect serve as outright prohibitions on marginally profitable firms.

"The buyers of a particular product may save a few cents or many dollars because the costs of producing it are passed along, involuntarily, to residents living close to the plant, but this does not justify the practice, nor do considerations of the comparative wealth of buyers and injured parties. Coercion in the form of unforeseen and injurious pollution can legitimately be met by coercion from the civil government.

"To reduce the costs of assessing injuries, *local* governments are best equipped to enforce pollution (cleanliness) standards. The larger the administrative or geographical unit, the more difficult it is to assess costs and benefits. Only when political boundaries are involved—county vs. county, state vs. state—should higher levels of civil government be brought in to redress grievances. Local conditions, local standards of cleanliness, silence, or whatever, involve local conflicts; these are best settled by local governmental units.

"The question of pollution, therefore, is a question of responsibility. The Bible affirms that each man is responsible for his actions. No man is to pass along the costs of any activity to his neighbor, apart from the latter's consent. Where there is ownership (legitimate sovereignty), there must also be responsibility."[8]

Safekeeping

7. When a man gives to his fellow money or articles to keep, and it is stolen from the man's house, then, if the thief should be found, he must repay [make it whole] double.

8-9. If the thief should not be found, then the owner of the house shall be brought to The God (or, the judges), [to determine] whether or not he has put his hand on the property of his fellow. (9.) For every matter of transgression with reference to an ox, or an ass, or a sheep, or a garment, or any lost thing concerning which one says, "Indeed, this is it"; to The God (or, the judges) the matter of both of them must be brought. The one whom God condemns (or, the judges condemn) must repay [make whole] double to his fellow.

10-11. When a man gives his fellow an ass, or an ox, or a sheep, or any beast to keep, and it dies, or it is injured, or it is driven away, no one seeing it, (11.) the oath of the LORD must be between the two of them. If he did not lay his hand on the property of his fellow, then its owner shall accept [the oath], and he will not make it whole.

12. But if it is certainly stolen from him, he will make it whole to its owner.

---

8. Gary North, "An Economic Commentary on the Bible, No. 36: Pollution, Ownership, and Responsibility," *Chalcedon Report* No. 130, June 1976. A much expanded treatment of this whole matter can be found in North's *The Dominion Covenant: Exodus* (Tyler, TX: Institute for Christian Economics, 1985).

13. If it is indeed torn by beasts, let him bring it as evidence. He will not make whole for what is torn.

If a man were to take a journey he might leave valuables or animals with his neighbor for safekeeping. The *first* case, which would also apply to animals, simply reminds us that if the goods are stolen, it is the thief who owes restitution, not the one with whom the goods were deposited.

The *second* case assumes that perhaps the man with whom the goods were deposited has stolen them, and then blamed a non-existent thief. Such a matter is to be taken before God's appointed judges (see Ps. 82:1, 6; Ex. 21:6; and for a specific instance 1 Ki. 3:16-28). The decision of the judges is final. (Rebellion against the sentence of the court merits the death penalty in Deuteronomy 17:12. Justice is imperfect in this world; we submit anyway, knowing that there is another more perfect Court which will try everyone at the last.)

The *third* case specifies matters in terms of things peculiar to animate property. The animal might wander off, or die, or be killed by wild beasts, or be driven off by raiders (as in Job 1:15, 17). Over such situations the keeper has no control. A simple oath before the LORD was to be acceptable to both parties. It was expected that God would curse the man who swore falsely (cf. Numbers 5).

The *fourth* case provides incentive for the man keeping the goods to catch the thief. "If it is *certainly* stolen" can only mean that the thief has been caught, because the context is dealing with animals, and the only way to know for sure that the animal was stolen rather than merely wandering off, is if the thief is apprehended. If the thief is caught while the owner is away, then the neighbor gets to keep half of the restitution, and the owner gets his property back. In the first case above, the thief is caught after the owner returns; in that case the owner gets the full double restitution.

An illustration might make this a bit clearer. John leaves his silver flatware with Bob while he takes a trip. One day a thief breaks into Bob's house and steals John's flatware, but nothing else. "Tough luck, John," thinks Bob, and forgets about it. Bob is not liable, after all. John will just have to accept Bob's oath (v. 11). Why should Bob even lift a finger to get John's stuff back?

Ah, but this law puts a different complexion on matters. If Bob manages to track down the thief, working with the police, etc., then Bob will get to keep half of the restitution. So, Bob calls the cops, and cooperates fully in getting John's flatware back. The thief is (wonder of wonders) caught. He is forced to make double restitution, returning the silver and also its equivalent in money to Bob. A few days later, John returns. Bob gives him back his silver flatware, and Bob gets to keep the restitution.

The *fifth* case specifies that no compensation is due if it can be proven that the animal was slain by a beast. The third case had already stated that an oath was to suffice in such a case, but in the interest of removing all suspicion, evidence should be presented when such is available.

This is a valuable principle in all of life. Since men want to play God, they like to insist that people should simply take them at their word. We are not God, however, and we should back up our statements with evidence wherever possible (without wearying other people, of course, and without disclosing confidences). Church rulers, to take an example, can have a tendency to maintain that people should believe what they say simply because they, the officers, say it. This is unwise, and creates suspicion.

Borrowing, Neighborliness, and Rent

14. When a man borrows something from his fellow, and it is injured or it dies, its owner not being with it, he will surely make it whole.
15a. If its owner is with it, he will not make it whole.
15b. If it is hired, it comes for its hire.

Full compensation is due for any damaged borrowed article. This ensures that the borrower will take care of his neighbor's property. If the owner is present, it is assumed that he will watch

out for his own goods, and if something happens, the man borrowing it is not obligated. Finally, if the article was rented and
breaks, nothing is owed.

Thus, if you loan me your lawnmower, and are standing by
while I start it, and I break it, I owe you nothing. But if I break it
and you are not present, I owe you another lawnmower. If I paid
you $5.00 for the use of it, then I owe you nothing more; you took
the risk. (It might be wise to pay for it anyway, if the rental fee is
only a token, like $5.00.)

These laws do not invalidate the practice of rental stores,
which generally have the customer sign a contract agreeing to
replace the item rented if they break it, or pay for repairs. Signing
this contract is part of the "hire," along with paying the rental fee.

Since this is the kind of thing that happens every day, a few
comments are in order. Let us assume that you borrowed your
neighbor's punchbowl and broke it. How should you make compensation? First, don't tell her in advance that you broke the
punchbowl, unless you have to. That only gives her an opportunity
to say she doesn't need a replacement. People say things like, "Oh,
well, forget it. It's not important," but in fact they don't forget. Second, don't just give her the money. She is likely to refuse to take
it. Also, why should she have to go to the trouble of purchasing a
new bowl, when you are the one who broke it? Third, don't buy a
more expensive punchbowl. It may not match her set. Let her use
the receipt and exchange it if she wants to. Fourth, don't neglect
the opportunity to witness for Christ. You are not doing this
because it seems nice and neighborly. You are doing it because
Christ your Lord tells you to. Let her know that.

If someone wants to make compensation to you, don't despise
him by refusing to accept it. Accept it graciously as from the
Lord.

What if you are visiting someone and you break something?
Technically, since they asked you in, and since they are present,
nothing is owed. Depending on the item and the persons involved, however, compensation might be the wise move.

What if your children break something? I think it depends on the circumstances. If your child is in the kitchen, and the lady of the house gives him a glass of water, and your child drops the glass, you don't owe anything because the lady of the house was present. (If she insists, you would be wise to replace it, out of courtesy and a desire to avoid conflict.)

On the other hand, if you are all in the living room, and your child wanders into the kitchen unsupervised, and breaks a piece of china, are you responsible? Technically, I think not. The hostess has a responsibility to keep breakables put up, if she invites children over. Also, the hostess has a responsibility to inform you to keep your children away from anything she fears might break. In a general sense, she is "with" everything in her house, since she knows her environment and you do not. After all, you have not borrowed anything; rather, you are her guest. All the same, it is frequently wiser to try to make compensation in these cases, to avoid resentments.

8

FAITHFULNESS (EXODUS 22:16-31)

The laws in this section are generally regarded as randomly thrown together, or arranged for mnemonic purposes. Originally I had placed these under the "Property" heading, because so many seem to have to do with the interplay between rich and poor. Further reflection, however, has caused me to believe that these are best seen as a section elaboration on the seventh commandment, "Thou shalt not commit adultery." Partly this is because we should expect a section on the seventh commandment, when the other commandments having readily applicable civil and social ramifications are dealt with (commandments five through nine). Also, the laws of vv. 16-17 indicate a bridge from property laws into marriage laws. Finally, and most convincing to me, all the laws in this section can easily be fit into the general Biblical view of the marriage between God and his people (on this, see Chapter 4, and Appendix F).

When God made covenant with Israel at Mt. Sinai, He married Israel. Israel was expected to be faithful to the Lord, as He was to Israel. Immediately, however, Israel played the harlot, and aroused the Divine jealousy (Ex. 34:14). The Divine Husband caused His faithless Bride to undergo the ordeal of jealousy (Num. 5; Ex. 32:20). In later years, God frequently was to refer back to His marriage to Israel—Ezekiel 16, Hosea 2, Malachi 2:11-16 being three prominent passages. The New Testament continues this imagery, explaining that Christ is the Husband of the Church (Eph. 5:22-33).

All the laws in this section have to do with covenant faithfulness, except the first, which could as easily have been categorized with the laws of property, and which forms a bridge into the laws against covenantal adultery. Except for this first section, the laws here are not set out as case laws, but as straightforward commands. Penalties are not always in view; God Himself is the One primarily offended, and He is the Avenger in most cases. There are four sections:

1. Two laws concerning the punishment of a seducer (vv. 16-17).

2. Three laws concerning the judicial punishment of blatant Spiritual adulterers (vv. 18-20).

3. Four laws concerning the way the helpless members of God's Bride are to be treated (vv. 21-27).

4. Six laws concerning the loyalty of the Bride to God (vv. 28-31).

Seduction

16. When a man seduces a virgin who is not betrothed and lies with her, he must certainly give the *mohar* for her and make her his wife.

17. If her father utterly refuses to give her to him, money must he pay, equivalent to the *mohar* for virgins.

The *mohar* is "wedding money," but there is dispute as to whose it was. Did the suitor pay the girl's father, or was the money for her? R. de Vaux has taken judicious ground: "This obligation to pay a sum of money, or its equivalent, to the girl's family obviously gives the Israelite marriage the outward appearance of a purchase. But the *mohar* seems to be not so much the price paid for the woman as a compensation given to the family, and, in spite of the apparent resemblance, in law this is a different consideration. The future husband thereby acquires a right over the woman, but the woman herself is not bought and sold. The difference becomes clear if we compare the *mohar* marriage with another type of union, which really was a purchase: A girl could be sold by her father to another man who intended her to be his own, or his son's, concubine; she was a slave, and could be re-sold, though not to an alien (Ex. 21:7-11). Furthermore, it is probably that the father enjoyed only the usufruct of the *mohar,* and that the latter reverted to the daughter at the time of succession, or if her husband's death reduced her to penury. This would explain the complaint of Rachel and Leah against their father, that he had 'devoured their money' after having 'sold' them (Gen. 31:15)."[1]

De Vaux comes close to the matter, but falls short, I believe. The simplest understanding of the *mohar* is that provided by R. North, as cited in Chapter 5 of this study: The money was for the wife. Only in the case of selling a girl into slavery did the money go to the father. In the case before us, if the man was unsuitable in the eyes of the father, the *mohar* had to be given to the girl anyway, so that her lack of virginity would be compensated for in the eyes of future suitors. The father could argue with a prospective suitor this way: "My daughter was seduced and thus is not a virgin. You do not need to provide her *mohar,* however, since she already has one from her seducer."[2]

The girl's father or brothers arranged for the *mohar.* In Genesis 34:12, Dinah's brothers dickered with Shechem for both a *mohar* and a gift. The gift probably was for the family, since on this interpretation the *mohar* was not. Notice that the servant of Abraham gave silver and gold to Rebekah, as well as gifts to her family (Gen. 24:53); this would be *mohar* and gifts. Both Saul and Caleb set tests of strength for prospective husbands, in lieu of the payment of *mohar* (1 Sam. 18:25-27; Josh. 15:16), but Caleb provided the financial equivalent of a *mohar* for Achsah (Josh. 15:18-20), though we don't read anything equivalent concerning Saul.

---

1. Roland de Vaux, *Ancient Israel* (New York: McGraw Hill, 2 vol. ed. 1965), p. 27.

2. R. J. Rushdoony, *Institutes of Biblical Law* (Phillipsburg, NJ: Craig Press, 1973), p. 178f. The payment of this money may well also be an equivalent to the required tokens of virginity, discussed in Appendix F. Payment of money does provide atonement in some cases, and is thus equivalent to the shedding of blood. See Exodus 21:30, and also the discussion of atonement money in Appendix D. Since the girl can no longer provide a blood-token of her virginity, the money, legally handed over, covers as substitute proof of her virtue.

Perhaps just one interesting note here. Apparently the free Israelite woman, with her *mohar,* had quite a bit of "independence" from her husband. This money would be her insurance policy, in case her husband died or divorced her (and so it is not the same as an insurance policy today). Also, however, it was money she could use and invest. It seems most likely that the money the woman in Proverbs 31:26ff. is using is her own money, not that of her husband (though perhaps it is money he has entrusted to her). Thus, if the husband were something of a fool when it came to money, the wife had her own which she could invest wisely to care for herself and her children.

Modern American Christian women are often more in the position of slave wives than of free ones, according to the Bible. They seldom have their own separate money. In the proper "Christian" home of today, the husband has *all* financial control. He has not provided his wife with money at marriage, nor later on (though he may adorn her with jewelry, which is hers to keep). If she takes a job, it is assumed that he will have ultimate say-so over the spending of her money. The Biblical marriage, however, while it may appear to entail more tension and negotiation between husband and wife, also produces people who are much more mature.

Turning directly to the law itself, the punishment for the seducer is that he must marry the girl, unless her father objects, and that he may never divorce her (according to Dt. 22:29). According to Deuteronomy 22:25-27, if the girl were engaged to be married, this would count as a case of adultery, and both would be put to death, unless it were a case of rape. There seems to be some latitude here, however, since we read in Matthew 1:19 that "Joseph, being a *just* man . . . was minded to put her [Mary] away privately." Here again we see a circumstantial application of the unchanging law of God; Joseph apparently regarded Mary as basically a good woman, who must have fallen into sin on one occasion, and so he determined that death was too severe a punishment for her. That this was perfectly just, the text itself tells us. This proves, by the way, that the death penalty is not mandatory in all cases where it is prescribed by law. It is the maximum penalty. The law of Deuteronomy 22:28-29 seems shocking to our ears:

> If a man finds a girl who is a virgin, who is not engaged, and seizes her and lies with her and they are discovered, then the man who lay with her shall give to the girl's father fifty [shekels] of silver, and she shall become his wife because he has violated her; he may not divorce her all his days.

At first sight, this seems to allow for rape of an unbetrothed girl. In Hebrew, however, the verb "seize" is a weaker verb than the verb for "force" used in the same passage (v. 25) to describe rape. This stronger verb is also used for the rape of Tamar (2 Sam. 13:11). Implied here is a notion of catching the girl, but not a notion that she fought back with anything more than a token resistance. Modern random rape would not be excusable under this law, and would have to come under the death penalty of Deuteronomy 22:25-27.

The Deuteronomy law specifies 50 shekels of silver, which gives us some idea of what the normal *mohar* for virgins must have been.[3] This is about 20 ounces of silver, but in terms of the value of silver then and now there is no way to determine about how much the *mohar* was. Christians would be wise to make some attempt to apply this law. The *mohar* given a girl at her wedding by her husband should consist of more than a diamond and a wedding band, but how much more it is difficult to say. Those who have very little to start with should set as their goal to adorn their wives with jewelry as the years go by, jewelry that would be the property of the wife.

Finally, a few remarks on the father's power to cancel the relationship between the young man and the daughter. We are not told all we should like to know about the legal side of marriages in Israel. Clearly there was a legal, civil aspect. De Vaux comments, "In Israel, acts of divorce were drawn up before the Exile (Dt.

---

3. Note that this amount is not the same as the purchase price for a woman of marriageable age (Lev. 27:4). This again shows that the *mohar* is not a "bride price."

24:1-3; Jer. 3:8), and it would be surprising if contracts of marriage did not exist at the same time. Perhaps it is merely by accident that they are never mentioned in the Bible."[4] The apocryphal book of Tobit shows the custom clearly: "Then he called his daughter Sarah, and taking her by the hand he gave her to Tobias to be his wife, saying, 'Here she is; take her according to the law of Moses, and take her with you to your father.' Next he called his wife Edna, and took a scroll and wrote out the contract; and they set their seals to it" (Tobit 7:13-14).[5]

The interest of the state in marriage is clearly seen in that the Bible distinguishes between bastards and legitimate children (e.g., Dt. 23:2). The state must have some way to recognize legitimate cohabitation. Also, the state is called upon to adjudicate in the case of the girl who is charged with not being a virgin (Dt. 22:13ff.). We have seen (Chapter 3) that there was a position in Biblical society called the "officer," and that his job in part was to record genealogies. Thus, we may easily conclude that contracts, such as Tobit and Edna sealed, were deposited or at least recorded by the civil authority, thus making a public record of the marriage.

Similarly, the interest of the Church is seen in that sexual relations within the prohibited degrees of consanguinity resulted in "cutting off," or excommunication from the Church in Israel (Lev. 20:17). Thus, the approval of the Church was needed for a marriage to be proper.

The difference between modern and ancient marriages seems to lie in the fact that the pronouncing of a couple man and wife was done by the girl's father, when he gave her to the son-in-law, and not by an official of the state or Church. Nonetheless, the marriage had to be approved by Church and state, in the sense that these agencies could be called in to punish offenses in the making of marriages.

Clearly, then, in the Biblical view, the approval of the girl's

---

4. De Vaux, p. 33.
5. Translation from *The Oxford Annotated Apocrypha* (New York: Oxford University Press, 1965).

father is all important. This is not to say, of course, that there are
no occasions when the officers of Church and/or state may have to
intervene and restrict the authority of the father. As we have
noted in the previous chapter, human covenants and relationships
are never absolute. Some men decide that their daughters will
never marry, but will remain their servants forever. In such a
case, the girls may appeal to the magistrates of Church and state,
and be delivered from the abuse. Sometimes the girl's brother or
mother may approve the marriage and the father disapprove.
Depending on the father's character and/or arguments, the courts
might rule against him.

What if a girl and boy elope? May the father properly annul
the marriage, if a Justice of the Peace has pronounced them man
and wife? Perhaps not under American civil law, but clearly in the
Church and under Biblical law he might do so. Except in unusual
circumstances, such as those mentioned in the preceding
paragraph, the approval of the father is essential to the making of
a marriage. The fact that the boy and girl have slept together, and
the fact that some civil officer in American society has declared
them man and wife, does not change this fact. Of course, it might
be very difficult for the father to get his way in the American
courts, and the wisest thing to do would usually be to bow to circumstances. The Church, however, must honor the father's decision, regardless of the decision of the state. In this case, the
Church would not recognize the marriage as legitimate, and
would have to excommunicate the couple for fornication, until
the approval of the father is forthcoming.

It is possible without difficulty to apply these provisions to
Christ and His Bride, the Church. In 2 Corinthians 11:2,3,
Satan's assault on Eve is explicitly compared to the seduction of a
pure maiden. In terms of this law, it is clear that the Father will
not permit the Bride to marry Satan, and thus that payment of
mohar money by Satan is required. Accordingly, the Bible
everywhere teaches that the wealth laid up by the wicked will be
given over to the righteous, partly as compensation for oppression. Indeed, in the exodus itself, the women of Israel were told to

demand payment from the Egyptians (Ex. 3:22). This should be seen as a demand for *mohar*. Appendix F points out that Christ's atoning blood provides the needed tokens of virginity for His Bride, so that she is declared innocent of her complicity in Spiritual fornication. Here we see that when the wicked are forced to pay *mohar* money to God's Bride, they are being forced to admit their guilt.

Spiritual Adultery

18. A sorceress you shall not allow to live.
19. Anyone lying with a beast most certainly shall be put to death.
20. One who sacrifices to a god, except it be to the LORD alone, must be devoted to destruction.

If we take this as the beginning of the section proper (after the bridge), we again see the laws arranged in descending order of punishment. We begin with three capital offenses, move to outright oppression of the poor, then to more subtle kinds of oppression, and close with warnings to be faithful to God.

Not only (female) witches but also (male) warlocks were to be put to death by God's law (Lev. 20:27). Gispen comments that "the feminine form used here could indicate the class as a whole (a well-known example is the Hebrew title of Ecclesiastes, *kohelet,* which is a feminine word, but indicates an office or completeness, 'preacher')."[6] I suspect that the feminine is used here because the faithfulness or unfaithfulness of God's Bride is in view. Any member of the Bride who turns to witchcraft is to be put to death.

A number of different words are used in Hebrew for that range of occult practices which can be called witchcraft. Unger states that the term used here denotes "one who practices magic by using occult formulas, incantations, and mystic mutterings."[7] He goes on to add that the "so-called 'witch of the Hebrews' did

---

6. W. H. Gispen, *Exodus,* trans. by Ed van der Maas (Grand Rapids: Zondervan, 1982), p. 222.

7. Merrill F. Unger, *Biblical Demonology* (Wheaton: Scripture Press, 1952), p. 153.

not rate higher than a fortune teller or a divining woman. Notwithstanding, hers was a crime deserving of death."[8] It is my opinion that the term used here is a general term, embracive of all the various practices listed in Deuteronomy 18:10f., and other places.[9] The two great examples of practitioners of witchcraft in Scripture are Jezebel (2 Ki. 9:22) and Manasseh (2 Chron. 33:6). Ezekiel 13:17-23 gives an instance of Israelite women using sorcery to kill people by magic.

The death penalty for witchcraft does not justify inquisition, since in Scripture the testimony of two or three witnesses is always needed for conviction (Dt. 17:6). As we argued at the beginning of this study, no society is religiously neutral. Biblical law protects the right of pagans to worship their own gods in secret, at times other than the times Christians worship,[10] provided they do not evangelize (Dt. 13:5). The Triune God alone is to be worshipped in public, however. Since social blessings come from God, the social relevance of such laws as this is obvious.

In context, this is a law for the Bride. She is to hearken to the word of her Lord, and not to the siren song of the seducer. Eve was corrupted by hearkening to the word of Satan, according to the marital analogy of 2 Corinthians 11:1-3. For the Bride to go off and seek power or knowledge from any source other than God is to commit Spiritual infidelity, and the punishment for adultery is death.

The second law here prescribes death for bestiality. The later occurrences of this law (Lev. 18:23; 20:15; Dt. 27:21) say "any"

---

8. *Ibid.*, p. 155.

9. Unger discusses these terms in *ibid.*, pp. 144ff.

10. I have defended this in my pamphlet, *Sabbath Breaking and the Death Penalty: An Alternate View* (Tyler, TX: Geneva Ministries, 1984). In brief, my position is that the reason the hearthfires of Israel were not to be "intensified" on the sabbath day, on pain of death (Ex. 35:3), is that only God's altar-hearthfire was to be intensified (by extra sacrifices) on that day. God's judgment, not man's, was to prevail. On that day, to build up one's own hearthfire was to stand in opposition to God's, and to set forth strange fire (Lev. 9:24-10:2). The more general meaning, which would apply to Christian culture today, is that while pagans might worship their false gods in private, they might not do so at the same time as true worship is offered. No competitive worship is permitted.

beast, clean or unclean. Sexual adultery, being so close to
spiritual adultery, merits the death penalty in Scripture, in all its
forms (Lev. 20; Dt. 22).[11] The specific form of fornication committed by Eve was bestiality — hearkening to the voice of a beast.
Accordingly, spiritual adultery is likened to bestiality, as the
heathen are likened to beasts (Lev. 20:24f.; Ezk. 23:20).

Finally, anyone publicly sacrificing to any god except the Lord
is to be put to death. Literally this reads, "put under the ban
(*ḥerem*)." According to Deuteronomy 13:12-18, when a whole city
committed this sin, the city was to be destroyed and burned "as a
whole burnt sacrifice." In other words, fire was taken from God's
altar, signifying his fiery justice, and applied to the city and its
corpses. Since they refused God's sacrifice, they themselves
became the sacrifices. In Leviticus 21:9, the daughter of a priest is
to be put to death, if she plays the harlot, and her body burned,
the implication again being with God's fire from His altar. Thus, I
take it that the intended application here is that an open idolator
should be put to death, and then his body burned with fire from
the altar.

Idolatry is specifically likened to spiritual harlotry in Exodus
34:

13. But you are to tear down their altars and smash their sacred
pillars and cut down their Asherah,

14. For you shall not worship any other god, for the LORD,
whose name is Jealous, is a jealous God,

15. Lest you make a covenant with the inhabitants of the land
and they play the harlot with their gods, and sacrifice to their gods,
and someone invite you and you eat of his sacrifice,

16. And you take some of his daughters for your sons, and his

---

11. From the *Diary of Samuel Sewell:* "April 6 [1674]. Benjamin Gourd of Rox-
bury (being about 17 years of age) was executed for committing Bestiality with a
Mare, which was first knocked in the head under the Gallows in his sight. *N.B.*
He committed that filthiness at noon day in an open yard. He after confessed
that he had lived in that sin a year. . . ." Since the crime was committed openly,
there was the testimony of two or more witnesses. Citation from the edition of
M. Halsey Thomas (New York: Farrar, Straus and Giroux, 1973), p. 4.

daughters play the harlot with their gods, and cause your sons to play the harlot with their gods.

17. You shall make for yourself no molten gods.

18. You shall observe the Feast of Unleavened Bread. . . .

We notice that the context of these remarks is the idolatry of Exodus 32, which was accompanied, apparently, by sexual sin (as indicated by the word "play" in Ex. 32:6, compared with Gen. 26:8). Notice that sharing a covenant meal with a false god is equivalent to adultery, so that sharing the covenant meal with the true God is equivalent to marital relations, symbolically. This is discussed in Appendix F.

Why these three laws? Obviously they are designed to sum up the demand for covenant fidelity, but what is the reason for their selection? I believe that it relates to the three offices of prophet, king, and priest. Offering false sacrifices is infidelity to God in the area of priesthood. Witchcraft is used to gain knowledge and information the false way (cf. 1 Sam. 28), infidelity to God in the area of prophecy. (But cf. Ezk. 13:17-23.) Bestiality is religiously an act of chaos, designed to obtain power,[12] and thus infidelity to God in the area of kingship or dominion. Man was made to rule animals, not to get power from them (Gen. 1:28). The suitable mate for a man is a woman, not an animal (Gen. 2:18-25). Bestiality entails a thoroughgoing reversal of dominion.

The Defenseless and the Poor

21. A stranger [sojourner] you (s.) shall not wrong or oppress, for you (pl.) were strangers [sojourners] in the land of Egypt.

22-24. Any widow or fatherless you (pl.) shall not afflict. (23.) If you (s.) afflict him at all, indeed if he cries out to Me at all, I will certainly hearken to his cry. (24.) Then My wrath will wax hot, and I shall slay you (pl.) with the sword, and your (pl.) wives will be widows, and your (pl.) children fatherless.

25. If money you lend to My people, even the poor who are with you, you shall not be to him as one bearing a burden [as a creditor]; you shall not impose upon him interest.

---

12. See the discussion in Rushdoony, *Institutes,* pp. 438ff.

26-27. If for any reason you take as a pledge the garment of your fellow, before the setting of the sun you shall return it to him; (27.) for that is his only covering; it is his mantle for his bare body. In what else can he sleep? And it shall come to pass when he cries to Me, then I will hearken, for I am compassionate.

I. *The Foreigner*

There is a thematic transition from v. 20 to v. 21, in that though foreign customs were outlawed, no oppression was to be visited upon foreign people. Indeed, the kindness shown to the stranger in the land was designed to win him to the true faith. Also, such persons, separated from their families and the strength of their clans, were in a very weak and vulnerable position. God here announces that anyone living in His land is under His protection.

At the time this law was given, the sojourners were the mixed multitude who came out from Egypt with the Israelites. Later on such strangers were traders from other lands who settled in Israel to sell their wares.[13] Also, in highly decentralized times such as those of the Judges, a fellow Israelite would be in the position of a stranger if he were laboring outside his own tribe.

This law is repeated in fuller form in 23:9, in the context of the ninth commandment. We shall have more to say about it in Chapter 9. Note the alternation of singular and plural here. The oppressor may be an individual, but the whole community has an interest in preventing this individual from continuing in his oppression.

II. *The Helpless*

Widows and orphans (or better, fatherless children) were frequently in a bad position in ancient cultures. If the woman did not have family to care for her, and no *levir* willing to marry her (Dt. 25:5-10; Ruth 3, 4), her *mohar* would not carry her very long

---

13. They would have had to settle in the towns, since the land was divided among the sons of Israel, and reverted to its original owners in the fiftieth year (Lev. 25). Thus, no outsider could ever settle in the land of Israel.

(assuming she really had one). Moreover, even though Biblical law is against it (Num. 27:1-11, e.g.), there is a tendency to treat women as legally inferior to men. Thus, it is frequently more difficult for a woman to get justice in court than it is for a man. As a result, widows have often been easy marks.

Verse 23 specifies the matter by dropping from the plural to the singular. Even one case of oppression will bring on the wrath of God against the entire society, as we see from the return to the plural in v. 24. All of society has an interest in protecting the weaker members of the Bride, as the plural in verse 22 implies. To stand by and allow a crime to be committed is to be guilty of that crime.

According to Leibowitz, "Rambam [Moses Maimonides] writes in his Guide for the Perplexed that we never find the expression of Divine wrath (*haron 'af*) in the Bible except in the case of idolatry. His commentators have been puzzled by this sweeping generalization, since we do find this expression of wrath used with reference to God's wrath against Moses (Ex. 4:14), Miriam and Aaron (Num. 12:9) and Baalam (Num. 22:22). They iron out the difficulty by limiting Rambam's statement to the Almighty's relations with the nation as a whole, leaving out the cases where only individuals are involved. . . . Malbim suggests another solution. He agrees that the expression *haron 'af* is only used in the Bible with reference to the whole people — when the offense in question is idolatry. In our case, the same expression is deliberately used in order to equate the affliction of the orphan and widow to idolatry, teaching us that there is no crime greater than this."[14]

We may say that the word *haron* means "kindled" in the sense of fire, and *'af* means "nostrils." Thus, literally this says that God's nostrils will be kindled against those who oppress the widow.[15] This is jealousy language. Potiphar's nostrils were kindled when he suspected Joseph of attempting to rape his wife (Gen. 39:19). The expression occurs four times in Exodus 32 (vv. 10, 11, 19, 22),

---

14. Leibowitz, *Shemot,* p. 395.
15. The created image of this attribute of God was visible to the ancients as the fire-breathing dragon; cf. Job 41:18ff.

as God responds to the Spiritual adultery of His people. In our comments above on Ex. 32-34, we established the connection between idolatry and harlotry; thus it is no surprise that *haron 'af* is used in both contexts. God, of course, is a consuming fire (Heb. 12:29), and He manifests his fiery judgment in the flaming sword of the cherubim (Gen. 3:24; Lev. 10:2; etc.), in the fire of sacrifice on the altar, in the lake of fire, and so forth. The particular burning anger of jealousy, however, is pointed to in this expression. God jealously guards His Bride. His nostrils flared against Moses when Moses did not want to deliver Israel (Ex. 4:14). His nostrils burned against Aaron and Miriam when they attacked the privileges of Moses (Num. 12:9). God's burning anger at Balaam (Num. 22:22) relates to Balaam's intention of cursing God's Bride, which in time he succeeded in doing (Num. 25; 31:16).[16]

This leads us to the observation that the widow in Israel was a type of the bride of Adam, whose husband God had killed for his sin. It was needful for a younger brother, the second Adam Jesus Christ, to take her as His wife. This widow typology is particularly prominent in the book of Ruth, and in the theology of Luke (Luke 2:37; 4:25f.; 7:12). The widow is under the especial protection of the Lord, until He comes to claim her as His own.

III. *Interest*

Interest may be charged on a business loan or investment (Matt. 25:27), but not on a personal or charity loan to a fellow believer (Dt. 23:19). Interest may be charged to an unbeliever (Dt. 23:20), because the Bible sees unbelievers as slaves by nature, and thus irresponsible. The added stimulus of interest is needed to galvanize them to repay the loan. In the case of fellow believers, if they do not repay the loan when they are able, the courts of the Church exist to help remedy the situation.

---

16. On the Balaam episode, see the excellent discussion in Gordon J. Wenham, *Numbers* (Downers Grove, IL: Inter-Varsity Press, 1981), pp. 164ff. Note that Balaam seduces Israel by means of sexual temptation—again the correlation between physical and Spiritual adultery. Phinehas's deliverance of Israel correlates physical and Spiritual fidelity.

Thus, if money is loaned to a Church or Christian non-profit agency, interest may not be charged. The many Churches, schools, etc., which invite "investments" and offer to pay back with interest, may well wind up paying the interest out of *tithes,* which is tantamount to robbing God. This is a most improper way to finance the kingdom of God.

The laws in Deuteronomy are in a section on the eighth commandment, and simply say that fellow believers are not to be charged interest. Here the poor are specified. Again we see God taking especial care of the weaker members of His Bride. No civil punishment is here specified. God is the Avenger, though doubtless social pressure would also help enforce these provisions. One could argue the propriety of civil punishment, however, by arguing that if any interest payments are extorted, double restitution would be required as penalty (and see Appendix G).

In an age of inflation, it would not be immoral to charge interest on a charity loan, provided the interest rate were fixed at the rate of inflation. It is real worth, in the form of paper money, which has been borrowed; and it is real worth, in the form perhaps of more paper dollars, which should be returned. Christians might agree, for instance, to tie the paper dollar value of the loan to the current price of gold (or some other agreed-upon commodity), so that the loan and repayment are understood to be in gold.

IV. *Pledges*

The law found here is elaborated on in Deuteronomy 24:

6. No one shall take a handmill or an upper millstone in pledge, for he would be taking a life in pledge.

10. When you make your neighbor a loan of any sort, you shall not enter his house to take his pledge.

11. You shall remain outside, and the man to whom you make the loan shall bring the pledge out to you.

12. And if he is a poor man, you shall not sleep with his pledge.

13. When the sun goes down you shall surely return the pledge to him, that he may sleep in his cloak and bless you; and it will be righteousness for you before the LORD your God.

As above, what we do not find in the Deuteronomy law is the threat of Divine vengeance.

The garment spoken of here is a heavy cloak, which a poor man would wrap around himself to sleep in at night. It is indeed permissible to take such a garment as a pledge, though not a handmill or millstone, since these are needed for the maintenance of life.[17] Each night, however, the garment must be returned to its owner again because it is then needed for the maintenance of life as Exodus 22:27 states. Leibowitz remarks: "We may well ask: What benefit accrues to the creditor from a pledge which he has to return to the debtor, whenever he needs it, and which he may only keep during such times as it is not needed by the owner?" Ibn Ezra, citing Se'adia Gaon, gave this reason: "The creditor would be afraid, otherwise, of the debtor borrowing from someone else against the same pledge. The Torah thus takes account not only of the interests of one party — the debtor, but of both, including the creditor as well (cf. 23:3: 'neither shalt thou favour a poor man in his cause')."[18]

Multiple indebtedness is thus restricted, because the poor man cannot put the same cloak up as collateral on several different loans. The cloak of a widow may not be used as collateral at all (Dt. 24:17). The modern fractional reserve banking system violates this principle, since the same money can be loaned out many times.[19]

The law here, as we have noted before, particularly has reference to the protection of the poorer and more helpless members of the Bride. It is God who has spread His cloak over his Bride in marriage (Ruth 3:9; Ezk. 16:8). In the symbolism of Scripture, the veil is removed from the face of the bride, removing the barrier of clothing between groom and bride (Gen. 24:65ff.).

---

17. To take a modern example, if a man needs his pick-up truck to conduct his business, then one must not take it as a pledge or use it as collateral.

18. Leibowitz, *Shemot,* p. 418.

19. On this see Gary North, *An Introduction to Christian Economics* (Phillipsburg, NJ: The Craig Press, 1973), pp. 12ff. See also Gary North, *The Dominion Covenant: Exodus* (Tyler, TX: Institute for Christian Economics, forthcoming), comments on Exodus 22:26f.

The two are one flesh, covered by one garment around them both. In terms of this, then, when God made His covenant with Israel, He spread his garment over them.[20] God gave the garment to the widow, and it may not be removed at all. God gave the garment to the poor man, and it is to be returned to him so that he can sleep in it.

The poor man, if oppressed, should cry out to God, who promises to avenge him (Ex. 22:27); but he may be tempted to curse God or the magistrates. The laws which immediately follow warn him not to do so.

Loyalty to God

28a. God you shall not curse [opposite of *honor*],

28b. And a ruler among your people you shall not curse [opposite of *bless*].

29a. The fulness of your harvest and the overflow of your presses you shall not delay [as offerings].

29b. The firstborn of your sons you shall give to Me.

30. So shall you do for your ox and your sheep; seven days will it be with its dam; on the eighth day you shall give it to Me.

31. As men of holiness shall you (pl.) belong to Me; and flesh in the field that is torn of beasts you (pl.) shall not eat; to the dogs you (pl.) shall cast it.

I. *Cursing God*

The verb used here is the same used in Ex. 21:17, meaning to make light of, to dishonor, not to pay what is due (see the fuller discussion in Chapter 6). Jesus showed the monetary implications of this in Mark 7:9-13, but it is spelled out here as well. The poor man must give the tithe (v. 29a), redeem his firstborn (v. 29b), and give the firstborn of his animals (v. 30), the same as everyone else. If he expects God to vindicate him, he must not repudiate the covenant.

---

20. The overshadowing of Israel by the glory cloud signified this. Also it is spoken of as the overshadowing by His wings. The edges of the garment are called wings in Scripture (Num. 15:38ff.; Dt. 22:12, 30; Dt. 32:11; Ruth 2:12; Ruth 3:9; Ezk. 16:8; etc.).

There is no penalty attached to cursing God in this sense. If, however, a man actively and openly repudiates the covenant, the punishment is death (Dt. 13:17). This is what Naboth was accused of in 1 Kings 21:10, 13 (and see Job 2:9). Also, public cursing of God with the tongue merits death, according to Leviticus 24:10-23. The man who "curses" (treats God lightly) will bear his own sin (Lev. 24:15), but the man who "blasphemes" (publicly attacking the Name of God) must be put to death (v. 16). From this I conclude that the man who simply decided to quit paying the tithe, or failed to give his firstborn, was not punished by the courts. It was left to God to deal with him.

II. *Cursing Rulers*

A different verb is used here, one which generally means to speak evil of someone. It is the opposite of "to bless," rather than of "to honor." The term for rulers (Hebrew: *nasi'*) here primarily designates a civil authority, though ecclesiastical rulers are not excluded. Even if rulers are evil, we are to pray for them, not curse them (Rom. 12:14). All authority is from God, and must be respected. "Even Michael, the archangel, when he disputed with the devil and argued about the body of Moses did not dare pronounce against him a railing judgment, but said, 'The Lord rebuke you' " (Jude 9).

Nothing in the Bible indicates that there is a civil penalty for the violation of this law. The Jews surely would have invoked it against Paul, had there been such: "Then Paul said to him, 'God is going to strike you, you white-washed wall! And do you sit to try me according to the Law, and in violation of the Law order me to be struck?' But the bystanders said, 'Do you revile God's high priest?' And Paul said, 'I was not aware, brethren, that he was high priest; for it is written, "You shall not speak evil of a ruler of your people" ' " (Acts 23:3-5).

The officers God has set in authority are not to be undermined by our words. Mothers are not to undermine fathers in the eyes of their children. Elders in the Church and officers of the state are not to be undermined. That is not to say that there is no place for resistance to tyranny, but it does indicate that attitude we are to take even in such an exigency.[21]

In this context, the rulers of the people are those who officially represent the Groom to the Bride.[22] To speak evil of them is to speak evil of God, whose appointed representatives they are.

There are financial implications here also. The same word for curse is used in Deuteronomy 28 with reference to financial losses (vv. 17-19). The man who speaks evil of rulers, cursing them with his breath, will be tempted to withhold taxes. We are told, however, always to pay tribute to whom it is due, and not to contest the power of the state in the area of taxation (Rom. 13:7; Matt. 22:21).[23] Indeed, in cases of doubt, we are to go the extra mile (Matt. 5:41). (This does not mean that we have to go out of our own way to pay taxes, but it means we are not to go far out of our way to avoid them either.)

III. *Tithes (22:29a)*

The tithe was to be brought in at the end of the harvest at the Feast of Tabernacles. The first noun in v. 29a literally means "fulness" and refers to grapes (Num. 18:27; Dt. 22:9). The second noun means "tears" or "weeping" and refers to the product of presses, perhaps olive oil, but most likely new wine.[24]

On tithing and the Biblical view of financing in general, see Appendices C and D.

IV. *The Firstborn (22:29b-30)*

Since God is the true Husband of all men, the firstborn always belongs to him. Eve confessed this when her first son was born:

---

21. On resistance to tryanny, see Gary North, ed., *The Theology of Christian Resistance,* Christianity and Civilization 2, and *Tactics of Christian Resistance,* C&C 3 (Tyler, TX: Geneva Ministries, 1983).

22. The wife of the high priest signified the Bride, so the officer himself signified the Groom. See Appendix F.

23. On the state's right to tax, see Appendix D.

24. Brevard Childs, *The Book of Exodus* (Philadelphia: Westminster Press, 1974), p. 450.

"And she said, 'I have gotten a man, from the LORD' " (Gen. 4:1). Moreover, the firstborn son represented the family line (Dt. 21:17), and the firstborn animal represented the family property. By claiming these, God claimed all. Also, God took Israel as His firstborn by redeeming them from slavery (Ex. 4:22), so that believers are God's property both by creation and redemption.

Unclean animals were to be redeemed or killed, since they might not be given to God (Ex. 13:13). Clean animals were given to Him directly (Ex. 13:12). Since men are unclean, in sin, they may not be given to God, and have to be redeemed (Ex. 13:13). The Levites had been substituted for the firstborn (Num. 3), but the requirement to give redemption to the Lord remained (Num. 18:15).

The eighth day was a day of death (circumcision, Lev. 12:3) and resurrection (Lev. 14:10, 23).[25] This was because it signified the beginning of a new creation. Just as there is a succession of generations in history, so there is a succession of weeks. Thus, the eighth day, which begins the second week, is also the day the child is removed (symbolically) from his mother and begins his (symbolically) independent life as the next stage in the succession (Ex. 22:30). The succession is defiled, unless redeemed by blood. Adam defiled man's first week by sinning on the sabbath, his first day. (Man proceeds from rest in God into work; rest (faith) comes before work.) The resurrection of the Son of Man, the Second Adam, on the eighth day inaugurated a replacement week, with rest again on the first day.

Jesus Christ is God's Firstborn, and all in union with him are counted in the community of the firstborn. He paid the price for them, that they might be redeemed. Since Christ is the fulfillment of these laws, ranchers do not owe their firstborn animals to the

---

25. For a fuller treatment of the significance of the eighth day, see Gary North, *The Dominion Covenant 2: Exodus* (Tyler, TX: Institute for Christian Economics, forthcoming).

Church any more than any of us owe a ransom for our firstborn sons.

V. *Holiness (22:31)*

God is the Source of life, and His blessing is life, not the curse of death. To belong to God, then, is to live in life, not death. Thus, Israel was ostentatiously to avoid death, and certain symbolic laws were given to the Old Covenant community to teach them this.[26] They were not to eat anything that had not been properly slaughtered. Dead meat found on the ground was "dirt," returning to the dust, and thus a sign of the curse and death (Gen. 3:19). It could be sold to "dogs" (unbelievers, Dt. 14:21).

In the Old Covenant, the stress in food laws was negative: "Do not eat what stands for the wicked, cursed way of life. Do not eat animals which resemble Satan in their lifestyles. Do not eat 'dirt' (including carrion). Let the dogs (unbelievers) eat such stuff, for it is like them. You avoid it." True, in the Passover and other communion meals of the Old Covenant, there was also the positive aspect of eating what incorporates you with salvation. Even here, however, the death-aspect predominates: It is the sacrificed lamb which is eaten, not a resurrected lamb.

The New Covenant food law incorporates all the Old Covenant food laws, and is wholly positive in aspect. We are to eat the flesh and drink the blood of the resurrected Christ. This is what it means to be men of holiness in the New Covenant.

In this law, the language switches to the plural, indicating that eating is a communal, social event. The paying of tithes and the dedicating of one's household (in the person of the firstborn) and one's property (in the firstborn of animals) are acts of individual devotion. Eating and refraining from eating what is forbidden are communal, social acts. It is Israel as a Church which is to eat the Lord's Supper. We have commented above on the analogy between the communion meal and marital relations.

---

26. For a fuller discussion of the laws of cleanness, see James B. Jordan, *Food and Faith* (forthcoming).

In conclusion, we may make a practical New Covenant paraphrase of verses 29-31 this way:

29a. Pay your tithes right away, laying up your vows on the first day of the week (1 Cor. 16:2).

29b. Live in union with Jesus Christ, God's Firstborn, thus dedicating yourself and your family to him in all you do.

30. Likewise, dedicate all your property to Him, for it all comes from Him.

31. Give visible testimony of your holiness and marriage to God, by regularly eating at the Lord's Table.

9

JUSTICE (EXODUS 23:1-9)

Our previous discussion has brought out the importance of language. Sins of the tongue are a very serious matter (James 3:1-12). Language can be creative or destructive, and gossip can destroy a man. Even worse is when the sin of the tongue occurs in a court of law.

Inseparably connected to the use of the tongue in court is the question of the impartiality of justice. God's law is impartial. It does not favor one person above another. (Grace does favor some, the elect; but law favors no one.) Modern law is increasingly partial. Special laws are passed to favor or protect business, unions, farmers, blacks, women, etc. Thus, our laws have become a means of warfare, with each group seeking legal favors over against other groups. The result is a warfare society.

These laws have to do with the ninth commandment. There are two sections. The first looks at matters from the standpoint of the individual called upon to testify in court, or bringing his grievance before the court. The second looks at matters from the standpoint of the magistrate, called upon to render judgment in court. Each section moves from the special to the general, from the courtroom to all of life. Thus, laws enjoining impartiality in all of life are appended to each of the two sections. We may divide the section as follows:

A. Seven laws dealing with individuals as they testify in court and as they live in community with others:

    1. Five laws concerning false witness before a court. (Special witness bearing before a court.)

167

2. Two laws concerning impartial dealings with personal adversaries. (General impartiality in all of life.)

B. Four laws dealing with magistrates as they rule in court and as they govern society:

3. Three laws concerning courtroom justice. (Special judgments before a court.)

4. One law concerning impartial dealings with non-believers. (General impartiality in all of life.)

Justice and the Witnesses

1a. You shall not carry about a false report.

1b. Do not clasp hands with a wicked man to be a malicious witness.

2a. You shall not follow a multitude to do evil;

2b. And you shall not bear witness in a suit so as to turn aside after a multitude, so as to pervert [justice].

3. And to a poor man, you shall not show partiality in his cause.

The first command forbids rumor mongering. The spread of rumor and gossip is one of the most serious problems in any community of people. Rumors subtly prejudice everyone who hears them, whether they wish to hear them or not. It is next to impossible to undo the damage done by gossip and the spread of hasty and premature judgments throughout a community or church. This command also implies that false reports are not to be given in court, since the Hebrew for "carry about" literally means "lift up," and thus also implies the giving of testimony before an authority.

The second command explicitly forbids conspiring to give false testimony in court. The "wicked man" referred to here is the guilty party. Deuteronomy 19:15-21 orders that a conspirator be given the same punishment as he intended for the party he hoped to convict: "Then you shall do to him just as he had intended to do to his brother" (v. 19a). See the discussion of this principle at the end of this chapter.

The third command reminds us that the majority is often, if not always, in the wrong. It is forbidden to consult social pressure or peer pressure in matters of truth, although such pressures are very difficult to avoid. It is not exactly the majority which is in view, but any group. Men find it easy to go with the crowd; we are told to check that tendency in ourselves. This is again a command against conspiracy, and against mob rule.

The fourth command specifies that we are forbidden to testify in court under the influence of social pressure. Here the man's testimony is perjured, but not as a result of malice (joining a conspiracy, verse 1b). In verse 1b, the malicious witness has joined in bringing the charge. In verse 2a, he has joined a mob in actively working to bring about an evil end. Here the untruthful witness is simply someone called upon to testify. He must again be wary of social pressure.

Finally, the fifth command orders us to be impartial. The poor can arouse sympathy, but emotion is not to influence truth and justice. Leviticus 19:15 states that partiality is to be given to no one.

Personal Adversaries

4. When you meet your enemy's ox or his ass going astray, you shall most certainly return it to him.
5. When you see the ass of one who hates you lying down under its load, then you shall refrain from leaving him; you shall most certainly release it with him.

Possibly the enemy spoken of here is one's adversary in a court situation, but even though we know that we are not to count our fellow believers as enemies, the fact is that antagonisms do develop within communities. The law is realistic: People have enemies, and this is how they should treat them. Clearly, if men obeyed the spirit of these laws, personal enmities would disappear. The act of helping and the act of receiving help go a great way toward breaking down hard feelings.

These laws forbid us to let hard feelings motivate our actions in life. God's law is realistic. It does not command us to feel a liking, in the modern sense of "like," for our personal enemies, which we may well be simply unable to do. Rather, it commands us to do good to them, which is well within our power. Doing good will bring about an emotional change in us, if such is needed.

The first case tells us that if we *meet* the beast of our enemy, we are to return it to him. If the beast wanders onto my land, I don't have absolute dominion over my own land, but must return it. We are not obligated, as in the second case, to go out of our way just because we *see* that the animal is lost. We don't have to chase it, though the verse implies that we should tell him about it.

The last phrase in the second case is difficult to translate. Gispen explains: "The Hebrew reads literally 'you shall refrain from leaving (it) to him; you shall surely loose (it) from him,' whereby 'leaving' and 'loose' are forms of the same verb. Some prefer to consider the second verb as deriving from a different root, which means 'to assist,' 'to help.' But it is possible to interpret the two verbs as 'leaving the work to the one who hates you,' and 'loosing, setting free, unloading of the donkey' respectively."[1] Whichever way we take it, the last clause orders us to stop and lend a hand in helping the man with his donkey.

In my opinion, these principles should also apply to Church and to state. It is quite common nowadays for a new church to be started in a town, and be made up of disgruntled persons from half a dozen other churches in town. Sheep-stealing, as this is often called, is wrong.[2] It is, of course, possible for people to transfer from one church to another, based on changes of theological opinion, or based on relocating from one part of town to another. Often, however, people misbehave in one church, and wander to another in order to avoid having to repent and shape up. How often are such persons told to go back and make it right with the first church, before being received into the second? In

---

1. Gispen, *Exodus,* p. 228.
2. It is also deadly. Building a church out of rebellious and self-willed people is a formula for disaster.

Scripture, oxen and donkeys signify people, and when an ox or an ass wanders into one church from another, the new church should not allow this without making certain that the individual is leaving the former church in peace.

Assisting the enemy in distress has implications for international relations. Government relief programs are no part of a Biblical agenda,[3] but the relief of suffering is part of the general duty of the Church. Even if those suffering are enemies, that is, non-Christians, we have a general duty to assist in alleviating their suffering. True, Hindus deserve to die, for they are under the wrath of God. True, Hindus deserve to starve because they abuse the land and refuse to eat the food (e.g., cattle) that God gives them. True, Christian churches today are too weak to be able to do much about it. Still, where and when the Church is able, she should endeavor to relieve suffering, even of the enemy. St. Paul says, "Do good to all men, especially to those of the household of faith" (Gal. 5:10). Thus our priorities are set, and we may not have the strength to do more than care for the household of the faithful today. When we can, however, we must do more.

The first five laws of Exodus 23 look at justice from the perspective of the ordinary citizen, called upon to testify. They naturally led to two commands to be impartial in all our dealings in all of life. We now switch to the perspective of the judges.

Justice and the Judges

6. You shall not pervert the justice due your poor, in his cause.

7. From a false charge stay away, and an innocent one and a righteous one do not slay, for I shall never justify a wicked one.

8. A bribe you shall not take, for the bribe makes officials blind and twists words of righteous ones.

---

3. Works of mercy are part of the peculiar work of the institutional Church, as an institution. For the institutional state to involve itself in this is for it to act as a surrogate Church. In America today, the national government combines many Church functions into itself; in fact, virtually all except formal liturgy (which plays little part in American Church life either). Simply warring against government welfarism without building up an ecclesiastical alternative, however, is fruitless and pointless, as well as possibly often cruel.

It is the judges who might be led to pervert the justice due to the poor. Just as the ordinary witness might tend to side with the poor, so the judges, drawn from upper strata of society, might tend to side with their friends, the rich. This is strictly forbidden.

In the second case, the judge is enjoined never to entertain a case he knows to be crooked. God states that He will avenge the innocent man who is set up and convicted by an evil judge.[4]

Finally, the judges are instructed never to take a bribe. Solomon implies that in an evil society, a bribe may be offered to a wicked judge (Prov. 17:8; 21:14). Bribery perverts the impartiality of judgment, but an evil judge has already forsaken impartiality. In such a situation, the elders of the Church should adjudicate the matter, and if a bribe to the pagan court is necessary, they should authorize its payment to protect the innocent. Scripture forbids receiving, not offering, a bribe.[5]

Is offering a bribe a form of temptation or seduction? Possibly. It could easily be sinful, thus, depending upon circumstances. If, however, the judge is known to be corrupt, and attempts to get him to deal righteously have failed, then paying the bribe upon the advice of Church elders is simply a way of submitting to oppression. One might view it as a court tax. If we call it a court tax, it does not seem evil to us. I believe, by the way, that this provision helps us with a present problem in America. The national government has determined to lay taxes directly upon the Church. This is a blasphemous sin, a way of stealing directly from God. We must protest it, and refuse to pay. If, however, the authorities come to close the Church down, we may decide to pay under protest, prophesying against their evil at the time, and viewing it as a form of theft. When the Babylonians despoiled the Temple, there was nothing faithful Jews could do but mourn. So

---

4. This phrase, "for I shall never justify the wicked," forms the foundation for Paul's theodicy in Romans, where he shows that it is possible for God "to be just and the justifier of the one who is of the faith of Jesus" (Rom. 3:26b). This is because Christ has died in the place of the faithful.

5. On this, see Gary North, "In Defense of Biblical Bribery," in Rousas J. Rushdoony, *The Institutes of Biblical Law* (Phillipsburg, NJ: The Craig Press, 1973), pp. 837-846 (and cf. also pp. 534ff.).

it is today in America. If the Church must use part of the tithe to bribe wicked judges, by paying into the social security system or some property tax, then she should do so, rather than perish. The decision to pay this bribe, however, should not be made lightly, and only when appeal and prophecy have failed.[6]

Some Jewish judges were so scrupulous that they would not hear a case if one party had ever done them a favor.[7] This is an example of the Pharisaical hedging of the law, condemned by Jesus repeatedly in the Sermon on the Mount. All the same, it raises an important question. Is a man obligated to disqualify himself from being a judge if he has had personal dealings with one or the other of the parties involved? Ideally this may seem desirable, but frequently it is not possible. In a church, for instance, the pastors (judges) will naturally know both of the people involved in a dispute. Doubtless they will have shared meals and other good times together. Does this mean that none of the pastors may sit in judgment? Are we obligated to obtain judges from some other church? Does their *ignorance* put them in a better position to render judgment?[8]

---

6. See Gary North, ed., *Tactics of Christian Resistance* (Tyler, TX: Geneva Divinity School Press, 1983). This 1983 Social Security tax on Church employees was repealed in 1984.

7. There are some interesting accounts of this in Leibowitz, *Shemot,* pp. 450ff.

8. To some extent these remarks have grown out of my knowledge of a recent Church court case. A conspiracy of rebellious and immoral persons, who had repeatedly been dealt with by their pastors, brought false charges against the entire company of pastors in their church. The charges were obviously false, and were easily proved so. Also, the congregation, knowing the characters of the men involved, had no difficulty in perceiving their true motivation.

All churches recognize that charges may not be lightly entertained against elders, because of the vulnerability of elders, and Satan's desire to discredit them. In this situation, the charges had but little surface plausibility, but the pastors who were charged decided that they wanted a public vindication. A Judicial Commission made up of other elders in the denomination was formed to hear the matter. Suddenly, the conspirators realized that these other elders were longtime friends of the men they had falsely charged. In any small, conservative denomination, all the pastors know each other. In the providence of God, this forms a check on the ability of Satan to discredit God's special office bearers. At any rate, the conspirators began to argue that these friendships constituted a bribe, and thus that *none* of these elders and pastors might sit in judgment on the case. One can see that the Pharisaical position would imply the total disqualification of the courts of any small denomination, and since virtually all

The answer to this concern is that if the pastors are so weak morally that they are incapable of assuming an objective stance, then they should not have been made elders in the first place. Contrary to B. F. Skinner, men are not machines, simply programmed by their environment. Men, particularly Christian men, have the ability to distance themselves psychologically from such influences. It may require an act of will to remain impartial, but it is hardly impossible. Moreover, human justice is not perfect, which is why there is a final and perfect Judgment at the end of history. If a man brings a matter to a human court, of Church or of state, he implicitly declares his willingness to abide by its procedures and judgments. If he rebels, he is to be put to death, or excommunicated, as the case may be (Dt. 17:8-13).

Indeed, God as our Ultimate Judge knows each of us with a fullness of intimacy which goes infinitely beyond our own self-knowledge. This does not disqualify Him from acting as Judge. He knows when we have offended Him, and when we have pleased Him with "sweet savor" offerings. On what philosophical basis, then, do we assert that a human judge, the analogue of God, must disqualify himself if he knows the men before the court? If a judge has been offended by one or the other of the men in the past, or has received gifts from them, does that disqualify him? If he knows the characters of the men involved, due to years of pastoring them, does this disqualify him? Why is ignorance a criterion of objectivity? I suspect that lying behind this correlation of impersonality with impartiality is the pernicious philosophy of Stoicism, not of Christianity.

In short, it is wrong for a judge to accept a gift or a bribe from

---

conservative denominations are quite small, no conservative denomination would be able to field a court! Finally, unwilling to trust in the providence of God, unwilling to trust in the objectivity of the elders they had sworn submission to, and under the advice of a modern Pharisee, all of the conspirators renounced the faith of the saints, and left the Church of Jesus Christ.

The question illustrated in this sorry concatenation of events is whether or not previous friendships (with all that entails) constitute a "bribe." The Pharisaical position says yes; the common sense (and Biblical) position, as this story illustrates, says no.

one of the parties in a matter before him. The law does not state that if he has ever received a gift from one party in the past, he must disqualify himself. To insist upon such as an implication of this commandment is to seek after perfect justice in this life, and is ultimately a denial of the limitations of man, and thus a denial of the prerogatives of God.

A bribe is not a tip. Tipping does not take place in a courtroom situation, and is considered part of the pay of the person serving you. People engaged in personal services tend to work harder if part of their pay comes in the form of tips. Thus, while tipping appears to be less efficient than simple payment, it is actually both more personal and results in greater efficiency in those kinds of jobs that entail personal service. In some places, a tip or bribe is expected before a relatively impersonal service is rendered. For instance, I am told that in some countries you may not be able to get an airline ticket without greasing the palm of the person behind the ticket counter. Here the requirement of the tip is offensive, because no personal service is being rendered.[9] The quality of performance in the transaction is the same in every case: selling a ticket. In the case of a waitress, however, the quality of performance can vary greatly, and a tip is an incentive to good performance.

The Sojourner

9. A stranger [sojourner] you (s.) shall not oppress; you (pl.) understand the life of the stranger [sojourner], for you (pl.) were strangers [sojourners] in the land of Egypt.

In context, this verse applies directly to the court, but the rationale of sympathy expands its application to all of life. Israel was located at the crossroads of the world. Caravans from Europe to Asia and Africa came down the Kings' Highway through Palestine, as did caravans from Europe to Asia, and from Africa to Asia, and vice versa. There were always strangers in the land. At

---

9. In fact, since it is practically required, is it simply a hidden cost, masquerading as a tip.

the time God gave this law, the sojourners were the mixed multitude which accompanied Israel out of Egypt.

They are enjoined to remember what it felt like to be strangers in Egypt. The threat implied is that if they deal harshly with strangers, God will return them to Egypt where they belong.

The alternation of singular and plural implies that since the entire community sympathizes with the stranger, the community should step in to prevent any individual from acting unjustly. It also implies that when a judge oppresses the stranger, the entire nation will suffer. The whole nation suffers for the sins of its leaders.

This verse, reminding the people that they had been strangers in Egypt, sets us up for the last section of laws, which again deals with sabbath rest, rest from the bondage in Egypt, and gives the laws for the feasts which had been God's rationale for demanding Israel's deliverance.

Judicial Procedure

As an addendum to this chapter, I wish to add some remarks about judicial procedure from Deuteronomy 19:15-21.

15. A single witness shall not rise up against a man on account of any iniquity or any sin which he sins; at the mouth of two or three witnesses a matter shall be confirmed.

16. If a malicious witness rises up against a man to testify against him of turning aside,

17. Then both the men who have the dispute shall stand before the LORD, before the priests and the judges who will be in those days.

18. And the judges shall investigate thoroughly; and if the witness is a false witness, and he has testified against his brother falsely,

19. Then you shall do to him just as he had intended to do to his brother. Thus you shall purge the evil from among you.

20. And the rest will hear and be afraid, and will never again do such an evil thing among you.

21. Thus your eye shall not show pity: life for life, eye for eye, tooth for tooth, hand for hand, foot for foot.

My purpose in taking up this passage is that it sheds light on Exodus 23:1-9. In verse 15, we are instructed that no man is to be convicted save at the "mouth" of two or three witnesses. This might seem to exclude the non-verbal testimony of fingerprints and the like, but in fact the Bible speaks of the testimony of non-human "voices," as in Genesis 4:10-11, "And He said, 'What have you done? The *voice* of your brother's blood is crying to Me from the ground. And now you are cursed from the ground, which has *opened its mouth* to receive your brother's blood from your hands.' " At least two lines of evidence are, however, required.

In a recent Church trial, questions were raised concerning verses 16-19. The precise matter at dispute was whether this passage means that a false witness is automatically to be counted as a malicious witness, or whether a witness who proves false must also be proven malicious before the Law of Equivalence can be applied to him. Mr. Jones (not the real name) brought charges against Mr. Smith. He charged that Smith had stolen $1,000 from him. Thus, Smith owed him double restitution, claimed Jones. The Church court informed Jones that if he lost the case, and Smith were declared innocent, then he would have to pay Smith $2,000. Jones countered, however, by asserting that the court would have to prove that he was *malicious* before he would be liable under Deuteronomy 19:19. If Jones were right, then a false witness would only be liable for his false charges if it could be proven that he was malicious in bringing them (according to modern American notions of what "malice" is).

Verse 16 states that if a "malicious" (*ḥamas*) witness rises up to accuse a man, then the matter is to be brought before the priests or the judges, according to whether the matter pertains to the LORD or to the civil realm (Dt. 17:9; 2 Chron. 19:11). In verse 18 we are told that if the witness is a "false" (*sheqer*) witness, one who has falsely (*sheqer*) accused his brother, then the Law of Equivalence applies.

As it stands, verses 18 and 19 state that an accuser need only be proven false (*sheqer*) in order for the Law of Equivalence to apply. In larger context, the *sheqer* witness has also been described as *ḥamas* (v. 16). *Sheqer* has to do with deception, disappointment, or falsehood. It is used for false or deceitful gods, for false witnesses, and for any form of lying. Thus, the overall meaning implies that a trust has been betrayed. A man trusted in a certain god, who turned out to be a fake; a man trusted the word of another man, which turned out to be false; a man swore an oath to speak the truth in court, and then told falsehoods. *Hamas* has to do with violence and wrong action. It is used for violent actions, as well as for injurious language and harsh treatment, ruthlessness, and the like: "a witness that *promotes* violence and wrong."

We might say that *sheqer* is a violation of the ninth commandment, while *ḥamas* is a violation of the sixth. By themselves, however, these terms do not help us to interpret the law at the point in question. Clearly, a man who goes to the trouble either to be deceptive or malicious is doing so self-consciously. Thus, intent may be presumed in such cases; and intent is what is at issue here.

The contexts of these passages also shed light on the matter. The man standing at risk in giving testimony is not simply any witness who may be called, but the man bringing the charges. In Exodus 23:2, he is a co-conspirator. In Deuteronomy 19, he is the equivalent of a murderer (vv. 11-13). Other witnesses may be misled themselves, and may give false testimony without intending to do so. Human psychology is quite complex. Investigation by the judges or lawyers may assist a "mere" witness in clarifying his testimony. There would need to be proof of conspiracy before a mere witness would stand at risk under this law. Not so regarding the man or men actually bringing the charges. The accuser is the one in view in this passage, and if the court finds him guilty of deception, then the Law of Equivalence applies to him.

So then, we are back to the main question: Must the court automatically find a man bringing false charges to be guilty of deception and malice? Or is it possible for such a man simply to back out scotfree by saying, "Well, I intended well, and I certainly was not malicious or deceitful. I honestly believed that this man was guilty." Now, in that case, the court would either have to prove, or have to entertain a second suit to prove, that the man *intended* to be deceitful or malicious. The problem with this notion is obvious: How do you prove intent?

Several other observations are relevant. First, Deuteronomy 19:18, 19 only require that the accuser be found false, not that he be found malicious, in order for the Law of Equivalence to be applied. On the basis of a narrow interpretation of the text itself, thus, there is no need to prove malicious intent.

Second, perjury is always a crime and must severely be punished. What is in specific view here, however, is not mere perjury (a man seeking to protect his wife, for instance), but perjury on the part of a man actually bringing charges and seeking specific punishment for the accused. Such a man can be presumed, without fear of doubt, to have carefully considered the matter beforehand. He is seeking a certain penalty (Dt. 19:19). He has not simply been called in to give testimony. He has gone out of his way to make a charge. When he is proven false (or rather, fails to prove his charge), it hardly squares with his actions for him to back off and say, "Well, I was confused, but I meant well."

Third, the general effect of these two viewpoints should also be considered. The understanding which requires *proof* of malice before a false accuser can be sentenced can easily be seen to open the court up to an infinity of false accusations from litigious persons. Men may freely bring false charges whenever they wish, without risk, unless it can be *proved* that their inner, subjective intentions are malicious. And how does one prove such a thing? What constitutes proof? On the other hand, the automatic-punishment view would tend to clear the court of such litigious persons. A man would think long and hard before conspiring to present a false charge, knowing that if his perjury were discovered, he would suffer automatic punishment.

Fourth, thus the tendency of the automatic-punishment approach is to impel men to settle matters out of court, which squares nicely with the teaching of Scripture elsewhere: "Make friends quickly with your opponent at law while you are with him on the way; in order that your opponent may not deliver you to the judge, and the judge to the officer, and you be thrown into prison" (Matt. 5:24; cf. Luke 12:58).

Finally, the Law of Equivalence only applies to the false accuser, not to any mere witness who may give false testimony. Other kinds of punishments would, however, be in order for the latter (cf., e.g., Dt. 25:3).

10

SABBATHS AND FESTIVALS (EXODUS 23:10-19)

The sabbath is one of the knottiest problems in Christian theology. Over the past 2000 years, opinions of great theologians have moved back and forth between a no-sabbath viewpoint and a strict sabbath viewpoint, as regards day-keeping. As a result, strange anomalies abound. Just to take one instance, the Presbyterian and Reformed churches, whose confessional statements enjoin strict sabbath keeping (of one variety), trace their theological lineage to Augustine, Calvin, and Knox. Yet these three theologians would not be permitted to take communion in many Presbyterian and Reformed churches because of their view of the sabbath![1]

I have dealt with this problem extensively elsewhere,[2] and here wish simply to summarize a few points relevant to this passage. Man was made a creature who needs a day of rest in a pattern of one in seven. Also, he needs times of festivity during the year. God has revealed to us a rest pattern and a festival pattern. In the New Covenant, in its fullest form (see Appendix A), men will be in continuous rest and festival, in the resurrection. Thus, the New Testament writers tell us that the sabbath day has been done away in the New Covenant; it has been fulfilled (Col. 2:16; Rom. 14:5; Gal. 4:9-10). In essence, the New Covenant entails a perpetual sabbath and festival. But as long as we remain in

---

1. On this see Richard B. Gaffin, Jr., "Calvin and the Sabbath" (Th.M. thesis, Westminster Theological Seminary, 1962).

2. In a series in "The Geneva Papers," a monthly publication of Geneva Ministries, P.O. Box 8376, Tyler, TX 75711.

the Old Creation, in bodies of the first Adam (pre-resurrection), the pattern of rest and festivity set out in the Old Testament is applicable to us.

I suggest the following formula: In the Old Covenant, men were to worship on the sabbath day (Lev. 23:3); in the New Covenant, men are to sabbath on the day of worship. The Lord's Day is not a "sabbath *day*," and properly should not be called such, except by extension. (We do not wish, however, to quarrel about words.) The day now is defined by worship and judgment, not by rest.

The typological aspects of the sabbath do not concern us here, though they bear on how we are to keep the Lord's Day in the New Covenant. The passage before us concerns the practical aspects of rest and the giving of rest. We shall, however, be concerned with the typological aspects of the festival calendar. We may divide the section into two parts:

1. Three laws concerning the observance of sabbaths (vv. 10-13).

2. Ten laws concerning the observance of festivals (vv. 14-19).

Sabbaths

10-11. Six years you shall sow your land and gather its produce, (11.) but the seventh year you shall let it rest and lie fallow, and the poor of your people will eat, and what they leave the wild beasts will eat. Thus you shall do to your vineyard and your olive orchard.

12. Six days you shall do your work, and on the seventh day you shall rest, so that your ox and your ass may rest, that the son of your maidservant and the stranger [sojourner] may be refreshed.

13. And in all that I have said to you (pl.), you (pl.) shall take care, and the name of other gods you (pl.) shall not mention nor let be heard out of your (s.) mouth.

When Israel was in Egypt, they were in the cruel bondage of pagan chattel slavery. They never got to rest. The wording of the sabbath laws here reflects the deliverance from slavery, in that the emphasis is on rest, and the giving of rest to one's subordinates, particularly to one's slaves.

In a sense, land is a living organism, composed of countless living organisms. The life of the land moves at a much slower pace than the life of men or animals, but even so, the land needs rest in order to be refreshed, just as men and animals do. To restore the land and keep it healthy, it is to be left fallow one year in seven. Any produce it may yield is free to any man or beast. The poor may freely take such produce from anyone's property. Here is one more practical social welfare law, of the gleaning variety (as opposed to the humanistic "hand-out" variety).

Even though the land was conquered in stages (Ex. 23:29), all the land was to rest simultaneously (Lev. 25). This required the Israelites to trust in God, and they failed to do so (Lev. 26:34, 43; 2 Chron. 36:21). God's promise was, however, that there would be a triple harvest in the sixth year (Lev. 25:20-22), which would make up any financial loss.

Even though we do not have such a guarantee of a miracle today, the principle of crop rotation, of letting the land lie fallow one year in seven, remains sound. The use of fertilizers to keep soil in continual production eventually destroys the earth.

The emphasis in v. 12 is on the giving of rest to one's subordinates, even down to the children of slaves and one's animals. The purpose is so that they might be refreshed. This word for "refreshed" implies catching one's breath, as well as reviving one's life (2 Sam. 16:14).

According to Leviticus 23:3, the sabbath day was also the time for worship in the local synagogue. The prophetic, teaching form of worship was decentralized in Israel, with local Levites teaching in local synagogues. The priestly, sacramental aspect of worship was centralized at the Temple, and highlighted by the three major festivals. Here we are dealing with sabbath day worship, and God enjoins them to pay close attention to His words as they are taught sabbath by sabbath, and to be sure not to give worship to any other gods. The plural in verse 13 implies corporate worship, and the return to the singular in the last phrase covers private devotion as well.

In my pamphlet, *Sabbath Breaking and the Death Penalty: An Alternate View*,[3] I have addressed the question of the death penalty for sabbath breaking, and some wider ramifications of sabbath keeping in general.

Festivals

14. Three times in the year you shall keep a feast to Me.

15a. The Feast of the Unleavened Bread you shall keep: For seven days you shall eat unleavened bread, even as I commanded you, at the appointed season in the month of Abib, for in it you came out of Egypt;

15b. And none shall present himself before Me empty-handed.

16a. And the Feast of the Harvest: of the first-fruits of your work, of what you sow in the field.

16b. And the Feast of Ingathering at the end of the year, when you gather in the fruit of your labor from the field.

17. Three times in the year all your males will present themselves before the Master, the LORD.

18a. You shall not offer the blood of My Sacrifice with leavened bread.

18b. And you shall not let the fat of My Feast remain until morning.

19a. The first of the first-fruits of your ground you shall bring into the house of the LORD.

19b. You shall not boil a kid in its mother's milk.

God's demand to Pharaoh was that His people be let go so that they might celebrate a worship festival to Him (see Chapter 2). It is most appropriate, then, that the Book of the Covenant closes with laws which specify this great privilege to the sons of Israel.

The festival calendar of the Old Testament is no more and no less binding on the Church today than is the sabbath day. Just as the Lord's Day has come in the place of the sabbath day, so the Church has devised voluntary festivals in the place of those of the Old Covenant. Just as the Old Covenant feasts followed the rhythmic pace of the natural year, giving typological meaning to

---

3. Forthcoming from Geneva Ministries.

it, so the Christian calendar also moves from the dark winter of the Nativity, through the rising of the sun, and the Resurrection of the world in the spring.[4]

There were to be three festivals, and the people were to attend all three. In Exodus 34:24, God guaranteed them that their lands would not be plundered while they were away at the festivals. In Exodus 23:17, the men were required to attend, but Deuteronomy 16:11 commands the attendance of all able to make the trip (cf. 1 Sam. 1:3, 9; Luke 2:41). Gifts were brought to the Lord at each feast, though tithes were brought in at the Feast of Ingathering (or Tabernacles; see Appendix C).

We are not told why all the males were to appear before God; thus, we are confronted with the fact itself. Like the wave offering, waved toward God and then received back from Him as a token of His ownership of the entire harvest, so all the men of Israel were waved before God as a token of His ownership of the entire people. Since verse 15b states that none shall appear empty-handed, and Deuteronomy 16:16 ties this directly to the thrice annual presentation, the men were to give an offering to the LORD at that time. Perhaps it was also a time of instruction in the law. The men would then teach their families (compare 1 Cor. 14:34-35). According to Deuteronomy 31:10ff., the law was to be read to everyone every seven years, which implies that women and children were not required except on that occasion.

I should like to make one comment on the ceremony required here. It was important that the men stand before God, formally presented to Him, and it was important that each ceremonially present an offering to Him. I draw from this that God wishes us to stand before Him, in a formal sense, in worship. The act of congregational standing for prayer is analogous to an army's passing

---

4. Christmas correlates to the Feast of Hanukkah, a mid-winter festival which originated during the period between the Old and New Testaments. It signified the restoration of the Temple after its defilement by Antiochus Epiphanes. Part of the ceremonies entailed the filling of the city and Temple with lights. It is easy to see how this relates to the coming of Christ, the light of the world and the true Temple of God. Jesus attended this feast in John 10:22.

in review before its Commander in Chief. Such formality is good
for us, and apparently required by God. I also draw from this that
it is important that tithes and gifts be presented to Him formally
as part of worship. It is better to put your gift in the plate as part
of the formal ceremony of worship before God's throne, than simply to mail it to the church.

I. *The Feast of Unleavened Bread*

All the leaven was to be purged out of the house for the feast of
Passover and Unleavened Bread. Leaven signifies growth and
maturation.[5] The old growth principle of Egypt had to be cut off.
When Israel arrived in Canaan, new leaven would be found in
God's land, and a new growth principle in righteousness would be
established. Each new year, at Passover, the old leaven was to be
cut off, and new begun. Thus, at the Feast of Pentecost (Harvest),
leavened bread was offered to God, leavened with the new leaven
of the new year (Lev. 23:17).

Leaven was not to be eaten for seven days. Why? Possibly as a
token of a new creation. God had made the world in six days.
Man was to have joined God in resting on the seventh, and then
on the eighth man would begin his work, kneading the dough of
creation and entering into the process of bringing it to maturity.
Man is the leaven of creation (cf., e.g., Matt. 13:33). Unleavened
bread for seven days would recapitulate the first week of creation,
before man began his leavening work. A new creation provided
man opportunity to begin anew, with the leaven of righteous labor
this time.

Where did the new leaven come from, since all leaven had
been purged for seven days? We are nowhere told. Possibly the
lees of wine were used to start the leavening process up again.
Also, leaven was made "from fine white bran kneaded with must;
from the meal of certain plants such as fitch or vetch; or from

---

5. Because the Bible so often speaks of the leaven of Adamic sinfulness, commentators have often linked leaven with evil. There were, however, leavened
offerings, most notably the one presented at Pentecost (Lev. 23:17), and the
kingdom of God is likened to leaven in Matthew 13:33.

barley mixed with water and then allowed to stand till it turned sour. As baking developed, leaven was produced from bread flour kneaded without salt and kept till it passed into a state of fermentation."[6] The new leaven came from the holy land.

The two commands in verse 18 refer to Passover. It was the death of the lamb which brought the old leaven to an end, and made new resurrection leaven possible. Thus, the old leaven had to be gone before the Passover sacrifice was made. (For a description of how Passover was conducted in the Temple, see 2 Chron. 35.)

The fat of the sacrifice was the choicest, juiciest part. Neither it nor any of the rest of the lamb was to remain until morning. The Passover meal was not ordinary food, and was not to be treated as such. Whatever was not eaten was to be burned up (Ex. 12:10). Historically, this has often been taken to indicate that leftover communion bread and wine should either be consumed or disposed of, but not retained. Protestants have generally not followed this practice, holding that after the communion, the bread and wine "revert" to common use. Protestants have manifested an aversion to consecrating material objects, based on the belief that in the New Covenant, all material objects have been definitively cleansed in Christ once and for all. Concerning communion, it has been felt that the ministers do not set apart the elements of bread and wine; rather, they are taken up and used by God in the very act of reception (eating). God does all the consecration, and leftover bread and wine has never been consecrated, for consecration takes place in the mouth.

Perhaps we can sidestep this debate (which takes us rather far afield from the focus of this study) by noting that nothing is to remain until *morning*. Generally speaking, the whole Old Covenant takes place at night. Evening precedes morning in Genesis 1, and by extension in the history of the world as well.[7] I believe that the

---

6. *The Illustrated Bible Dictionary* (Wheaton, IL: Tyndale, 1980), p. 891.

7. See my essays on sunrise in my series "Christianity and the Calendar," in *The Geneva Papers*, a monthly publication of Geneva Ministries, P.O. Box 8376, Tyler, TX 75711. A complete file of these is available for a contribution.

meaning of this stipulation was to point to the fact that Passover was simply a figure of the salvation to come. It sustained the people annually, but would be superseded at the Resurrection of Christ, when the Sun of Righteousness would arise on Easter morning. Similarly, the peace sacrifice was not to be consumed after the *third day* (Lev. 7:17), pointing to its supersession in the third-day resurrection of Christ.

Eating signifies application and identification. The death of the substitute lamb was applied to the people as they ate it. Just so today, the sacrifice of Jesus Christ is applied to his people as they eat the sacramental bread and wine. The action of the sacrifice is long since over and done with, and Christ has been raised and is seated in heaven; but the food of the sacrifice is still being taken from the altar and eaten, thus applying His death to His people.

On the day after the sabbath that came during the Feast of Unleavened Bread, the first sheaf of picked grain was waved before the Lord (Lev. 23:10-14). This was the first of the first-fruits, and is probably referred to in Ex. 23:19a. This ties the Feast of Unleavened Bread to the Feast of the Harvest. Just as soon as the Lamb has been offered for the people, immediately the land begins to blossom with new life and fruitfulness. There is no delay in the progressive enjoyment of the Kingdom of God.

A parallel symbol will help us understand this better. In John 7:37-39, "Jesus stood and cried out, saying, 'If any man thirst, let him come unto Me and drink. He that believes on Me, as the Scripture has said, out of his belly shall flow rivers of living water.' But this He spoke concerning the Spirit, which they that believe on Him were to receive." Now, what is the water? It is clearly, first of all, the influence of Christ and the Spirit. It also, however, flows from individual believers out into the world.

So it is with leaven. The leaven inserted into the world at the first creation was humanity. Adam and his descendents would leaven the world, and bring it to fulfillment. This leaven (humanity) was corrupted. Thus, the Second Adam came to begin the New Creation. First and foremost, the leaven inserted into the Church is the Holy Spirit, who came and leavened the bread of the Church at Pentecost (Lev. 23:17). Secondarily, the leaven is the redeemed humanity, the Church, now inserted into the three measures of meal (the world). This symbolism is most appropriate, since leavened meal is what is normally used as starter in leavening more meal. A baker reserves a small part of his leavened dough, and uses it to start more. Thus, the insertion of leaven (the Holy Spirit), is done once and for all, and then spreads from dough to dough day by day.

Thus, the Feast of Unleavened Bread required a week of unleaven before the leaven is reinserted into the bread. This can more clearly now be seen as a sign of the re-creation of the world in seven days, followed by the new leavening of the new humanity beginning on the eighth.

II. *The Feast of the Harvest*

Also known as Weeks or Pentecost, the one-day Feast of the Harvest was the time at which the first-fruits of the field were presented, baked in a leavened loaf (Lev. 23:17), to the Lord, in recognition that it was He who gave the harvest.

The Feast of the Harvest also fell on the day after a sabbath, seven weeks after the waving of the first sheaf (Lev. 23:15-21). The seven days of re-creation have issued in seven weeks of true righteous maturation and growth, for it was a leavened loaf which was waved to God. Jesus arose on the day of the first sheaf, and imparted the Holy Spirit to his disciples on that day (John 20:22), though the full outpouring of the leaven of the Spirit did not come until seven weeks later (Acts 2).

From this we see the progressive growth of the kingdom of God. Immediately after the Sacrifice, the first-fruit sheaves become available for eating (after they have been waved before God). Seven weeks later, there is enough to bake into a loaf to wave before God. But there is still more growth to come, which will be made manifest at the Feast of Ingathering.

The liturgy of the first-fruits is found in Deuteronomy 26:1-11.

III. *The Feast of the Ingathering*

Also known as Booths or Tabernacles, this eight-day feast climaxed the festival year for Israel, coming seven months after Passover. It was here that the tithe was presented (see Appendix C). All the people were to make shelters of branches and live in them all week (Lev. 23:39-43). It also signified the ingathering of all the nations of the world (Num. 29:12-34 — 70 bulls for the 70 nations of Genesis 10).

Since the Feast of the Ingathering was a celebration of the fullness of life, prosperity, and joy, it was not to be mixed or associated with death. The prohibition on mixing life and death is the theme of Deuteronomy 14 (see Appendix B). Just as Ex. 23:19a encapsulates the Feast of the Harvest (tying it with Passover), so v. 19b summarizes the meaning of the Feast of the Ingathering. It is sometimes thought that boiling a kid in milk was a magic ritual used by the Canaanites, and that this is why it was forbidden. The text, however, does not forbid boiling a kid in milk, but in its own mother's milk. The reason is that life and death must not be mixed. That milk which had been a source of life to the kid may not be used in its death. Any other milk might be used, but not its mother's.

This law is thrice stated in the Torah (Ex. 23:19; 34:26; Dt. 14:21). It is obviously quite important, yet its significance eludes us. There are many laws which prohibit the mixing of life and death, yet we wish to know the precise nuance of each. There is no example of the breaking of this law in Scripture, unless we go to a metaphorical application, seeing the kid as a symbol for a human child.

We notice that the kid is a young goat, a child. The word only occurs 16 times in the Old Testament. In Genesis 27:9, 16, Rebekah put the skins of a kid upon Jacob when she sent him to masquerade as Esau before Isaac. Here the mother helps her child (though Jacob was in his 70s at the time). In Genesis 38:17, 20, 23, Judah pledged to send a kid to Tamar as payment for her services as a prostitute. In the providence of God, this was symbolic, because Judah had in fact failed to provide Tamar the kid to

which she was entitled: Judah's son Shelah. Judah gave his seal
and cord, and his staff, as pledges that the kid would be sent, but
Tamar departed, and never received the kid. When she was found
pregnant, she produced the seal and cord and the staff, as
evidence that Judah was the father. The children that she bore
became her kids, given her by Judah in exchange for the return of
his cord and seal and his staff.[8] Finally, when Samson visited his
wife, he took her a kid, signifying his intentions (Jud. 15:1).

These passages seem to indicate a symbolic connection between the kid and a human child, the son of a mother. (Indeed,
Job 10:10 compares the process of embryonic development to the
coagulation of milk.) The kid is still nursing, still taking in its
mother's milk in some sense, Jacob and Rebekah being an example of this. The mother is the protectress of the child, of the seed.
This is the whole point of the theology of Judges 4 and 5, the war
of the two mothers, Deborah and the mother of Sisera. Indeed,
the passage calls attention to milk. The milk of the righteous
woman was a tool used to crush the head of the serpent's seed
(Jud. 4:19f.; 5:24-27). How awful if the mother uses her own milk
to destroy her own seed!

Victor P. Hamilton has written that "in the husbandry of
Israel a young male kid was the most expendable of the animals,
less valuable than, say, a young lamb. The young males were
used for meat; the females kept for breeding. Thus, a kid served
admirably as a meat dish: Gen. 27:9, 16; Jud. 6:19; 13:15; 15:1; 1
Sam. 10:3; 16:20. . . ."[9] Accordingly, one of the most horrible
things imaginable is for a mother to boil and eat her own child.
This is precisely what happened during the siege of Jerusalem, as
Jeremiah describes it in Lamentations 4:10, "The hands of compassionate women boiled their own children; they became food
for them because of the destruction of the daughter of my people."
The same thing happened during the siege of Samaria, as recorded
in 2 Kings 6:28f. In both passages, the mother is said to *boil* her

8. Even in English, the term "kid" is used for children.
9. *Theological Wordbook of the Old Testament* (Chicago: Moody Press, 1980), p. 150.

child.

We are now in a better position to understand this law, and its placement in passages having to do with offerings to God. The bride offers children to her husband. She bears them, rears them on her milk, and presents them to her lord as her gift to him.[10] Similarly, Israel is to present the fruits of her hands, including her children, to her Divine Husband. She is not to consume her children, her offerings, or her tithes, but present them to God. The command not to boil the kid in its own mother's milk is a negative command; the positive injunction it implies is that we are to present our children and the works of our hands to God.

Jerusalem is the mother of the seed (Ps. 87:5; Gal. 4:26ff.). When Jerusalem crucified Jesus Christ, her Seed, she was boiling her kid in her own milk. In Revelation 17, the apostate Jerusalem has been devouring her faithful children: "And I saw the woman drunk with the blood of the saints and with the blood of the witnesses of Jesus." Her punishment, under the Law of Equivalence, is to be devoured by the gentile kings who supported her (v. 17).[11]

The New Covenant

These three festivals come together in the Lord's Supper for Christians. Whether we use leavened bread, signifying that we live after Pentecost, or unleavened bread, signifying that we get a new start in life each time we partake of Holy Communion, it remains that the only feast God has commanded us to celebrate is the Lord's Supper. That is the occasion for us to drink wine and make merry before Him (Dt. 14:26).

Because these festivals are fulfilled in the Lord's Supper, we have no more required feasts. Man is still a creature of festivity,

---

10. Notice that Abraham gave a feast the day Isaac was weaned from his mother's milk, and that it was on this occasion that Isaac, now weaned, had to confront the threat of Ishmael. Sarah, presenting her child to Abraham, took measures to protect him.

11. On this passage in Revelation, see David Chilton's forthcoming *Exposition of the Book of Revelation*.

however, and where the Church refuses to set up a festival calendar, men simply use whatever pagan calendar surrounds them. Churches which attack Christmas and Easter as "pagan" holidays (because pagan cultures also celebrate feasts at these times of the year) generally wind up making a big to-do about Thanksgiving, New Year's Day, and the Fourth of July, festivals which tend to partake of the genuinely pagan idolatry of nationalism.

11

CONCLUSION (EXODUS 23:20-33)

Since our study is focused on the laws of the Book of the Covenant, we shall only look briefly at its epilogue. The other places where the law of God is presented end with blessings and curses (Lev. 26; Dt. 28). The blessings and curses here consist of warnings to obey the Angel of the Lord, the Captain of the Lord's hosts. God's pillar-chariot of fire and cloud would go before them (cloud = chariot, Ezk. 1) and bring them into the promised land (Ex. 23:20-23).

They were not to prostrate themselves in worship before any of the Canaanite gods, but were to destroy all of their places of worship, including their frequently-phallic memorial pillars (v. 24). If they served the Lord only, He would remove from them all sickness, and there would be no miscarriages or barrenness in the land (v. 25). He would make it easy for them to defeat their enemies, by sending rumors of fear into the land before them (see Josh. 2:11), and by sending hornets ahead to drive out the people (vv. 26-27).

So that the wild beasts would not multiply in a deserted land, God promised to drive the Canaanites out little by little (v. 29-30). Man was created to take dominion over the animals, and even the dominion of wicked Canaanites was preferable to complete wildness.

All the Canaanites were to be driven out. Israel was not to ally itself with any of them, lest they be taken in a snare (vv. 31-33). Sadly, we see from Judges 1 and 2 that Israel was not consistent with this promise, and thus God repeatedly had to chastise them.

194

Indeed, right away in Exodus 32 they fell away, and received the implied curse of this passage, as the God Who had promised to protect them if they were faithful turned against them because of their faithlessness.

Practically, we see from this a program of Christian conquest. We are advised that we should not expect to take over society as a Christian minority, but to work at influencing and changing society little by little. We have no mandate to exterminate whole races of people today, except as we "exterminate" them by means of converting them into the Christian race. The roots of the tares are intertwined with those of the wheat (Matt. 13: 24ff.), and the former cannot be uprooted without also destroying the latter. Gradualism, therefore, is the order of the day.

We may expand on this to point out that Christians frequently do not know how to run society. Suppose all non-Christians resigned from all government posts tomorrow, and invited Christians to take over. Do we have Christians in our local community who know the ins and outs of running the water department, or the sanitation department, or how to use firearms against criminals? Probably not. Christian infiltration and influence must, therefore, be gradual.

The promise not to drive out the Canaanites all at once, then, is most gracious of God. He will not leave His children in dire straits. He will use the Canaanites to protect us from the "wild beasts," until we are mature enough to take over on our own. Here, then, is the method by which Christians may work to impose these righteous civil laws upon societies in the world today.

Appendix A

OLD AND NEW COVENANT

Theologians use the terms 'Old Covenant' and 'New Covenant' in a variety of ways, and so it is necessary for me to spell out how I am using the terms.

It is sometimes assumed that man was created to be a covenant-receiver, but which of the covenants man receives has nothing to do with his fundamental nature. Man is always "in" some covenant, but by nature he is not in any particular covenant. I reject this idea. It seems to me that a Biblical philosophy of man and covenant should be worded this way: that Adamic flesh is definitively linked to the Old Creation and to the First (or Old) Covenant. The placement of the sabbath in the First Covenant (with Adam) indicated that the goal of history was a transfigured condition, with new flesh, a new creation, and a new covenant.[1] Because of sin, this consummation comes through death and resurrection, so that we speak not of a transfigured body, but of a resurrection body.

The New Covenant cannot, then, arrive in history apart from the resurrection body, for the New Covenant is tied to the condition of man in resurrection and in the new creation. Jesus Christ alone is in the resurrection body, and in the perfect environment of heaven, so that He alone is in the New Covenant in this full sense.

Christians still live in the Old Creation, in Old Adamic flesh,

---

1. I have dealt with this more extensively in my essays on the Sabbath in "The Geneva Papers." These are available from Geneva Ministries, P.O. Box 8376, Tyler, TX 75711.

and must still keep the terms of the Old Adamic Covenant (take dominion, rest on one day in seven, etc.). The Holy Spirit, however, has come into the middle of history to overlay the *essence* of the New Covenant upon the Old Covenant situation.[2] Thus, Christians are in the New Covenant by faith, and by the experience of the Holy Spirit. They eat Christ's resurrection flesh and drink His resurrection blood, and thereby (by faith) come to have resurrection life in themselves (John 6:53-58; Luke 22:15-20). They are in union with the resurrected Christ. Historically speaking, in the resurrection of Jesus Christ the New Covenant *came*, once and for all. The essential dividing line in history is at Jesus' resurrection, not at the end of history when the rest of us are resurrected. In a phrase, Christians are in the New Covenant, but still live in Old Adamic flesh, in the Old Creation, and still must perform the Old Covenant tasks of dominion.

This opens up the question of the status of believers before the resurrection of Christ. They lived in the New Covenant by anticipation. The New Covenant was provisionally administered to them. Since Christ had not been raised, however, the New Covenant had not *come* definitively to them, and so all their covenants were extensions and specifications of the original Old Adamic Covenant.

Since the Old Adamic Covenant had in it a type of the consummation (the sabbath), a place of meeting (land, the Garden) and a sacrament of fellowship (the Tree of Life), after the Fall all the ceremonial pointers to the work of Christ were added to these three things. The ceremonial law of the Old Testament is sabbatical, geographical, or sacramental in character, and falls away with the definitive coming of the New Covenant in the resurrection of Jesus Christ.

All the post-Fall specifications of the Old Covenant, then, are made on the basis of the sureness of Christ's coming work, and point to that work. Thus, these covenants *reveal* the New Covenant, but do not *bring* the New Covenant.

---

2. This ties to the third day/seventh day pattern, discussed in Chapter 3.

No one can be saved under the Old Covenant, for the sin of man brings only the curse of that covenant. Abraham and David were saved by faith in the New Covenant, in the Christ to come, even though they lived *under* the Old Covenant. Christians live *under* the New Covenant, but in the Old Creation.

In this chart, I have graphed this view, showing how people were to live under each covenant (the mode of life), what the essential nature of the period of history is, and what the condition of the creation is.

Specific Covenant	Condition of the Physical Creation	General Covenant (Covenantal Nature of the Period)	Mode of Life (Which General Covenant the Power for Life Proceeds From)
Adamic (Pre-Fall)	Old (First) Creation	Old Covenant	Flesh (Power of the First Creation proceeding from the First or Old Covenant)
Adamic (Post-Fall)	Old Creation	Old Covenant	Spirit (*Provisional* Power of the New Creation, proceeding from the New Covenant)
Noachic	Old Creation	Old Covenant	Spirit (provisional)
Abrahamic	Old Creation	Old Covenant	Spirit (provisional)
Mosaic	Old Creation	Old Covenant	Spirit (provisional)
Davidic	Old Creation	Old Covenant	Spirit (provisional)
New (pre-consummational)	Old Creation	New Covenant	Spirit (definitive)
New (consummational)	New Creation (New Heavens and Earth)	New Covenant	Spirit (consummational)

Appendix B

THE CASE LAWS CORRELATED
WITH THE TEN COMMANDMENTS

Reformed scholars, particularly in the Netherlands, have suggested ways to categorize the laws of the Pentateuch in groups connected with each of the Ten Commandments. I am indebted to Dr. Hendrick Krabbendam, of Covenant College, Lookout Mountain, Tennessee, for initially suggesting this to me, although I have modified the scheme he employs at certain points.[1]

The Two Givings of the Law

Moses, when sermonizing at the second giving of the law (Deuteronomy, from the Greek "deuter" = second, "nomy" = law), is able to follow the order of the Ten Words. The first giving of the case laws, however, was mixed in with historical circumstances, responding to needs, and thereby showing how necessary the laws were.

Ex. 21:1-11	4th
Ex. 21:12-36	6th
Ex. 22:1-15	8th
Ex. 22:16-31	7th
Ex. 23:1-9	9th
Ex. 23:10-19	4th

---

1. A fine study of the structure of Deuteronomy by a scholar unfamiliar with the Reformed work in this area is Stephen A. Kaufman, "The Structure of Deuteronomic Law," *Maarav* 1/2 (1978-79):105-158. I have also departed somewhat from Kaufman's structure. Walter Kaiser tends to follow Kaufman closely; cf. *Toward Old Testament Ethics* (Grand Rapids: Zondervan, 1983), chapter 8.

Ex. 23:20-33	1st
Ex. 25-Lev. 10	2nd
Lev. 11-24	3rd
Lev. 25	4th
Lev. 27	10th
Num. 1-4	5th
Dt. 6-11	1st
Dt. 12, 13	2nd
Dt. 14	3rd
Dt. 15:1-16:17	4th
Dt. 16:18-18:22	5th
Dt. 19:1-22:8	6th
Dt. 22:9-23:14	7th
Dt. 23:15-24:7	8th
Dt. 24:8-25:4	9th
Dt. 25:5-26:19	10th

The First Commandment

The first commandment speaks of the uniqueness of Yahweh, the LORD, and reminds the people of their redemption from Egypt. In Ex. 23:20-33, the people are exhorted to worship the Lord only, and to do so with a view to his bringing them into the land of Canaan. The Lord Who brought them out will bring them in. Deuteronomy 6-11 makes the same points over and over again.[2]

The Second Commandment

"There is one God, and one Mediator between God and man," says Paul in 1 Timothy 2:5. The second commandment concerns the uniqueness of the Mediator, by affirming that there is no contact between God and man except in the way *God* has instituted. No image of anything at all can be *made by man for the purpose* of regarding it as a contact point between God and man (see Judges 17 for a clear instance of this). The laws concerning the construction

---

2. Kaiser combines the first and second commandments and sees Deuteronomy 12 as dealing with them both.

of the Tabernacle and of the sacrificial system all fit in here (Ex. 25-Lev. 10). The sin of the people in Ex. 32 was a violation of the second commandment, for they made an idol and regarded it as the contact point with God.

Deuteronomy 12, 13 can be divided as follows:

12:1-14 There is to be only one place of mediation and special worship.

12:15-28 Animals may be slain for food anywhere, unlike during the wilderness wanderings when they were to be slain only at the sanctuary (Lev. 17:3, 4); but tithes and sacrifices only at the sanctuary.

12:29-31 Do not imitate the rituals (service) of the pagans.

12:32-13:5 The uniqueness of God's mediating Word.

13:6-18 The punishment for enticement of apostasy and idolatry.

The Third Commandment

The third commandment orders us to wear God's Name properly, not in a way connected with vanity and death, but in a way connected to life. Thus, the third commandment has to do with ceremonial life and death, cleanness and uncleanness. These are the concerns of Lev. 11-24:

11:1-47 Unclean animals involve identification with death, not with God.

12:1-8 The woman's loss of blood in childbirth is a sign that the child is born ceremonially (and Spiritually) dead, until God's Name is placed on him by circumcision (v. 3).

13-14 Leprosy signified a living death. Death was not allowed in the presence of God, where His Name was placed, so the leper had to stay away.

15:1-33 Any discharge from the private parts was a loss of life and an exposure of nakedness. The naked dead are not clothed in the Name of God.

16:1-34 The atonement, or covering, for sin, which was spreading death even to the sanctuary.

17:1-16 Life is in blood, but man is not to try to get life from

the blood of the creature, but solely from God. Life is to be
returned to God, Who gave it.

18:1-30 Uncovering nakedness through abominable practices.
When Adam and Eve sinned, their nakedness was exposed, and
they were cast out of God's presence, where His Name had been
placed (the garden).

19:1-37 Various laws, all predicated on the need to fear the
Name of God. Rationale for obedience: "I am the LORD." That is,
fear my Name.

20:1-27 Punishments for uncovering nakedness.

21:1-24 The priests are especially associated with God's
Name, and thus must especially separate from ceremonial death.

22:1-33 The sacrifices offered must not "profane My holy
Name" (vv. 2, 32).

23:1-44 Worship in the presence, before the Name, of God.

24:1-9 The light of God and the Name of God.

24:10-23 The punishment for cursing the Name of God.

Similarly in Deuteronomy:[3]

14:1-2 Excessive mourning not compatible with wearing God's
Name.

14:3-20 Unclean animals.

14:21a Do not eat dirt, flesh rotting and returning to dirt.

14:21b Do not confuse life and death by cooking a kid in its
own mother's milk, which had been its source of life.

14:22-29 Rejoice at the place where God has established His
Name (v. 23).

The Fourth Commandment

The fourth commandment has to do with rest, festivity, and
release from bondage. The Ordinances in Exodus 21 - 23 begin
and end with laws related to the fourth commandment:

21:1-11 Release of slaves from bondage into dominion-rest.

23:10-13 Sabbaths.

---

3. Kaiser puts Deuteronomy 13 and 14 under the third commandment. I
believe that he and Kaufman have not located the precise ethical perspective of
the third commandment properly.

23:14-19 Festivals.

Leviticus 25 also connects with the fourth commandment, following as it does immediately after the stoning of the man who cursed the Name of the Lord.

In Deuteronomy:[4]

15:1-11 Release of debts.

15:12-18 Release of Slaves.

15:19-23 Consecration to God; rest in God.

16:1-17 Festivals.

The Fifth Commandment

The fifth commandment has to do with submission to God in the form of submission to His earthly authorities. In Numbers 1-4 the leaders are set up for battle, and the Levitical authorities are established. In Deuteronomy:

16:18-20 Judges.

16:21-17:1 Submission before God.

17:2-13 The judgments of the judges.

17:14-20 Kings.

18:1-8 Levites.

18:9-22 Prophets.

The Sixth Commandment

The sixth commandment has to do with preserving life from violence. This is different from the third commandment, which has to do with avoiding death in the presence of God. In Deuteronomy:

19:1-13 Cities of Refuge and the regulation of the Avenger of Blood.

19:14 Violence against covenant life and property.

19:15-21 Murder as attempted by the tongue.

20:1-20 Laws of war, regulating violence.

---

4. Kaiser starts this section with 14:28, because of the mention of the festival and tithing. I think that the emphasis in 14:22-29 is on the *presence* (Name) of the LORD.

21:1-9 Laws for unsolved acts of violence.

21:10-14 Laws protecting the warbride from violence.

21:15-17 Laws for protecting the firstborn from violence.

21:18-21 Laws removing incorrigible criminals before they turn to violence.

21:22-23 Laws against degradation in death; violence to God's image.

22:1-8 Laws to promote life:

vv. 1-4 Return lost property.

v. 5 Distinguish male and female, promoting sexual life.

vv. 6-7 Preserve environment for future generations.

v. 8 Protect against accidental violence and harm.

The Seventh Commandment

The seventh commandment has to do with chastity and purity, in the bride of Christ and in the earthly marriage. In Numbers:

5:1-4 Chastity and Covenant membership.

5:5-10 Chastity and faithfulness to God.

5:11-31 The "ordeal" of jealousy.

6:1-21 The vow of the Nazirite, especially chaste and separated to God.

In Deuteronomy:

22:9-11 Covenant chastity, signified by not mixing things that differ symbolically. The ox is clean, and the ass unclean. Wool causes sweat, while linen does not (Ezk. 44:18; Gen. 3:19).

22:12 Reminder of covenant chastity (Num. 15:37-41).

22:13-21 Laws to protect the integrity of marriage.

22:22-29 Laws against adultery and rape.

22:30 Law against incest.

23:1-8 Chastity and the bride of the Lord.

23:9-14 Chastity and the warcamp, seen as the house of the heavenly Bridegroom.

The Eighth Commandment

The eighth commandment has to do with the preservation of propriety, the preservation of what is proper to one sphere or another. It is difficult to establish the boundary in Deuteronomy between the seventh and eighth commandments, because covenant chastity and covenant propriety are so close conceptually as to overlap. Moses may be deliberately blending the two commandments here:[5]

23:15-16 Foreign slaves who covenant with God become God's property (or, become part of His chaste bride).

23:17-18 It is improper to contribute a harlot's wages to God (or, a harlot cannot be part of God's bride).

23:19-20 Interest.

23:21-23 Money vowed to God.

23:24-25 Respect of the neighbor's property.

24:1-4 Propriety in divorce.

24:5 Newlyweds may not be "stolen" from one another.

24:6 Pledges.

24:7 Man-stealing.

The Ninth Commandment

The ninth commandment has to do with justice, impartiality, and false witness. In Deuteronomy:

24:8-9 Libel and leprosy.

24:10-13 Justice for the debtor.

24:14-15 Justice for the hired man.

24:16 Impartiality in punishment.

24:17-22 Justice for the stranger, orphan, and widow.

25:1-3 Justice in punishments.

25:4 Justice for all creatures.

The Tenth Commandment

The tenth commandment prohibits coveting of the neighbor's wife and house. It refers to any attempt to obtain something to which one has no right, even if one avoids violating the letter of the law. In Deuteronomy:[6]

---

5. Kaiser puts 23:15-18 with the seventh commandment.
6. Kaiser stops the tenth commandment with 25:16.

A. Not coveting the neighbor's wife (Dt. 5:21a):

25:5-10 So far from coveting the other man's wife and children, one should do good to the neighbor (in this case a brother), and build up his family as much as possible.

25:11-12 Any attack on the neighbor's ability to give pleasure to his wife and build up his family is to be severely punished.

B. Not coveting the neighbor's house, etc. (Dt. 5:21b):

25:13-16 The Christian is not to have the tools of a thief, lest he be tempted to use them.

25:17-19 The punishment of the envious Amalek. (On the grounds for this envy, see Numbers 24:20.)

26:1-19 The cure for covetousness: confession of grace and free payment of required moneys. (Compare Paul's advice, Eph. 4:28, "Let him that stole steal no more, but . . . . share.")

Leviticus 27 also has to do with paying vows.

Appendix C

TITHING: FINANCING
CHRISTIAN RECONSTRUCTION[1]

The Bible sets forth tithing as the principal means of financing the kingdom of God. Apart from a return to systematic, Biblical tithing, there will be no Christian reconstruction in America.

There is a great deal of confusion in the area of tithing in the Church at large today. Some hold that tithing is not clearly taught in the New Testament, and that we are not permitted to establish it from the Old. I have dealt with this theological viewpoint in the early chapters of this book.

Among those willing to take a "whole Bible" view, there is also confusion. This is partly due to the influence of a book called *Tithing and Dominion,* by Rousas J. Rushdoony and Edward A. Powell.[2] While there is much of value in this study, it suffers from a failure to grasp properly the nature of the tithe system set up in the Bible. To be specific, Powell and Rushdoony assume that there were three separate tithes, when in fact there was only one with several aspects. They also permit the tithe to be given at random to various kinds of Christian activities, when Scripture requires that it be given to the ecclesiastical order. To a great extent, the essay which follows is designed to correct the faults in Powell

---

1. This essay, with slight modifications for audience, appears in Gary North, ed., *Tactics of Christian Resistance.* Christianity and Civilization No. 3 (Tyler, TX: Geneva Divinity School Press, 1983). An earlier and less complete form of this essay was published in newsletter form by the Institute for Christian Economics in 1981.

2. (Box 67, Vallecito, CA: Ross House Books, 1979).

207

and Rushdoony's study. With these things in mind, however, I can recommend the examination of their study, since it does contain much of value.

The problem in the Church at large is due to the evil influence of "grace giving." The notion of grace giving places men in bondage, for they never know when they have given enough. It also dishonors God in that it encourages men to give as *they* please instead of as *He* has ordered. Also, in point of fact, men seldom give anywhere near ten percent of their net business income to God, so that grace giving usually means robbing God (Mal. 3:8-12). Tithing liberates men because it tells them exactly how much God requires, and leaves them free to use the remainder in dominion tasks.

I have set this discussion out in a series of numbered propositions. This is because it makes the various points easier for the reader to isolate, and because it condenses the essay by eliminating transitional sentences and paragraphs. We shall first of all consider the nature and rules concerning Biblical tithing, and then make some practical observations on how these might be implemented in our day.

The Melchizedekal Tithe

1. The Old Covenant was a provisional administration of grace and law, while in the New Covenant the kingdom of God and the law of God are established definitively (Rom. 3:31). The Cultural Mandate was restricted under the Old Covenant (Gal. 4:1ff.), but fully republished in the New. The restrictive nature of the Old Covenant was due to the fact that the Spirit was not yet given, because Jesus was not yet glorified, and thus power for dominion was limited (John 7:38, 39).

2. Part of these restrictions was a system of laws which kept the people closely tied to an agricultural economy. The Old Covenant laws of tithing are couched in this framework, and they cannot directly be applied to all New Covenant situations.

3. Moreover, the Levitical tithe system was intimately tied to the sacrificial system and the centralized sanctuary of the Old

Covenant. The Levitical tithe system is, however, preceded, under-girded, and succeeded by the Melchizedekal tithe system (Heb. 7).

4. The Melchizedekal tithe system is permanently obligatory. Abraham paid tithes (10%) to Melchizedek, and all the true sons of Abraham (Rom. 4; Heb. 7) will also pay the tithe to the greater Melchizedek, Jesus Christ. In return for the tithe, Melchizedek gave Abraham bread and wine. Anyone who refuses to pay a tenth to Christ should also be refused the bread and wine of the Lord's Supper (Gen. 14:18-20).

5. The Melchizedekal priestly order was connected to sonship (Heb. 7:3), especially the privileges of the firstborn.[3] God very meticulously superseded the Melchizedekal order with the Levitical order in Numbers 3. Thus, the Melchizedekal order always underlay the Levitical order throughout the Mosaic period. The Levitical tithe, then, is an extension and specification of the Melchizedekal tithe.

6. The Melchizedekal order was typologically reasserted in the Davidic Covenant (2 Sam. 7), which spoke of the king as a son. Psalm 110 and the book of Hebrews must be understood in the light of the Davidic Covenant. Again we see the Melchizedekal order as the foundation for the Levitical, especially as the Davidic kings supported and reformed the Levitical system from time to time. Indeed, the plans for the Temple and the building of the Temple were not given to and accomplished by the Levitical priests, but by the Davidic kings. (See 1 and 2 Chronicles.)

7. The fact that the Levitical tithe is built on the Melchizedekal means that an examination of how the Levitical tithe functioned in the Mosaic period can provide useful pointers as to how the fully established Melchizedekal tithe should be used in the New Covenant period.

The Levitical Tithe

8. Because of the restrictions on the cultural mandate, and

---

3. As a type of Christ, Melchizedek is seen as unique. Psalm 110:4 and Hebrews 5:6 speak of the "order of Melchizedek." This is our concern at present.

because of its typological nature, the Levitical tithe is always spoken of in terms of the agricultural year. The tithe is seen as collected annually, and given to a centralized Church order. In the New Covenant, the tithe is given to local churches, and the emphasis is on weekly rather than annual contributions (1 Cor. 16:2).

9. Of course, agriculturalists and self-employed persons may and probably should continue to tithe on annual increases. Wage earners, however, should tithe on their paychecks as they arrive, weekly if possible.[4]

10. The stress in 1 Corinthians 16:2 on laying aside the tithe on the first day of the week gives a New Covenant focus to the first fruit offerings of the Old Covenant. The time-honored custom of paying the Church before paying anything else is based on this.

11. How many tithes were there? Deuteronomy 12:17 and 14:23 speak of a tithe on "grain, new wine, and oil." Leviticus 27:30, 32 speaks of a tithe on seed, fruit, and animals. If we take these as two different tithes, we should notice that they do not overlap. Together they do not constitute 20% of the whole $[.10(a + b) + .10(c + d) = .10(a + b + c + d)]$. Thus, the total tithe remains at 10%.

12. More likely, however, these specifications should not be taken to mean different tithes, but different aspects of one tithe. We must beware of an overly nominalistic hermeneutic, which assumes that because different terms are used for the same thing, different things are in fact meant. Leviticus 27 is concerned with vows and their redemption, and the tithe is here seen as a form of vow (cf. Gen. 28:20, where Jacob's tithe is seen as a vow). The fact that Numbers 18 speaks of the tithe as going to the Levites does not contradict Deuteronomy 14:22-29, which tells us that the tithe was used to finance participation in the feast before being turned over to the Levites. The expression "grain, new wine, and oil" is used in Deuteronomy 7:13 as significant of all the blessings of the land.

---

4. Wages must be seen as income, since the *power* to earn wages comes from God, just as the yield of a field or vineyard comes from Him. Thus, clearly a tithe is owed on wages.

13. The term 'poor tithe' to refer to the command in Deuteronomy 14:28, 29 is a misnomer. The money was given to the elders of the gate, which today are the elders of the local churches (1 Cor. 6:1-5). They determined its use. Part of it went for the poor, but part also for the salary of the local Levite.

14. Contrary to popular ideas, Levites were found in the towns of Israel as teachers in proto-synagogues. Worship was conducted every sabbath and new moon (Lev. 23:3; Dt. 18:6; Jud. 17:7; 18:30; 19:1; Neh. 10:37f.). The third-year tithe was, then, not a poor tithe, but a local as opposed to a national tithe.

15. In the New Covenant, since there is no longer any central sanctuary, all tithes go to the "elders of the gate." We are in a perpetual third-year tithe situation, until God's great seventh year comes at the Last Judgment. A study of the third-day and third-year concept in the Bible reveals that just as Christ arose on the third day, we are living in the third day until the seventh day arrives (Gen. 22:4; 42:18; Ex. 19; Num. 19; Hos. 6:2; Jonah 1:17).

16. Under the Old Covenant, in the first and second years the people took their tithes to the sanctuary to celebrate the Feast of Booths (cf. Dt. 14:22-27 with 16:13-14). They used the tithe to finance their participation in the feast. What was left over, the larger portion by far, was given to the national Levites.

17. In the third year, the people took part of their tithes to the sanctuary to celebrate the Feast of Booths (cf. Dt. 26:14), and then returned to their locales, depositing the remainder of the tithe with the elders of the gate.

18. During the year, as various crops came in, and as various animals gave birth to their firstborn, the tithe and firstborn offerings would be laid up. These were apparently delivered in the festival of the seventh month, the Feast of Booths. (Cf. 2 Chron. 31:7.)

19. The tax of the firstborn was also used first to help finance participation in the Feast of Booths, and then the remainder given to the Levites (Dt. 14:23 + 15:19-20).

20. The Lord's Supper and the Love-Feast of the New Covenant corresponds to participation in the Feast of Booths (1 Cor.

11:33f., Jude 12). Some churches have occasional Love-Feasts (Agapes, or covered dish meals). Others have them monthly (new moons) or weekly. It is appropriate to use the first part of one's tithe to pay for the dinner you bring to these suppers. The poor, of course are to be sponsored by those better off.

21. Ordinarily, the tithe went to the Levites. The New Covenant affirms that all the Lord's people are Levites (Dt. 33:9 + Matt. 10:35-37, etc.). This does not mean that the Old Covenant people, under the provisional administration of law and grace, were not also priests. Indeed, the Levites came into being as substitutes for the firstborn of all Israel (see #5 above), so that foundationally every household in Israel was a priestly community. What this means is that the Levites were ecclesiastical specialists, called to special office.

22. The Biblical view of special office is neither democratic nor aristocratic. Every Christian has the general office. The rationale for special office is in terms of gifts and in terms of the need for good order (1 Cor. 12; 14:40), not in terms of priesthood in any pagan (aristocratic) sense. In times of distress, any general officer may teach, baptize, and administer communion (cf. Ex. 4:25).

23. The tithe went to the Levites because they were ecclesiastical specialists. The elders of the gate governed the use of the synagogue's money. Churches which distinguish between preacher-teachers and ruling elders have an analogous system today.

24. The Levites tithed to the high priest and his family (Numbers 18). Analogous to this, since the high priest was the high court of the Church (Dt. 17:8-13), there is a place for a tithe of the tithe to be passed from the local church to larger courts for their purposes.

25. The local tithe was administered by the elders for two purposes: the salary of the synagogue Levite and care for the poor (including the widow, fatherless, and alien). The national tithe was used by the Levites for a number of purposes, principally educational or cultic in character. An examination of these will show us what the tithe should and should not be used for today.

26. A study of the temple taxes of the Bible shows that the sac-

rificial system was not maintained solely by the tithe, and so the use of the tithe under the Old Covenant cannot differ greatly from its proper use in the New. (See Appendix D.)

27. Part of the tithe did, of course, go to maintaining the sacrifices, offered daily, sabbatically, monthly, etc. We might think the Church needs less money today since it no longer has this expense. In the New Covenant, however, there is a great expense connected with missions which was not present in the Old Covenant. In the Old Covenant, God located His people at the crossroads of the world, and brought the world to the Church. In the New Covenant this is reversed, and money is needed for missions.

Education

28. It is frequently remarked that one of the duties of the Levites was education (Lev. 10:11; Dt. 17:18; 31:9-13; 33:10; 2 Chron. 17:7-9; Neh. 8:9). It is clear from these passages that this education was training in the Word of God, not in other matters. Unfortunately, this all-important point has been obscured.

29. Some branches of Christian philosophy have in the twentieth century picked up on a shibboleth called 'sphere sovereignty.' Supposedly, social life is divided into a series of separate spheres, one of which is the sphere of education. This pattern of thought has led and continues to lead to confused practices across the Reformed world in the area of education.[5] There is, in fact, no such thing as a 'sphere of education'; rather, education is simply the training arm of each aspect of life.[6]

---

5. In other words, each social sphere is unique and separate from the others in its government. This is true of Church, state, family, and economy. These Reformed thinkers apply this also to the school, so that the school is not under the control either of parents or of the Church. The school must have its own "educational creeds." And so forth. In some Calvinistic circles this has resulted in schools which use fruitcake teaching techniques and teach radical humanist ideas, but which are immune from criticism from parents and clergy because of "sphere sovereignty."

6. Those readers aware of the thought of Herman Dooyeweerd will realize that I am not (at this point) criticizing his notion of theoretical law-spheres, but certain radical social applications of a, possibly perverted, understanding thereof.

30. Training of small children in the basics of life in a given culture is not the duty of the Church (Levites), nor of some "school sphere." It is the duty of parents, and is to be financed by parents. For parents to use the tithe for this purpose is to rob God. The tithe is for education in the law-Word of God, not for teaching small children to color, read, write, and add. Mothers and fathers took care of this task in Israel, and if they deputize the task to teachers, it is to be a free contractual arrangement, not the business of the Church.

31. Powell argues that children do not belong to parents, but to God, and so the tithe should be used to educate small children.[7] This is not a sound argument, because it is true of everything. Everything belongs to God, including my own private business; therefore, I may use the tithe to build up my private business. Not so. God has instructed parents to educate children, not only in the basics of life but also in theological and religious matters (Prov. 1:8; 6:20; 31:1; Ex. 10:2; 12:26; 13:8; Dt. 4:9; 6:7, 20f.; 32:7, etc.). Thus, under normal circumstances, not even the religion class in a grade school should be paid for by the tithe. It is the parents' job.[8]

32. A second aspect of education is education in a calling. This is the duty of the family and also of the individual himself (herself). Again, it is robbing God to use the tithe for this purpose. A man's family might help him with college, and there is always room for charity, but it is not the business of the tithe to finance education in carpentry, medicine, or French literature. After all, this is capital investment with a pay-off. Christian colleges should not ordinarily (see #35 below) be financed by the tithe.

33. A third aspect of education is in the sphere of the state. Military schools have a place, but not financed by the tithe.

34. The fourth form of education is education in the law-Word

---

7. Powell and Rushdoony, p. 106f.

8. On the subject of children's education in Israel, see Roland de Vaux, *Ancient Israel* (New York: McGraw Hill, 1965), pp. 48ff. De Vaux is a liberal, and is often untrustworthy. These few pages, however, simply summarize Biblical information.

of God. This was the duty of the Levites and of the Church today. This is what is to be financed by the tithe. At the high school and college level, religion classes may be taught by professional "Levites," and their salaries probably should be paid for by the Church and the tithe. This would be analogous to the way the state pays the salary of R.O.T.C. instructors. In some countries, various churches sponsor theological colleges on the campuses of secular universities.

35. Remember, however, that the tithe also goes for the poor, and paying the tuition for a poor child to go to a Christian school is entirely appropriate. Education in a calling was accomplished by apprenticeship in the ancient world, and the poor were trained by becoming temporary indentured servants (Dt. 15:12-15). Thus, the tithe probably should not be used to help poor college students, though gifts over and above the tithe are entirely proper. Helping to get a Christian college started might call for tithe money, considering how this builds up the Church. There are some grey areas here; elders must decide. Seminary students (future "Levites") should be sponsored by the tithe. Only in this way will older, more responsible family men be enabled to receive professional theological training.

36. Remember also that in times of persecution many functions must "hide" under the Church. In the United States today, it may be necessary for some Christian schools to declare themselves as part of the ministry of a local church in order to avoid persecution by the secular state. This temporary measure is not, however, normative.

37. One result of throwing grade school education wholly on the purses of parents is that Christian schools will not have as much money. Is this really a problem? Rushdoony has pointed out that education has a Messianic function in our society.[9] As a result of this salvation function, vast and unnecessary amounts of money are poured into education. Christian schools, having a more limited and proper role in life, should be less expensive and

---

9. *The Messianic Character of American Education* (Phillipsburg, NJ: The Craig Press, 1968).

smaller than Messianic schools. There is much in the Messianic curriculum which need not be in that of the Christian schools.

38. To take one example, experimental science. Science in the Christian school should take the form of naturalism, the study of the "ways" of animals, building on the proverbs and observations of Solomon. Experimentation and dissection are specialized and technical studies, and have more to do with education for a calling than education for the whole of life.

Medicine

39. Because of the involvement of the Levites in the cleansing rituals of the leper (Lev. 13, 14), it has sometimes been maintained that medicine is a proper use of the tithe. In the Bible, however, there is a difference between sickness as such, which is "healed," and leprosy, which is "cleansed." A woman on her period is unclean, but not sick. A child with measles is sick, but not unclean. A leper is both sick and unclean. Uncleanness is "ceremonial" in nature, not medicinal. Also, the Bible clearly distinguishes between the ritual healing work of Church elders (James 5:14) and the labors of a physician such as Luke.

40. Most "medicine" in Scripture is preventative, a side benefit of the "ceremonial" law, and still instructive for us today. Childbirth and general care of the sick was accomplished by midwives and other semi-professionals within the community. There is really no reason to see the Levites as a class (in part) of professional healers. Medical care should be under free enterprise, and its expenses covered by insurance policies, as we have it today.

41. Care for the poor, in the area of medicine and health in general is, of course, a proper use of the tithe.

Advisors to the State

42. The Levites in Israel served as advisors to the state (Dt. 17:9, 18) and they sat in on court cases to help render judgments by giving professional advice concerning the law of God (1 Chron. 23:4; 26:29-32; 2 Chron. 19:8-11). They were the closest thing to a

professional lawyer class that existed in Israel, for they were experts in the law of God.

43. Thus, the tithe should be used to maintain a corps of professional theologians and legal experts, as well as educators. The Church must ever advise the state regarding its duties before God. Rightly do the confessions of the Reformation state that the civil magistrate has the power to call Church synods to advise him. In light of this, it would be proper for a church to use part of its tithe to assist men in law school, so that they will "know the enemy" better.

Worship

44. The Levites were professional musicians within the Church. Worship in the Bible centers around teaching, the sacraments, and the response in singing and dancing. The Bible shows us that it is God's will for his people to be trained in proper worship, and to be led by skilled professionals (1 Chron. 15:16-24; 25:1-7; Ps. 149:3; 150:4). This use of the tithe is almost completely overlooked by the conservative and platonic Reformed and fundamentalist churches. The result has been the secularization of music, the reduction of dance to an exclusively erotic function, and the fragmentation of life; not to mention the fact that people do not know what to do with themselves on the sabbath. The reintroduction of wholistic worship to our dying churches will take time, but it is part of the work of the tithe to pay for it.

The Foundation of Society

45. The purpose of the tithe, in sum, is to provide the financial underpinning for the foundational work of society. As such, it finances Christian reconstruction. Society is founded and reconstructed only on the basis of the forthsetting and implementation of the Word. The capitalization of all of life is made possible when the tithe is properly paid and directed.

46. The tithe finances the reconstruction of society indirectly, through the proclamation of the Word. This is the meaning of

Judges 17-21. All the disorders in society arose because the Levites were not doing their job. Every man did that which was right in his own eyes because the Levites were not keeping society conscious of the nearness of the presence of the King (the LORD) and of the demands of His law. They were seeking riches wrongly (Jud. 17). They did not love the people as Christ loves the Church, willing to sacrifice themselves for the bride (Jud. 19). As a result, the people were in open violation of the laws pertaining to the love of God (Jud. 17) and of the laws pertaining to the love of the neighbor (Jud. 19, 21).

47. Thus, the use of the tithe to pay for the work of the Church does not compromise its social use; rather, it constitutes its indispensable social character. Training in the Word and the response of worship are together the bottom line of civilization. Without the forthsetting of the Word, nothing can be accomplished.

48. The confrontation of God with Pharaoh was precisely over the issue of worship (Ex. 3:18; 4:23; 5:1-3; 8:1). So was the confrontation at the time of the Reformation, and the Puritan confrontation with the state church a century later. The tithe finances social renewal by financing special worship in all its fulness. People who sing and have memorized the psalms, for instance, are equipped to conquer the world.

49. I cannot go into it here, but the reader should be apprised of the fact that the central religious disposition of any civilization is revealed in its sacramental theory. The fact that great religious movements and wars were fought out over transubstantiation, the Real Presence, and theories of baptism — such seems very strange to modern secular man. If we were not so blind to the foundations of our own culture, however, we would realize that the question of how God makes Himself known, and whether He can be controlled, is the central question of civilization. Eastern Orthodoxy believes that the world is kept in existence by the proper recitation of the liturgy. Roman Catholicism believes that the world is kept in existence by the perpetuation of the substitutionary dying of Christ. Calvinists believe that the world is kept in order (not in existence) by the work of the Spirit, who cultivates obedience to the law and

who makes Christ specially present at His sacraments. Baptists have no theory of social order, for they have taken Western nominalism to its extreme of almost total individualism; for them the sacraments are mere symbols.[10]

50. The reconstruction of society means that foundational attention must be paid to the reconstruction of worship. Hard thinking must be devoted to architecture, building churches that can accommodate true love feasts, orchestras and choirs, sacramental worship in the round, and even places for sacred dancing. Work needs to be done in music, training in psalm singing and chanting, the development of competent choirs and orchestras, writing music truly worthy of the worship of God (as opposed to the cheap junk of the last century or so). The development of a professional class of theologians and Biblical lawyers, who can speak to the legal questions of our day and retrain our civilization in the Word of God, is also a task of the tithe. And of course, the general care and retraining of the poor and helpless is a task of the tithe as well.

Should the Tithe Always Go to the Church?

51. Because of the incredible failure of the Church in our day, it is very easy to make a case for giving the tithe to parachurch organizations (non-sacramental teaching orders). I believe that the question here must be approached with care. My thesis is that the elders of the gate (the local church) should in normal healthy times administer the tithe, and they may use it in part to support various agencies; but that in times of apostasy the tithe must go to the Lord, and this may mean giving it to non-sacramental teaching organizations.

52. It will not do to say that the general office of all believers means that the tithe may be given wherever the individual wants. Nor will it do to say that the special office in the Church is to be given the tithe under any and all circumstances. Rule in the

---

10. See James B. Jordan, ed., *The Failure of the American Baptist Culture.* Christianity and Civilization No. 1 (Tyler, TX: Geneva Divinity School Press, 1982).

Church, including the disposition of the tithe, is representative or covenantal. *Ordinarily,* the elders of the gate (Church) should determine the disposition of the tithe. Members should not try to designate where their tithe is to be used. They may, of course, give gifts above the tithe for certain purposes.

53. When the special officers in the Church apostatize, or become so delinquent that the general officers (members) come to believe that the tithe properly should be redirected, then the power of the general office comes into play. Of course, ideally what should happen is that the true Christians should form a true church, and direct their tithes there. This is not always possible, and people rightly choose to give part of their tithe to the local church and part of it to faithful prophetic organizations outside the strict parameters of any particular church.

54. The tithe goes to the Lord (Lev. 27:32; Mal. 3:8). When a church ceases to set forth the law of the King, to make present the reality of the Lord, we are obliged to cut off giving it the tithe. To give the tithe to apostates is to rob God. Thus, in some seasons of the history of the Church, the tithe will need to go to parachurch institutions, but only because these are really more fully Levitical than the so-called Church itself.

55. Sometimes 2 Kings 4:42-44 is pointed to in this regard. The people evidently brought the tithe to the prophets in Northern Israel. This is interpreted as due to an apostasy on the part of the Levites. While I think that this situation is roughly analogous to what has been set forth in paragraphs 53 and 54 above, it is not as parallel as it might seem. Northern Israel was cut off from Jerusalem and the central Levitical work. It was a separate nation. Many if not most of the Levites migrated from Northern Israel to Judah. The prophets and the schools of the prophets were simply the churches of Northern Israel. Of course, they were not the national Church, for the officially approved cult of Northern Israel was calf worship, Baalism (1 Ki. 12:26 - 13:34). The prophets formed a remnant Church, not a parachurch organization.

56. It was the elders of the gate who directed the local tithe to the poor and to the local Levite (Dt. 14:28f.). Similarly, in early

America, the churches contributed part of the tithe to support the American Tract Society, the American Bible Society, and various other tithe-agencies, such as those dedicated to missions among immigrants. As the churches became more institutional and less evangelical, local churches were expected to give only to denominational benevolences. With the splitting of the traditional and now apostate churches in the early years of the twentieth century, the fundamentalist groups frequently returned to the practice of supporting "parachurch" tithe agencies. Thus, God's general principles have been applied in varying ways due to circumstances.

How to Tithe

57. Since all life and strength comes from God, we owe a tithe on whatever our hands produce. The tithe is a return to Him for the strength and capital He has given us. The tithe is paid on the increase, what we make with what we have been given. Those who are paid wages and salaries have little problem calculating 10% of their gross income and paying it to God.

58. The laws of tithing are phrased in terms of a man's business. Thus, if a man has a herd of sheep, he tithes on all the newborn of the year, not just on the sheep he takes out of the field to eat (Leviticus 27:30-33). Thus, a businessman must tithe not simply on what he removes from his business for his own salary, but on what the business itself produces.

59. A man is to tithe on his increase. The flock as it exists at the beginning of the year has already been tithed on.[11] The tithe is on the newborn. They are not bred before they are tithed; just so, money is not to be used before it is tithed on. I have known men who sought to increase their money by investing it, before tithing on it. This is clearly a violation of principle.

60. How about housing and electricity, and other expenses? God provided these things for Israel in guaranteeing each man a

---

11. In other words, God does not tithe on capital. He grants it by creation. He demands a tithe on the return of capital, on the increase. Application: no property taxes in a Biblical law system.

plot of land. In terms of agricultural production, God provides the sun and rain. Thus, it may well be argued that the modern businessman may regard housing and power as part of his capital, and subtract these expenses from his gross income before tithing. These are not part of his profit. At the same time, he must tithe on his profit (increase) *before* moving his company into a newer bigger building. Tithing must come before expansion.

61. We can see that applying the tithe principle to modern business leaves us with some grey areas. Thus, we must be careful in judging others, and leave room for God's assessment. If a man has an attitude of seeking to minimize his tithe by including everything under the sun as a capital expense, God will deal with him. On the other hand, God does not desire men to decapitalize themselves in tithing. What can fairly be counted as foundation capital, and thus expenses necessary to the production of the profit, should be paid before the tithe is calculated.

62. What about advertising? Advertising has two purposes: to set forth a business before the eye of the market, and to expand the business to provide an increase in profit. The first function is a necessary capital investment, and should be paid before the tithe is calculated; but the latter is an expansion, and should only be engaged in after the tithe has been paid. What would be a fair way to calculate the difference? I suggest the following. First, a businessman should subtract his advertising expenses from his gross income for the year. Then he should work out the percentage of his capital expenses over against his profit. Then, that percentage of his gross income which went to necessary capital expenses is the same percentage of his advertising which was necessary to keep him at last year's level, and should be deducted from his net profit before he tithes.

To take a simple example: Christian Enterprises took in $100,000 last year. During the year, CE spent $10,000 in advertising. CE had $45,000 in capital expenses (rent, power, raw materials), and thus $45,000 in profit. Thus, CE can properly assume that of its $10,000 advertising, half was necessary to get the money to pay for capital expenses, and half contributed to profits. Thus, half of the $10,000 was a capital expense, and so $5,000 should be added to overall capital expenses. This leaves profit at $50,000, so that a tithe of $5,000 is owed to God before the business makes any moves to expand.

63. What about taxes? Clearly a man owes God His tithe before he owes the state a tax. On the other hand, confiscatory taxation, more than 10% of income, can be viewed as a plague of locusts or as the damage caused by an invading army. (See 1 Samuel 8, where tyranny is expressed as a government which takes 10% or more in taxes, thus making itself a god.) Increase for the year can only be calculated in terms of what is left after the locusts have damaged the crop. In terms of this, it might be proper to consider taxes as part of basic capital expenses, rent paid to the invading army, and pay the tithe on what remains after taxes. I suggest, however, that a man include in his capital expenses only that amount of tax that goes over 10% of his taxable income. In that way, his conscience can be clear, for he is ascribing to tyranny only what tyranny takes in excess of what the state might properly take.

64. All of this entails a certain amount of juggling. After all, what the state considers taxable income will not be exactly what a Christian might consider titheable income, so that 10% of tax is only a rough way to do service to the principle outlined in paragraph 63 above. Also, the state permits deductions from tax based on tithing, up to a certain amount. Thus, precision in tithing is almost certainly impossible. What God honors, however, is more the intention to tithe than the actual amount. After all, God has infinite resources. He can finance Christian reconstruction at any time He chooses. In terms of that, the widow's mite, faithfully given, does more to honor God and bring about Christian reconstruction than does a large tithe calculated by a niggardly businessman seeking to tithe as little as possible.

65. Finally, we should note that tithing is inescapable. God will have his 10%, and either we will pay it over voluntarily, or it will be extracted from us forcibly. Men who do not willingly tithe a generous 10% will find that God does not prosper them. They

will find that God gives them over to a spirit of folly, and they make bad business decisions, and lose money. (The book of Haggai deals with this.) When men do not tithe willingly to God's Church, God takes the tithe and gives it to His enemies, to raise them up as a scourge to the Church. When Christians return to the practice of faithful tithing, God will begin to decapitalize the wicked, and will give dominion back to His people.

Appendix D

STATE FINANCING IN THE BIBLE[1]

The Mosaic Head Tax

The head tax in Exodus 10:11-16 is sometimes thought to have been a civil tax in ancient Israel. Since each man paid the same amount, it is argued that modern Christian states should employ the same poll tax principle.[2] There are problems with this view, and in the first part of this essay we need to explore the Mosaic head tax to discover its actual purpose.

Exodus 30:11-16 reads as follows:

11. The LORD also spoke to Moses, saying,

12. When you take a census [literally, sum] of the sons of Israel to number them [lit., for their being mustered], then each one of them shall give a ransom for himself [lit., his soul or life] to the LORD, when you number [muster] them, that there may be no plague among them when you number [muster] them.

13. This is what everyone who is numbered [who passes over to the group which is mustered] shall give: half a shekel according to the shekel of the sanctuary (the shekel is twenty geras), half a shekel as a contribution [heave offering] to the LORD.

14. Everyone who is numbered [who passes over to the group

1. An earlier and less complete form of this essay was published in newsletter form by the Institute for Christian Economics in 1981. I have revised my opinion on a couple of points since that time, so this version should be regarded as my latest thinking on the subject.

2. This is the position of R. J. Rushdoony, *Institutes of Biblical Law* (Phillipsburg, NJ: The Craig Press, 1973), pp. 281f., 492, 510, 719. Rushdoony is not alone in this opinion, however.

which is mustered], from twenty years old and over, shall give the contribution [heave offering] to the LORD.

15. The rich shall not pay more, and the poor shall not pay less than half shekel, when you give the contribution [heave offering] to the LORD to make atonement for yourselves [your souls or lives].

16. And you shall take the atonement money from the sons of Israel, and shall give it for the service of the tent of meeting, that it may be a memorial for the sons of Israel before the LORD, to make atonement for yourselves [your souls or lives].

The Meaning of the "Atonement"

The half shekel of silver was collected as a "ransom" for the life of the men mustered, as an "atonement" (covering) for them, so that God would not strike them with a plague. It has been suggested that this ransom and atonement have reference to the protective covering of society provided by the civil order. The money was used, it is suggested, to pay for the civil government and to pay for the military.

Examining the passage, we find in the first place that the atonement is to prevent a plague from God. We might see this "plague" as the civil disorders that accompany anarchy, failure to support the state; but 2 Samuel 24 stands against such an interpretation: When David wrongfully numbered the people, God struck Israel with a literal plague.

Moreover, secondly, 1 Peter 1:18 refers to this ransom money when it says, "you were not ransomed with perishable things like silver and gold from your futile way of life inherited from your forefathers, but with the precious blood . . . of Christ." In other words, the payment of ransom silver, properly part of the lifestyle of the forefathers, is superseded by the blood of Christ. The ransom and atonement of Exodus 30, then, is not simply a political covering, but a type of our redemption in Jesus Christ.

This will become even clearer as we look at the circumstances of the money's collection, and at the use to which it was put.

The Circumstances of Collection

The word used for "number" is *paqad,* which means to muster an army. The word is also used throughout the prophets to mean "visit" or "punish." There are other words in Hebrew which refer to numbering in the sense of counting up or adding up, as Exodus 30:12 aptly illustrates ("When you take a *sum . . .* to *muster* them"). Thus, the numbering spoken of here in Exodus 30 is not a mere counting census, but *a visitation or judgment designed to see who is on the LORD's side.* Those who pass over into the camp of the mustered men are thereby declaring themselves to be in the army of God, as opposed to the army of Satan. When the LORD comes, he comes to visit and punish, to muster all men and see who has and who has not passed over into his army.

In 1 Samuel 15:4, we read that Saul "gathered the people and mustered them." Thus, merely calling the people together for battle is not the same as mustering them. Mustering involves an actual counting, which is why in the passages which show Israel mustered for battle, we are always given at least a round number indicating how many men were present. The mustering is always for battles (Jud. 20:15, 17; 21:9; 1 Sam. 11:8; 13:15; 2 Sam. 18:1; 1 Ki. 20:15, 27; 2 Ki. 3:6). In Numbers 1, the men were mustered to conquer Canaan; they refused to fight, and God destroyed them in the wilderness.

Now this shows us two things. First, whenever the army mustered, each man was to bring a half shekel in his hand as atonement money. Second, the mustering was *not an annual census,* but an *occasional* mustering for battle whenever needed.

Why was David visited with a plague when he mustered the people in 2 Samuel 24? We are not given as much information as we might like, but the following points should be kept in mind. First, the decision to muster the people was arbitrary on David's part, since there was no occasion of war (nor any need, apparently, to repair the house of God—on this, see below). There was no justification for this peacetime census. His actions show David to have been a man of war, a man of excessive blood, who wanted to keep up an army when there was no need. This is why God would not let David build the Temple (1 Chron. 28:3). Second, since a plague broke out, it is possible that David did not subscribe the head tax.[3] When the plague was lifted, David insisted on paying for the future site of the Temple with fifty shekels of silver, which I take to be a token payment of the ransom demanded by Exodus 30. (The connection between the silver and the building of the house of God will be taken up below.)[4]

Why is *atonement* required when a mustering census is taken? Some believe that the very act of taking a census shows a lack of trust in God. To trust in numbers is faithlessness. Clearly this might be the case, but in Exodus and Numbers, it is God Himself who orders the census. Obviously, we cannot accuse Him of sin. Moreover, it is the men themselves who need atonement, not the one who orders the census.

I believe that the reason is that God is very near to His people in war, and his presence threatens to kill them unless they are

---

3. Just before this book went to press, another dimension of 2 Samuel 24 was called to my attention. David here seems to act like Pharaoh, trying to take control of the population. The Angel who struck Egypt strikes Israel in turn. Though a different Hebrew word is used, the Angel's stretching forth His hand in v. 16 reminds us of Moses' stretching forth his hand to bring plagues on Egypt. The silver David paid toward the Temple, thus, might correspond to the spoils the Egyptians gave to the Israelites, which was to go toward building the Tabernacle. Perhaps the passage conflates both the atonement money and the spoils of Egypt motifs.

4. It seems also that David's purpose was to incorporate the voluntary Israelite militia into the standing army. Note the distinction between "Joab's servants" and "all Israel" in 2 Sam. 11:1 and 12:26-31. David's years in exile had formed a professional army around him, distinct from the Israelite militia, which fought when summoned, but only for causes it believed just (as we see in the book of Judges). As Mendenhall has pointed out, the intent of David's census was "to incorporate the levies into the royal army officered by royal appointees about whose competence and loyalty the king would have no doubts. In contrast, the old folk militia was not reliable, since they would not answer a call to arms issued by an unpopular king, or for a war they felt to be unnecessary (see 1 Kings 12:21-24)." George E. Mendenhall, "The Census Lists of Numbers 1 and 26," *Journal of Biblical Literature* 77 (1958):58f. This view receives corroboration from the fact that it was Joab and the commanders of the army who opposed David in this (2 Sam. 24:2, 4), possibly because they viewed this as a weakening of the professional army by dilution, and as something which would cause great resentment among the people.

atoned for.[5] It is always God Who is seen as the Captain of the army (for instance in Josh. 5:13 - 6:5 and 2 Sam. 5:22-24). God walks in the midst of the army camp (Dt. 23:14). Thus, the camp must be holy. The collection of the atonement money protects the militia from harm, and covers for their sins. The fact that the money is used for the upkeep of the Tabernacle/Temple indicates a connection between the environment of the Temple (God's House) and that of the army camp (God's War Camp). Both are especially holy, and thus especially threatening to sinful man. Under the Old Covenant, each had to be especially sanctified, and the men who entered each had to be especially sanctified, as we shall see later on.

There is no evidence that this mustering with taxation was annually repeated. Exodus 30 does not say that there is to be an annual census, nor does any other passage of Scripture.

"Three times a year all your males shall appear before the Lord GOD" says Exodus 23:17. This is repeated in Exodus 34:23, and again in Deuteronomy 16:16, where it is added "and they shall not appear before the LORD empty-handed." Conceivably this gathering of the LORD's men was accompanied by the payment of atonement money, which would mean that the head tax was collected thrice yearly. This possibility is eliminated by the next verse, "Every man shall give according to the gift of his hand, according to the blessing of the LORD your God which He has given you." The members of the host are to give gifts, not heave offerings as in Exodus 30. The Hebrew terms and concepts are different. Also, it is not a "mustering" but an "appearance." Moreover, the gift was in proportion to God's blessing, not a fixed amount (cf. the language of Dt. 16:10).[6] Thus, the only annual gatherings

---

5. In the first edition of this essay, published in newsletter form by the Institute for Christian Economics, I stated that I believed that the reason is that the spilling of blood in warfare renders men unclean and in need of cleansing or purification. That cleansing, however, is taken care of under the laws in Numbers 19, as seen applied in Numbers 31.

6. Since the giving is according to the LORD's blessing, perhaps the proportional rendering of tithes and first fruits is what is in view here. This is the more likely, since these two vows were paid at the three annual feasts, especially at the Feast of Booths. See Appendix C.

of the host of the LORD are not seen as censuses, and no head tax is taken. There simply is no evidence of an annual head tax.

There seems to have been one peacetime occasion for collecting the half shekel tax, and that is when the house of God needed repairs. When Joash repaired the Temple, he called for the Levites to collect money from three sources (2 Kings 12:4). These were (1) "money that *passes*"; (2) assessment money from trespass offerings and vows; and (3) goodwill gifts. The first category seems to be a reference to Exodus 30:13 and 14, money from those who "*pass* over to the ranks of the mustered." Keil and Delitzsch argue for this understanding in their *Old Testament Commentary* on 2 Kings 12:4. More evidence for this interpretation is provided by the parallel account in 2 Chronicles 24:6, where the tax is called the "levy of Moses." Just as a shepherd lines up his sheep and counts them as they pass under the rod (Lev. 27:32), so the Lord counts his people (Ezk. 20:37). As each man passed the counter, he deposited his half shekel in a receptacle, and joined the ranks of the mustered.

Joash was not going to war, so this peacetime muster was solely for the purpose of raising money to repair the house of God. We have argued from the use of the term *paqad* (muster) that the tax was collected before battle. These are the only hints in the Old Testament that the half shekel tax was ever collected in the history of Israel after the events recorded in Exodus 30 and Numbers 1.[7]

Use of the Tax

Since the money was collected just before battle, it might be supposed that the money was used to finance holy war. While this

---

7. In 2 Chronicles 24 we read about the apostasy of Joash, how he murdered Zechariah the son of Jehoiada, and how God judged him by bringing in the Syrians against him. In 2 Kings 12, however, Joash's apostasy is not mentioned. Rather, the theology of 2 Kings 12 turns on an ironic point in connection with the atonement money. When the Syrians invaded, Joash bought them off by giving them the gold and silver of the Temple (2 Ki. 12:18). Thus, instead of defeating God's enemy, and using the atonement money and the war spoils to build up the Temple, Joash uses God's Temple money to buy off the enemy! This is all 2 Kings 12 needs to say in order for us to realize that Joash has apostatized.

is a bare possibility, I think it is very unlikely. The following considerations should be kept in mind.

First, the initial collection of the tax, which definitely is connected to the military function in Numbers 1, was used to build the Tabernacle (Ex. 38:25ff.). Of course, the Tabernacle was the ultimate political as well as ecclesiastical center of Israel, but the point is that the head tax was not used to finance warfare or for public works. (The pure silver of God's kingdom-house stands in contrast to the reprobate silver of wicked men, Jer. 6:29-30).

Second, the census under Joash went to the repair of the Temple, and as mentioned above, the Temple was founded on land purchased by silver shekels given by David after cessation of the plague brought on by his evil census.

Third, even though we are not told what was done with the money from battle-muster (indeed, we are not explicitly told that such money was ever actually collected), we do see a great deal of war booty going to the building and provisioning of the Temple. The wealth of the ungodly, acquired through holy war, goes to build the Kingdom of God. Money connected with *war* goes to build the house of *prayer* (Is. 56:7).

Fourth, when men were summoned for war, they brought along their weapons. Provisions for the army were raised from the people themselves (Jud. 20:10). The tax was not needed for the prosecution of war.

Finally, even if we were persuaded that the tax went to help defray expenses connected with holy war, that would still not make it a civil tax. The military was not necessarily a state function over against a Church function in the Old Covenant. Indeed, *holy war* was a specifically *priestly function*. The torching of cities is to be understood as taking God's fire off from His altar and applying His holy fiery wrath to his enemies. Thus, the torched cities were called "whole burnt sacrifices" in the Hebrew Old Testament (Dt. 13:16; Jud. 1:17; 20:40, in Hebrew). During the holy war, the men became temporary priests by taking the Nazirite vow (Num. 6; 2 Sam. 11:11 + Ex. 19:15; Dt. 23:9-14; Jud. 5:2, "That long locks of hair hung loose in Israel. . ."). This is all to say that the

rendering of specific judgments is a sabbatical and priestly function, not a kingly one. The kingly function in the Bible is in the
area of leading, cultivating, and shepherding, especially through
the skillful serving of one's subordinates (Mark 10:42-45). *The
sword of the state executes according to the judgments rendered by the priests.*
(In the New Covenant age, every believer is a priest, just as the
Old Covenant believers became priests by taking the Nazirite
vow. In our system, the priests render judgment by sitting on a
jury, and then the state executes the judgment.)

Thus, the military duty is priestly, and a duty of every
believer-priest. Both Church and state are involved in it, since the
Church must say whether the war is just and holy, and the state
must organize the believer-priests for battle. The mustering of the
host for a census is, then, not a "civil" function as opposed to an
ecclesiastical one, and the atonement money of Exodus 30 is not a
poll tax, as some have alleged.

Summary

The Mosaic head tax cannot be said to have had any explicitly
or even implicitly civil function in the Old Covenant. Its purpose
was to cover men from the wrath of God when they drew especially
close to him in His Temple/War Camp. It seems to have been collected whenever Israel was mustered for battle, and on one occasion at least it was subscribed to raise money to rebuild the Temple. It had no other purpose than to pay for the building and
maintenance of the house of God. As seen in 2 Kings 12 and 2
Chronicles 24, it was collected by the Levites and administered by
the priests.

Of course, one might argue that the house of God (Tabernacle, Temple) is a microcosmic representation and concentration
point for the whole kingdom of God, inclusive of the civil function
as well as the ecclesiastical. In Christianity, however, the focal
point of civilization is not the state, as it is in paganism, but worship in the presence of God, organized by the Church. Thus, the
house of God is preeminently a house of prayer, not a political
center (Is. 56:7; Jer. 7:11; Matt. 21:13).

The Temple Tax in the New Testament

During the period between the closing of the Old Testament and the coming of Christ, the Hebrew civilization developed an entire social structure based on the teachings of the Mosaic law. In time this system hardened into what we see among the Pharisees at the time of Christ: a great many extra rules which distorted and often negated the principles of the Mosaic instruction.

One custom which developed was the payment of a half-shekel head tax to the Temple on an annual basis. As we have seen, this was not prescribed in the Old Covenant itself. Edersheim points out that this money was used to pay for the upkeep of the Temple and for the national sacrifices (daily, weekly, monthly, etc.)[8] In this respect, the Temple Tax is based both on the Mosaic head tax and on the self-imposed levy of Nehemiah 10:32-33, which was designed to pay for the sacrifices. Edersheim points out that so much money was taken in that some was used for public works, but this was not the design or purpose of the subscription.

Jesus was asked to pay this tax in Matthew 17:24-27.

> 24. And when they came to Capernaum, those who collected the two-drachma (tax) came to Peter, and said, "Does your teacher not pay the two-drachma?"
> 25. He said, "Yes." And when he came into the house, Jesus spoke to him first, saying, "What do you think, Simon? From whom do the kings of the earth collect customs or poll tax, from their sons or from strangers?"
> 26. And upon his saying, "From strangers," Jesus said to him, "Consequently the sons are exempt [free].
> 27. "But, lest we give them offense [cause them to stumble], go to the sea, throw in a hook, and take the first fish that comes up; and when you open its mouth, you will find a stater [or, shekel]; take that and give it to them for you and Me." (NASV)

It is important to note how Jesus treats this tax. Peter's hasty reply to the question of the tax collectors meets with a mild rebuke from Jesus. Just a few days before, Jesus had given Simon the

---

8. *The Temple: Its Ministry and Services* (Grand Rapids: Eerdmans), pp. 72ff.

name "Peter," as a sign of his faith. Now Jesus addresses him as "Simon," an indication that Peter was not thinking in terms of the principles of the faith when he told the tax collectors that Jesus was bound to pay the Temple Tax. Jesus does agree to pay the tax, so as not to cause offense, but not before He demonstrates that he and his followers are not obligated to pay it.

Jesus always respected and kept the Old Covenant law. His purpose in coming into the world was to take the Old Covenant to Himself and, in His own death and resurrection, to transform it into the life-giving New Covenant. If the Temple Tax had indeed been part of the Mosaic order, Jesus would have been bound to pay it. This proves that the annual Temple Tax was not a proper understanding of Exodus 30.

Jesus goes on to say that taxes are a form of tribute levied on conquered foreigners, so that citizens of the kingdom itself are not subject to them. This principle shows why the Old Covenant Tabernacle and Temple were built and maintained primarily on the spoils of war and on freewill offerings from the people. The Mosaic head tax was, however, a tax levied occasionally on God's own people. To this extent, the members of the Old Covenant were still "strangers" to the kingdom; they were "afar off" and had not yet been "brought nigh" in the full New Covenant sense (Gal. 4; Heb. 9:7; 10:1-3, 19-22; 11:39, 40).

With the coming of the New Covenant, however, there can be no head tax levied on sons of the kingdom for maintenance of religious worship. This is not to say that the tithe is abolished, for it is not a head tax or tribute money but is a (mandatory) votive gift (Gen. 28:22) and a privilege of kingdom citizens. Moreover, this is not to say that a Christian state may not levy a head tax for civil purposes. It is to say that a church may not levy a head tax.

As Peter himself was later to write (1 Pet. 1:18), payment of ransom silver in the Old Covenant was "futile," for it did not effect definitive redemption or atonement (cf. Heb. 10:4). The redemption and atonement wrought by Jesus Christ makes men true sons of the kingdom, and eliminates forever the Mosaic head tax of Exodus 30.

In conclusion, the Mosaic head tax was never a civil tax. It was a religious tax and has been fulfilled definitively in Christ.

The Prince's Tax in Ezekiel

A passage which speaks of a tax collected by the state is Ezekiel 45:13-17.

> 13. "This is the offering that you shall offer: a sixth of an ephah from a homer of wheat; a sixth of an ephah from a homer of barley;
> 14. "and the prescribed portion of oil (*namely,* the bath of oil), a tenth of a bath from *each* cor (*which* is ten baths, *or* a homer, for ten baths are a homer);
> 15. "and one sheep from each flock of two hundred from the watering places of Israel—for a grain offering, for a burnt offering, and for peace offerings, to make atonement for them," declares the Lord GOD.
> 16. "All the people of the land shall give to this offering for the prince of Israel.
> 17. "And it shall be the prince's part to *provide* the burnt offerings, the grain offerings, and the drink offerings, at the feasts, on the new moons, and on the sabbaths, at all the appointed feasts of the house of Israel; he shall provide the sin offering, the grain offering, the burnt offering, and the peace offerings, to make atonement for the house of Israel."

In short, each citizen in Israel was to pay to the state proportional taxes on his various capital assets, and the state was to use this money to pay for the maintenance of the sacrificial system. This does not seem to correspond to any conceivable New Covenant civil duties, since the sacrificial system has been fulfilled in Christ. Conceivably, this means that the state should pay for the bread and wine used in the Lord's Supper, but by itself that is the most this could mean (and even this strikes us as most unlikely). Salaries for Church officials are accomplished through the tithe.

Notice that this is not a head tax, nor is it an income tax like the tithe. It is a proportional assessment of capital, though very minimal.

The pattern described in Ezekiel is ideal. It was never intended to be implemented, and indeed could not have been implemented because of its many strange features (for instance, dividing the land up into symmetrical strips of land, or building a Temple the size of a mountain). Ezekiel 40-48 is like a parable, designed for instruction but not for implementation. At any rate, with the coming of the New Covenant the magistrate has no duty to provide sacrifices, for the repeated sacrifices have ceased.

Was this the pattern earlier, for Solomon's Temple? We know that God gave David instructions as to the building of the Temple, and this doubtless included instructions regarding provisions for sacrifices (1 Chron. 28:11ff.). It is not said what these were, however. There is some evidence that the kings provided the sacrifices, on some occasions at least (2 Chron. 31:3; 35:7ff.), but these seem to have been personal freewill offerings, not the direct result of taxes.

The evidence is scanty, and it seems to me most likely that the sacrifices were usually paid for out of the tithe. In the first, second, fourth, and fifth years, the tithe went to the national (as opposed to the local) Levites, and a tithe of the tithe went to the priests. The Levites had their own cities and fields, and thus were not by any means solely dependent on the tithe for their livelihoods. They could easily have raised the animals necessary for the daily, weekly, monthly, etc. sacrifices, or they could have eaten the animals they themselves raised and used the tithed animals for the sacrifices.

Why did the kings ever get involved in providing sacrifices at all, and why does Ezekiel speak of it as the prince's duty in his figurative vision? I believe it is because the king in Israel was not only a normal office, but also a figurative one. The Davidic Covenant (2 Sam. 7) points to the symbolic nature of the sons of David. They would be somewhat like Melchizedek, priest-kings whose position was established on the basis of sonship. As a result of their symbolic function, the kings of the Davidic line were very closely connected to the maintenance of the sacrificial system. They were not to usurp the special duties of the priests (2 Chron. 26:16ff.), but so closely connected were they to the maintenance of the cult that they could be said to have offered sacrifice themselves (for instance, 2 Sam. 6:17; 2 Chron. 7:5).

Nehemiah's Head Tax

When Israel was restored from captivity there was no king, for the nation was a vassal state to other powers. The house of David continued to have preeminence in the society (cf. Haggai 1:1; Zerubbabel was a descendent of David), but there is no recorded statement of any taxes being paid to them.

Nehemiah led the people to place themselves under a covenant to support the rebuilt Temple and its sacrifices. This is recorded in Nehemiah 10:32-33, "We also placed ourselves under obligation [literally, imposed commandments on ourselves] to contribute yearly one third of a shekel for the service of the house of our God: for the showbread, for the continual grain offering, for the continual burnt offering, the sabbaths [i.e., sabbath offerings], the new moon [i.e., new moon offerings], for the appointed times [i.e., the seasonal festival offerings], for the holy things, and for the sin offerings to make atonement for Israel, and all the work of the house of our God."

This rule has not infrequently been connected to the head tax of Exodus 30, under the erroneous impression that the Mosaic head tax was an annual assessment. Notice, however, first of all that it is not a half-shekel but a third of a shekel that is collected. Second, note that the passage does not say, as Nehemiah 10:29 and 34 do, that this was done in accordance with the law of God given through Moses. Rather, it expressly says "we imposed commandments on ourselves." What was done here was surely right, and in accordance with the general rules God had given, but it is not purely and simply an application of the Mosaic head tax.

Money was needed to rebuild and maintain the Temple, and there would be no more mustering taxes collected from holy war. Nehemiah's provision took up the slack. Also, there were no longer any kings to provide the sacrifices, and people were not in a position to reinstitute the entire Levitical order overnight, so again Nehemiah's provision was a needed accommodation to the situation.

Again, this was not a civil tax at all. Its purpose was wholly cultic.

To summarize what we have found thus far: The only kind of civil taxes spoken of in a normative (as opposed to descriptive) fashion in the Bible were those given to the prince for the special purpose of providing sacrifices, and this is only clearly seen in Ezekiel's parabolic Temple teaching. We must conclude that the Bible gives no explicit instruction regarding how the state is to be financed.

Implicit Teaching

How about implicit instruction? Well, throughout the books of Kings and Chronicles we see the kings of Israel and Judah levying taxes and exacting tribute from the people. This is, however, normally regarded as oppressive and as a fulfillment of the curse pronounced by Samuel in 1 Samuel 8. According to Deuteronomy 17:17, if the people decided to call for a king, the king was not to engage in *excessive* accumulation of wealth. Samuel in 1 Samuel 8 regards it as a great sin for the king to take ten percent of the income of the people, for to do so was for the king to put himself in the place of God, taking a tithe. Indeed, as Rushdoony has pointed out, "they are told that the taxation of their new order will be a ruthless tithe of *capital* as well as income."[9] We may draw from this that the king may exact a head tax, a small proportionate capital tax (Ezk. 45), or an income tax, but that it must not be "oppressive."

During the period of the Judges, which is far more normative for a Christian commonwealth than the quasi-symbolic period of the Davidic monarchy, there is no indication of any monies going to the state at all. The "state" mostly consisted of the elders of the gates. These dispensed the tithe in the third year, paying the salary of the local Levite and caring for the poor. Their salaries apparently came from their own work. The husband of the excellent woman of Proverbs 31 was able to devote a lot of time to political service because of the financial shrewdness of his wife. In time of warfare, the people were summoned to fight. They sup-

---

9. Rushdoony, *Institutes,* p. 798 (emphasis added).

plied themselves with needed weaponry. The roads to the cities of refuge were to be kept up (Dt. 19:2), but we are not told with what money.

Because of the instinctively statist character of modern thought, many Christian writers and thinkers, including very conservative ones, look to changing the civil order as the most important aspect of Christian reconstruction. Thus, there is a continual drive to find in the Bible specific legislation for the state. If the Bible clearly teaches that the only legitimate form of civil taxation is a head tax, for instance, then perhaps it is proper for Christians to refuse on principle to pay any income taxes. This present essay demonstrates the invalidity of this approach. Indeed, since the Church is God's model government, and God has instituted an income tax (the tithe) for its financing, we might easily argue that the Christian state should be financed in an analogous manner, by an income tax of less than ten percent (not making itself equal with God).

In conclusion, God has not seen fit to legislate exactly what should go for the financing of the state. He has seen fit, however, to demand a tithe for the financing of the Church. In those times of history when the tithe is given properly and the Church does her work with integrity, the state will greatly shrink in size and will require only a minimum in taxation. On the other hand, in those seasons of history, like our own, when the people refuse to tithe, and the Church is not faithfully proclaiming and educating in the Word of God, then the state will grow to massive size, and will exact a terrible tribute. The reformation of the state, then, awaits the reformation of the Church and the proper use of the tithe.

Appendix E

SALVATION AND STATISM

The biblical concept of salvation is basically restoration to covenant fellowship and life with God based on the redemptive work of Christ. The Old Testament word for salvation, however, specifically focuses on restoration to the garden of Eden, in that it means literally "to put into a large, open place."[1] The name 'Joshua' comes from this word, and Joshua was a savior in this sense indeed. Jesus' command to make disciples of all nations, (i.e., to conquer all the places of the world), shows Him to be the Savior, and indeed the name 'Jesus' is simply the New Testament form of 'Joshua.'

Thus, Biblical salvation entails not simply the establishment of the Church, but entails the restoration of the whole fabric of life, including social life. Perhaps then we should expect to find God giving us a blueprint of the perfect civil government, of the Christian state. Some people in history have thought that the Bible, in the Mosaic law, was doing just that, but in fact there is no corpus as such of judicial laws in the Bible. The reason why so many people have erred in looking at the Old Testament laws as if they were judicial laws designed for some state is that since the rebellion of man, the human race has been infected with Statism, and thus men tend to look at the Bible through glasses tinted with

---

1. The root is *yasha'*. "The root meaning in Arabic is 'make wide' or 'make sufficient'; this root is in contrast to *tsarar* 'narrow,' which means 'be restricted' or 'cause distress.' That which is wide connotes freedom from distress and the ability to pursue one's own objectives. To move from distress to safety requires deliverance." John E. Hartley, in *Theological Wordbook of the Old Testament* (Chicago, Moody Press, 1980), p. 414.

240

this Statism.

What is Statism? Satan's offer to mankind was that man should be like God. Specifically, man would not have to learn God's ways and pass judgments in terms of God's word, but man would issue judgments out of himself, reshaping the world to fit his own desires.[2] Thus, man's sinfulness consists essentially of his desire to exercise sovereignty over God's universe — a direct sovereignty, answerable to no one, rather than a derivative dominion in terms of God's law. When God rules over a man, He provides him with his (external) Word, and influences him to obedience by His (internal) Spirit. When one man tries to rule another man, the situation is different. He provides him with an external word of command, but he cannot reach within his neighbor to influence him within. Thus, he must influence him externally, by force, by threat of violence. It is the state which is the repository of force, the threat of the sword. Sinful man, then, turns to the state to enforce his attempted sovereignty.

The world is full of problems, which are the consequences of sin, and sinful man would like to be rid of these problems, so that he can enjoy the good life. The wicked know that some type of salvation is needed. People need to be changed (especially those Christians who refuse to go along with the wicked's plan of salvation). Again, sinful man can only rely on force, on the state, to effect this salvation. The wicked state is thus not only sovereign but also Messianic. Sinful man's social order is state-centered, or Statist. The Bible sets its face against Statism, from Babel to the Beast.

Biblical social order is not state-centered but God-centered. The solution to human ills is not government spending but Divine grace. Protection from the enemy is not guaranteed by the state, though it plays a part here, but by God. Society is not reformed by state-directed education, but by the Gospel of God. The civil government is not to serve (rule) as a savior.

This explains why we do not find a set of judicial laws in the

---

2. See Jordan, *Trees and Thorns* (forthcoming).

Bible. All the laws of Scripture, including the social laws, are religious. The social laws are God-centered. Some of them relate to Christian civil government, but there is no corpus of civil law or judicial law because the Bible is not a Statist document.

Appendix F

PROLEPTIC PASSOVER (EXODUS 4:22-26)

In Exodus 4:22-26 we have the seemingly curious incident of God's attack on Moses as he reentered Egypt:

22. [God said,] "Then you shall say to Pharaoh, 'Thus said the LORD, "Israel is My son, My firstborn.
23. "So I said to you, 'Let My son go, that he may serve Me'; but you have refused to let him go. Behold I will kill your son, your firstborn." ' "
24. Now it came about at the lodging-place on the way that the LORD met him and sought to put him to death.
25. Then Zipporah took a flint and cut off her son's foreskin and touched it to his leg, and she said, "You are indeed a bridegroom of blood to me."
26. So He let him alone. At that time she said, "a bridegroom of blood," with reference to the circumcision.

A Survey of Interpretations

This passage has a history of arcane explanations, most of which ignore the matters that are clearly stated or implied in the text. Before going into my own thinking on the matter, I should like to survey previous interpretations, some helpful, some not.

An early comment is found in *The Life of Moses* by Gregory of Nyssa (c.335 - c.395). "Moses went down to Egypt and he took with him his foreign wife and the children she had borne him. Scripture says that an angel[1] encountered him and threatened

---

1. The Greek Septuagint (LXX) translation substitutes "angel" for "LORD" in this passage. Gregory would have been using the Greek, not the Hebrew original.

death. His wife appeased the angel by the blood of the child's circumcision."[2] Gregory comments further, "since his son had not been circumcised so as to cut off completely everything hurtful and impure, the angel who met them brought the fear of death. His wife appeased the angel when she presented her offspring as pure by completely removing that mark by which the foreigner was known."[3] From all this Gregory learns that the Christian philosophy may marry pagan philosophy (the wife) provided that the offspring (a synthesis) has the corruption of pagan thought removed (circumcision), so that only the good remains. Clever as this is, it has nothing to do with the theology of Exodus.

Turning to the Reformation, we find that Calvin's comments are also speculative and do not derive from the text. God was angry, says Calvin, because Moses had not circumcised his son, and Moses had not circumcised him because Jethro and Zipporah opposed it. The text nowhere indicates this latter notion; indeed, as a descendant of Abraham, Jethro doubtless did know about circumcision, whether we understand it as a rite applying only to the seed people, Israel, or to all believers. Calvin goes on to assume that Zipporah was angry, threw the foreskin at Moses' feet, and "fiercely reproaches him with being 'a bloody husband.' "[4] Nothing in the text indicates any anger; the phrase "bridegroom of blood" is not the same as "husband of blood"; the Hebrew word for "touch" does not mean "throw." Finally, we have to say that Calvin, like Gregory of Nyssa, ignores the context, which is God's announced threat against the firstborn sons of all persons living in Egypt.[5]

---

2. Book I, para. 22. Trans. by Abraham Malherbe and Everett Ferguson (New York: Paulist Press, 1978), p. 35.

3. Book II, para. 38, p. 63.

4. *Commentaries on the Last Four Books of Moses*, trans. by Charles W. Bingham (Grand Rapids: Baker, reprint 1979), comments *ad loc.* See also Calvin, *Institutes*, Book 4, Chapter 15, Section 22, for further comments on Zipporah.

5. Calvin's approach illustrates a danger in the Antiochene or "grammatical-historical" approach to exegesis. The Antiochene school, under the influence of Theodore of Mopsuestia, a quasi-Nestorian, can fairly be said to have erred in the direction of naturalism, at the expense of the literary structures of Scripture. The problem lies not in the "grammatical" side of the method, but in the "historical" side. Modern evangelical Bible commentaries, using this method,

The same unhelpful approach is taken by Matthew Poole, although Poole does mention in passing the correct approach. Speaking of the statement "a bloody bridegroom," he says, "Yet some make these to be the form or solemn words used in circumcision, *Thou art a spouse,* or *a son of bloods, to me,* i.e., made so to me by the blood of circumcision. But it doth not appear that this was the usual form. Nor was it likely that she, being a Midianitish, not a Hebrew woman, and doing this suddenly, and in a rage, should be so expert to know, and so punctual to use, the right form of words, when she did not use a fit and decent carriage in the action, as appears by her casting it as his feet."[6] Again, the notion that Zipporah "threw" the foreskin is based on a mistranslation, and the idea that she was ignorant of God's ways, though a daughter of Godly Jethro and a wife of 35 or so years to Godly Moses, is not credible. Again, like Calvin, Poole takes no note of the context.

There is little improvement in the remarks of Matthew Henry. Like Poole, Henry mentions but dismisses the interpretation that the phrase "bridegroom of blood" refers to the child's coming into covenant with God. He prefers to see Zipporah as acting in fury. He also wrongly states that Moses was "unequally yoked with a Midianite," based on the clearly wrong assumption that Jethro was a pagan.[7]

---

frequently have much more to say about archaeology and the customs of the Ancient Near East than they have to say about the text. No conservative denies that the events recorded really happened; the question is rather where we go to find the context and meaning of the events *as recorded by the Holy Spirit.* Calvin here invents an historical and an emotional (psychological) context, and explains the text in terms of it, instead of explaining the text in terms of its own literary Biblical context. The modern "Biblical-theological" approach to exegesis is a needed corrective to the Antiochene method. On the Nestorianism of Theodore of Mopsuestia, see Rowan Greer, *Theodore of Mopsuestia: Exegete and Theologian* (Westminster, England: The Faith Press, 1961); and Rousas J. Rushdoony, *The Foundations of Social Order: Studies in the Creeds and Councils of the Early Church* (Nutley, NJ: The Presbyterian & Reformed Pub. Co., 1968), pp. 98-111.

6. *A Commentary on the Holy Bible* (London: Banner of Truth Trust, 1962), comments *ad loc.*

7. *Commentary on the Whole Bible* (countless editions available), comments *ad loc.*

There is no need to rehearse in detail the comments of later expositors who make basically the same assumptions in interpretation. These include G. A. Chadwick,[8] George Rawlinson,[9] Alfred Edersheim,[10] A. W. Pink,[11] James G. Murphy,[12] Keil & Delitzsch,[13] S. G. De Graaf,[14] W. H. Gispen,[15] and Homer C. Hoeksema.[16] This is an impressive array, but it must be born in mind that this passage had not been subjected to careful scrutiny in the way that, say, Romans chapter 5 has been. These expositors basically rehearse the opinions handed to them by their forefathers, and that interpretation is every bit as flawed at the end of many repetitions as it was when first dreamed up.

There have been, however, expositors who dealt more carefully with the text. John Gill, for instance, notes that Jethro and Zipporah, descendents of Abraham, would have known about circumcision, and thus cannot be blamed for Moses' failure to circumcise his son. Gill holds that Zipporah touched the foreskin of her son to Moses, and called him a "bloody bridegroom," in the joy of receiving him back from the dead, her husband anew. He also mentions the possibility that Zipporah was addressing her son with this phrase, which would be a way of congratulating him

---

8. In *The Expositor's Bible* (Grand Rapids: Eerdmans, 1940; originally published in the late 19th century), comm. *ad loc.*

9. In *Ellicott's Commentary on the Whole Bible, ad loc.*

10. *Bible History* (Grand Rapids: Eerdmans, [1876] 1972) I:57f.

11. *Gleanings in Exodus* (Chicago: Moody Press, my edition dated 1971, but originally published in the early 20th century), p. 40. Sloppy publication data plagues the evangelical publishing world.

12. *Commentary on the Book of Exodus* (Minneapolis: Klock & Klock, [1866] 1979), comm. *ad loc.*

13. *Old Testament Commentaries* (several editions available), comments *ad loc.* K&D make one improvement, in speculating that Zipporah called Moses (n.b.) a "bloody bridegroom" because in this act she got him back from the dead as a new husband. This is still erroneous, however; Zipporah was addressing her son.

14. *Promise and Deliverance,* trans. by Evan and Elizabeth Runner (St. Catharines, Ontario: Paideia Press, 1977) I:262f.

15. *Exodus,* trans. by Ed van der Maas (Grand Rapids: Zondervan, 1982, original Dutch version early-mid 20th century), comments *ad loc.*

16. Class Syllabus: The Bondage and Exodus (Grandville, MI: Theological School of the Protestant Reformed Churches, 1975), p. 51.

on his covenant-marriage to the LORD. Gill thinks this is more unlikely, however. The advantage of Gill's approach is that he does not read into the text any anger on the part of Zipporah. His approach, thus, is somewhat less speculative.[17]

The same basic interpretation is offered by Cunningham Geikie[18] and Hywel R. Jones.[19] G. A. F. Knight takes the same view, except that he speculates that Moses had not been circumcised, and that Zipporah touched her son's foreskin to Moses' genitals (Hebrew "feet" taken euphemistically).[20] There is no evidence for the notion that Moses had not been circumcised; indeed, Joshua 5:5 says that "all the people who came out [of Egypt] were circumcised."

Utterly worthless interpretations are found in *The Interpreter's Bible* (not surprisingly). The writers, Rylaarsdam and Park, agree that this story is a hold-over from some earlier myth or saga having to do with the dangers of the wedding night and the possibility of demonic attacks on newlyweds. They also think that the purpose of the story is to show that circumcision came from the Midianites.[21] Similar nonsense is found in the commentary on Exodus by J. P. Hyatt: "The original story may have concerned a demon or deity of the boundary between Midianite territory and Egypt whom Moses failed properly to appease. Some scholars have suggested it was a night demon contesting with Moses for the "right of the first night.""[22] Hyatt also calls attention to the treatment of the passage by Kosmala, discussed below.[23]

---

17. *Exposition of the Old Testament* (Grand Rapids: Baker, [1852] 1980), comments *ad loc.*

18. *Hours with the Bible* (New York: James Pott & Co., 1884), Vol. 2: From Moses to the Judges, p. 123.

19. In *The New Bible Commentary: Revised* (Grand Rapids: Eerdmans, 1970), comments *ad loc.*

20. *Theology as Narration* (Grand Rapids: Eerdmans, 1976), p. 35.

21. (Nashville: Abingdon-Cokesbury Press, 1952), comments *ad loc.*

22. In The New Century Bible Commentary series (Grand Rapids: Eerdmans, 1971), comments *ad loc.*

23. Other weird liberal views are summarized in Brevard Childs, *The Book of Exodus* (Philadelphia: Westminster, 1974), pp. 95-101. Childs's own contribution to the discussion is taken up below.

R. Alan Cole is the first of the expositors we have come to who actually takes note of the context of this incident. In discussing whether God was attacking Moses or his son (which is not clear, as we shall see), he notes that "if the 'him' refers to Gershom, then there is a closer link with the context (death of the first-born), as showing how Moses' first-born nearly died."[24] Cole goes on to point out that the Hebrew of verse 25 should be translated "*touched* it to *his* feet," rather than "*threw* it at *Moses*' feet." Cole is unable to find an explanation for the phrase "bridegroom of blood." Even though he is unable to explain the passage fully, Cole at least takes the text at face value, without inventing imaginary scenarios to explain it (e.g., Zipporah's convincing Moses not to circumcise his son; Zipporah's rage at Moses; etc.).

Like Cole, Umberto Cassuto in his *Commentary on the Book of Exodus* also notices that God threatens Moses immediately after threatening all the firstborn sons living in the land of Egypt. In other words, he takes note of the context of this pericope. Cassuto holds that God attacked Moses (though in context it is more likely that God attacked the son), and that Zipporah touched the blood of her son's foreskin to Moses as though to say: "Let the one take the place of the other. Just as the first-born son sometimes suffers on account of his father (this is the link with the preceding paragraph), so shall the shedding of a few drops of the blood of Moses' first-born son, which consecrates the infant to the service of the Lord, serve as an additional and decisive consecration of his father to the Lord's mission."[25] Cassuto believes that the expression "bloody bridegroom" is addressed to Moses, because Zipporah has received him back from the dead. I shall argue that Zipporah is addressing her son.

Childs investigates the passage carefully, and while I believe he has not gotten every aspect correct, I wish to call attention to several points he makes.[26] First, he correctly notes that Zipporah

---

24. *Exodus* (Downers Grove, IL: InterVarsity Press, 1973), *ad loc.*
25. Trans. by Israel Abrahams (Jerusalem: Magnes Press, [1951] 1967), comments *ad loc.*
26. Childs, *Exodus,* pp. 98-101, 103f.

did not throw the foreskin at Moses' feet, but touched it to her son's feet. Second, he remarks that "the smearing of the blood serves as a visible demonstration that circumcision had indeed been performed." Sadly, Childs fails to connect this with the visible smearing of blood at the Passover. Third, Childs confesses to being unable to understand why the expression "bloody bridegroom" is used in connection with circumcision. He assumes that its meaning has been lost to time.

As we draw to the conclusion of this survey, I should like to call the reader's attention to the remarks of George Bush, whose *Notes on Exodus* was published in 1852.[27] First of all, Bush notes the context, and determines that it was Moses' firstborn son, Gershom, who was attacked. Second, he states that it is most likely that Zipporah did not cast the foreskin down, but "that she made it to touch his feet, or rather his legs, in the act of cutting, for the original term is by no means that which is ordinarily employed to signify *casting* or *throwing down.*"

Finally, Bush investigates the meaning of the phrase "bloody bridegroom." He states that "a far preferable construction, in our opinion, is to consider the words as addressed to the son, now grown up, from his being *espoused,* as it were, to God by the seal of circumcision. Aben Ezra remarks, 'It is the custom of women to call a son when he is circumcised *a spouse (ḥathan).*'[28] Kimchi in his Lexicon, under *ḥathan* concurs in the same view, which is also adopted by Schindler, Spencer, Mede, and others. The idea that Zipporah intended to upbraid her husband with the cruelty of the rite which his religion required him to perform, seems hardly tenable; for as she was a Midianitess, and so a daughter of Abraham by Keturah, it is not easy to imagine her altogether a stranger to the ceremony of circumcision, which had been from the earliest ages perpetuated in all the branches of the Abrahamic race. . . ." The only thing Bush does not take notice of is that Zipporah actually says that her son is *her* bloody bridegroom, not

---

27. Reprinted by James & Klock (Minneapolis, 1976).
28. This is not quite accurate enough. *Ḥathan* means either "son-in-law" or "bridegroom," not simply spouse—J.B.J.

God's: "Surely you are a bridegroom of blood *to me*" (verse 25). It is not Gershom's covenant-marriage to God that is in view.

In closing, we turn to an essay written by Hans Kosmala, entitled "The 'Bloody Husband.' "[29] Kosmala's study has two major flaws. First, he adopts the liberal critical view which sees the Book of Exodus as compiled from various sources. Second, he invents a speculative "Midianite theology" background to explain the phrase "bridegroom of blood." At the same time, Kosmala very carefully and meticulously studies the text as it is, noting that in context this incident comes immediately after God has threatened the firstborn sons of Egypt. Clearly, then, the one attacked by God in the lodging place is the son of Moses, not Moses himself.

Most importantly, however, Kosmala notices the connection between this incident and the Passover, a connection already established by immediate context. He argues that there is an obvious parallel between Zipporah's smearing of the foreskin's blood on her son's legs, and the smearing of the Passover lamb's blood on the doorposts of the houses in Egypt. In both cases the firstborn son is under attack. In both cases God calls off the attack when He sees the blood.

Kosmala points out that nowhere in the whole Bible does the verb translated "touch" have the meaning of "cast." It is utterly impossible to read that Zipporah cast the foreskin at someone's feet. "The only possible literal translation is: 'she made it touch (with regard to) his feet,' meaning 'she touched with it his feet or legs.' "[30] And since Moses has been nowhere mentioned in the paragraph describing this incident, there is no warrant for believing that she touched Moses with it; she touched her son's legs with it. (The Hebrew word for foot, *regel,* often simply means 'leg.')

Kosmala comments: "It is important, therefore, to make the sign on the child *visible*. It must be *seen*. That is necessary for any blood-rite. When God commanded the Israelites to smear the blood of the slaughtered animal on the lintel and the door posts, it

---

29. *Vetus Testamentum* 12 (1962):14-28.
30. *Ibid.*, p. 23.

was done in order that it might be seen: 'When I *see* the blood, I will pass over you . . . and not smite you' (Ex. 12:13, 23)."[31]

Concerning the phrase "bloody bridegroom," Zipporah is clearly addressing her son, not Moses. Moses is not in view in this story. Moreover, Moses had been a bloody bridegroom years before, on their wedding night. It would make no sense to address him thus on this occasion. Kosmala, however, has no explanation for Zipporah's use of this phrase, except to suggest that it was part of "Midianite theology." This, however, is wholly speculative on his part.

A Suggested Interpretation

What actually is happening here? God has just stated that His wrath against sin is going to take the form of killing the firstborn of men. This is because the firstborn male inherits preeminence, blessing, and a double portion from the father (Gen. 25:23,31; 27:4ff; 48:14ff.). Also, the firstborn acts as priest in the home, under the father's oversight (and thus, the Levitical order came into being by the Levites' being substituted for the firstborn of all Israel, Numbers 3). Thus, *the firstborn son signified the center and future of the family.* To spare the firstborn was to spare the family; to kill the firstborn was to kill the family.

Where was the "lodging place on the way?" We are not told. One might be inclined to think it is the border of Egypt, but immediately after this incident (if the text is in chronological order here), Aaron meets Moses at Mount Sinai. Thus, the lodging place would have to be near the mountain of God. On the other hand, possibly the lodging place incident is set here, out of chronological order, because of the theological context set up by verse 23, God's threat against the firstborn sons. In that case, it could easily be the border of Egypt.

I think the best way to resolve this difficulty is to take note of the vagueness of the text. Moses is drawing near to Egypt, a land

---

31. *Ibid.,* p. 24. Of course, for Kosmala there is not the idea of substitution in this blood-rite. Rather, its purpose is superstitious: to avert evil.

defiled with blood which has called up the Divine Blood Avenger. Moreover, he is drawing near to God's Holy Mountain, resting place of the Divine Blood Avenger. God, the Avenger, is going to visit Egypt, accompanying Moses. God (perhaps) joins Moses' party here at the lodging place, and when He does so, He finds that Moses has not heeded His warning regarding the firstborn sons. God is going to go with Moses to bring blood vengeance on Egypt, but before doing so, He is going to make Moses an object lesson to the Egyptians, by giving Moses a proleptic experience of Passover.

God attacks "him." The logical reference for the "him" in verse 24 is the word "firstborn" in verse 23. If we assume that God attacked the firstborn son, and Zipporah circumcised him, then we simply assume that Moses was not present at the time (which is entirely possible, since he might have been watering the animals, obtaining food, paying the bill, etc.). In this case, we see that God is attacking Moses' family by attacking his firstborn. Possibly, God was attacking Moses, and only the salvation of Moses' firstborn would save his family, and therefore Moses himself. The text is deliberately vague; God could have made it clear for us if it were important. Theologically, Moses and his son are in the same position, under the threat of death, and the simplest way to take the text is to hold that God was attacking Gershom.

In order to avert destruction, Zipporah circumcised her firstborn son. Then she smeared the blood on "his" legs (not "threw it at his feet," which is an indefensible translation). On whose legs? Most likely, on her son's legs. This made the atoning blood visible to God, and He stopped His attack. (If God were attacking Moses, it would still have been more practical for Zipporah to smear the blood on her son's legs, than to get near a possibly struggling Moses.)

Then, Zipporah addressed "him" and called him a "bridegroom of blood" (not a "bloody husband," a mistranslation).[32]

---

32. The Hebrew term, *ḥathan*, means either "son-in-law" or "bridegroom," as in Psalm 19:5; Isaiah 61:10; 62:5; Jeremiah 7:34; 16:9; 25:10; 33:11; and Joel 2:16. It never means simply "husband." The two Hebrew words for "husband" are *'ish* (man) and *ba'al* (lord).

Since Moses had been a bloody bridegroom on their wedding night years before, it is unlikely that Moses was the "him" addressed here by Zipporah. Also, it is expressly said in verse 26 that the phrase "bloody bridegroom" has reference to the circumcision, and it was the son (who was probably grown up by this time)[33] who was circumcised.

In summary, the most likely reading of the passage is this: Moses had not circumcised Gershom in Midian. God's wrath was expressed against all who dwelt in the land of Egypt, and that wrath was pointed against the firstborn sons. When God joined Moses on the way into the land of Egypt, God tried to kill Gershom. For some reason, Moses was not able to perform the circumcision, and Zipporah did so. She smeared the bloody foreskin on her son's legs. God saw the blood, and passed by. Zipporah stated that circumcision had made her son a "bloody bridegroom."

What does all this mean? To get at this question, let us look first at why God would attack Moses' family at all, and then at the meaning of "bridegroom of blood."

In Chapter 6 of this study we discuss the avenger of blood. Blood defiles the land, and calls up the avenger. The land of Egypt was defiled by blood. The aorta of Egypt was the Nile, and into the Nile had been tossed the murdered Hebrew babies (Ex. 1:22). To symbolize this defilement, the Nile was turned to blood (Ex. 7:17ff.). This called forth the Divine Avenger of Blood, the Angel of Death. Since the entire land was defiled, all those living in the land, including the Hebrews, were threatened by the Avenger. Only those who hid in cities of refuge would be spared. On Passover night, each faithful home became a city of refuge, by smearing blood on the doorposts and lintels.[34]

---

33. Moses had lived in Midian 40 years. Since Zipporah was a young woman at the time he arrived, their marriage probably occurred early in his sojourn. Thus, Gershom may have been as old as 35 years at this time.

34. Bear in mind that the Levites were not yet the priests of Israel. When the Levites were later substituted for the firstborn, it followed that the place of refuge moved from the homes of the firstborn to the homes of the Levites, the six designated Levitical cities of refuge. At this stage in history, however, the fathers

This is exactly parallel to what happened to Moses' family at the lodging place. The blood of the Passover smeared on the doorposts corresponds to the blood of circumcision smeared on Gershom's legs. It had the same effect. The lodging place became a place of refuge, just as the Hebrew homes in Egypt did later on.

Kosmala has rightly pointed out, as we noted above, that in both cases the blood was made visible to God, and that this is the reason God ceased attacking the household. Possibly the imagery is more specific. We find in Canticles 5:15 that the legs of a human figure are compared to pillars, or doorposts. The human body is compared to a house frequently in Scripture, as in Ecclesiastes 12, and there is nothing fabulous in seeing a comparison between legs and doorposts.[35] Indeed, even apart from these other passages the parallel between the circumcision of Gershom and the Passover all but explicitly states the analogy.[36]

We may ask why God attacked Moses' family at this point, rather than simply waiting for the Passover. There are two possible answers. First, Moses had killed a man (Ex. 2:12), and possibly it is his blood in particular which called up the Avenger. Possibly; but Moses was a civil magistrate in Egypt, being a member of

---

and firstborn were the priests, and so the home was the place of refuge.

Also, just as a man under threat of death could leave the city of refuge only when the high priest had died, so Israel under the threat of death could leave Egypt only on the basis of the death of the Passover lambs.

35. On the comparison in general, see M. G. Kline, *Images of the Spirit* (Grand Rapids: Baker, 1980).

36. We shall note in footnote 37 below that doorposts are a place of birth, and the comparison between coming out of a doorway and coming out of the womb between the legs is obvious. Western rationalist man is frequently blind to the visual images of Scripture, and to visual analogies which Scripture expects men to see without difficulty. There are architectural parallels among the forms of the Garden of Eden, the Tabernacle, the Temple, the New Jerusalem, the Glory Cloud, the Temple of Ezekiel, and the human body. The Bible expects us to note these, and to draw proper inferences from them. To limit God's revelation to the kinds of linear logical structures favored by modern rationalist man is to make oneself deaf to the Word of God. It is not necessary, in other words, for God to say explicitly somewhere, "The East Gate of the Garden, guarded by Cherubim, is parallel to the three Eastern Curtains of the Tabernacle, embroidered with Cherubim." Nor is it necessary for God to say, "Now, human legs are parallel to the doorposts of a house." But, in fact, see Canticles 5:15.

the royal household and 40 years of age, and his action in judging and executing the Egyptian was not an act of lawless violence, but an execution of lawful justice. The Bible never criticizes Moses for this, but presents his action as righteous and faithful (Acts 7:24ff.; Heb. 11:24ff.). The execution of criminals is never said to defile the land, or to require atonement; such execution is itself the atonement required. Thus, in my considered opinion, I think it unlikely that it was Moses' killing of the Egyptian which called forth the Avenger.

The other possibility is that God acted here to teach Moses the basic principle that He was about to use in the Passover. Thus, Moses came to be in a better position to explain God's ways to the people: The land was defiled, and all men were living on borrowed time, for the Avenger was coming soon. Substantiation for this opinion comes from the context in which this incident took place. The LORD referred to the "wonders" He was going to perform in Egypt (v. 21). The "miraculous signs" are referred to in verse 28. These two paragraphs bracket the incident at the lodging place. Thus, this incident was one more sign to Israel of how God was going to deal with them. The things that happened to Moses were types or shadows of what would happen to those in union with Moses. The experience of the head precedes that of the body. Moses' flight from Egypt, his forty years in the wilderness, his rearing sons there, and their circumcision at the time they draw near to God, are recapitulated in the experience of the Israelites, though with some differences. (The reader should remember that the Hebrews did not practice circumcision in the wilderness, but their sons were circumcised by Joshua when they entered the Land of Promise.)[37]

---

37. The Bible indicates, by this, a connection between the rite of circumcision and Israel's position as a priest to the nations. There is no indication that true believers outside Israel were supposed to practice circumcision. It was tied to Israel as the seed-throne-sanctuary people. When Israel was out of the sanctuary land, or away from God's special presence, they did not practice circumcision, it seems. Thus, Moses was not necessarily at fault for not having circumcised his sons. But, once he came into God's special presence, circumcision was again necessary. In the New Covenant, there is no longer a division of labor between seed-

Let us now turn to the meaning of the phrase, "bridegroom of blood." Since the Passover-exodus was the preeminent redemptive type of the Old Covenant, it embraces all the different figures for salvation used in Scripture. We have mentioned the avenger of blood/city of refuge pattern. We may also say that substitutionary atonement was clearly in view. Additionally, the exodus was Israel's birthday, and coming out of the bloodied doorways in the morning was equivalent to exiting the womb. Furthermore, it was Israel's adoption as sons of God.[38] We could go on, but the precise figure used here is of marriage. The exodus was Israel's marriage to her Divine Husband, as Ezekiel 16 and Hosea 1-3 make clear.[39] This is a common enough theological point. We also see that circumcision also refers to marriage, as the passage before us demonstrates.

What is unusual, and strange to our ears, is the reference to

---

people on the one hand, and those faithful on the other hand, who dwell outside the land but at the "east gate," the place where offerings are brought to the seed-people. Now all are holy to God, and all are baptized. On the bipolarity or division of labor and purpose between the seed-people and the other faithful, see Genesis 2:10-14 with 25:1-6, 18 and Isaiah 60:4-9. I believe that Zipporah fully understood the purpose of circumcision as a sign that the Seed-Savior would come through Israel, but that it was not practiced among the believing Midianites. This explains, by the way, the legitimate presence of uncircumcised God-fearers in the New Testament era, Acts 10:1,2 with 11:3. (This footnote may be challenged by pointing out that Ishmael and Esau were circumcised, and they may have maintained the practice down through the generations. On the other hand, Jethro, another descendent of Abraham, apparently did not practice it, though he knew about it. More work is needed in this area, I readily confess.)

38. On doorways and birth (or its ironic opposite, death), see Gen. 18:10; Jud. 11:31; Jud. 19:27; 1 Sam. 1:9; 1 Ki. 14:17; John 10:1-9, and the discussion in Chapter 5 of this study.

39. Did God marry Israel at Passover or at Mount Sinai? Ezekiel 16:8 is not precise. It would be wrong to try to separate Passover and Mt. Sinai into two different events. Rather, they are part of one complex of events. Moreover, there is nothing problematic in seeing both events as wedding nights, just as there is nothing problematic in the fact that animal sacrifices were not offered only once in the history of the Old Covenant, but over and over again. Neither Passover nor Mt. Sinai were *definitive* redemptive events. The definitive redemptive event was in Jesus Christ. Both Passover and Mt. Sinai were proleptic revelations of the then-future redemptive event, and were only provisional in character. That there is an overlap of meaning between the two is, thus, to be expected.

blood. In polite society, we do not usually discuss the blood of the wedding night,[40] but what other possible meaning is there for the phrase "bridegroom of blood"? Somehow, the blood of circumcision is equivalent to the blood of the wedding night. How shall we understand this?

The answer is that God demands His bride be a virgin.[41] This is clear from 2 Corinthians 11:2,3: "For I am jealous for you with a godly jealousy; for I betrothed you to one husband, that to Christ I might present you a pure virgin. But I am afraid, lest as the serpent deceived Eve by his craftiness, your minds should be led astray from the simplicity and purity (of devotion) to Christ." We see from this that Eve lost her Spiritual virginity when she hearkened to the voice of the serpent, and as a result she began to bear his seed alongside her own (Gen. 3:15).[42] The bride has played the harlot.

The bride, thus, can provide no blood on the wedding night. She is condemned to death, by the law of Deuteronomy 22:13-21, which states that a woman must have a token of virginity, a bloodstained wedding sheet, to prove that she is not a whore. What will be done for such a woman, if her husband truly loves her? He will provide his own blood to stain the sheet, to provide her with tokens of virginity. Just as it was blood from her "private parts" which would have been her token, so it must be blood from his, for it is at this part of their bodies that they become "one flesh." The blood of the wedding night is the visible token of their oneness, blood which flows from the very place at which they become one flesh. Since the woman cannot provide it, the circum-

---

40. Possibly Ezekiel 16:9, taken in context, makes direct reference to the blood of the wedding night. At the very least, the blood washed away here conflates that of birth and marriage.

41. To symbolize this, the wife of the high priest had to be a virgin, Leviticus 21:13. See also the parallel between the destruction of Jerusalem, God's wife, and the death of the wife of acting high priest, Ezekiel, in Ezekiel 24:16ff.

42. After all, angels do not marry or give in marriage. The seed of the serpent must come, thus, through the woman. We see the fulfillment of this in Genesis 4, where the two sons are the two seeds.

cision of the man does.[43] The groom circumcises himself on the wedding night, painfully, in order to provide legal covering for the bride he loves, and as a token of their union.

Thus, one of the (many) meanings of circumcision was this: Since Israel was a harlot, her Husband would give His blood for her covering and as a sign of their union. The circumcision of each male child provided a continuing reminder to Israel that she deserved to be put to death for playing the harlot in her father's house, and that a substitutionary atonement was the only way she would find judicial righteousness. Also, circumcision provided not just a reminder, but an actual covering until the crucifixion of her Lord would provide the final circumcision, and her definitive justification.

Zipporah, we are told, "cut off *her* son's foreskin" (Ex. 4:25). Why does the text not say, "Moses' son's foreskin"? Doubtless it is because of the bride theology of this passage. It is Israel-Eve as the Mother of the Seed who must be saved here. It is her son whose circumcision will deliver her from death. The conflation of husband and son seems to be a mixed metaphor, but while mixed metaphors are not permitted in college English classes, the Bible abounds in them. At this point, let me call attention to the book of Ruth, in which Boaz is clearly the kinsman-redeemer. Yet, in Ruth 4:14, 15, Obed is called Naomi's kinsman-redeemer. The son is conflated with the husband.[44]

---

43. Thus, Adam and Eve felt their shame especially in their private parts, and made aprons. Illicit sexual activity is called "uncovering nakedness" in Leviticus 18. Discharges from the genitals, life flowing away, cause uncleanness (Lev. 15). R. J. Rushdoony has called attention to the symbolic parallel between the human body and the garden, with fountain in the center: "To understand this meaning we must remember that a fountain is a source, a place on earth where living water comes forth. There is an obvious analogy to the woman's ovulation." *The Institutes of Biblical Law* (Phillipsburg, NJ: The Craig Press, 1973), p. 429.

44. This is in terms of the Biblical theology of *succession*. Repeatedly in Genesis it is seen as important that each bride be succeeded by another true bride, and each seed by another true seed. Thus, it is immediately upon the death of Sarah that Abraham moves to provide a bride for Isaac (Gen. 23, 24), and when Rebekah arrives, Isaac takes her into Sarah's tent (24:67). Similarly, when Jacob is sent to Laban to get a righteous wife (replacement bride), this is

We are now in a position to say why God dealt with Zipporah rather than with Moses in this situation. It is because Zipporah could more fully signify Israel as God's bride, in need of a token of virginity. Thus, Moses is simply absent from this narrative. Where he was and what he was doing, it is not important for us to know.

This passage also explains the reference in Revelation 19:7,9 to the "marriage supper of the Lamb." The blood of the lamb was the sign of Israel's marriage to the LORD, at Passover. The Passover feast, thus, was a marriage feast. Passover was the marriage feast of the lamb. In the New Covenant, the Lord's Supper fulfills Passover (and all the other feasts and meals of the Old Covenant as well). Thus, the Holy Eucharist of the Church is the marriage supper of the True Lamb of God. Since the Book of Revelation is arranged in the order of a worship service,[45] we expect the Lord's Supper to come at its climax, as here it does. In a very precise way, then, the phrase "marriage supper of the Lamb" refers to the fulfillment of Passover.

In paganism, the marriage relation between a man and his god is seen in sexual terms. Thus, sexual relations are sacramental in pagan religions, and repeatedly in Scripture this "fertility cult" form of religion is warned against (for an example, see 1 Sam. 2:22). Because of the Creator/creature distinction, there is no sexual relationship between God and man. The sexual relationship between man and woman symbolizes the Spiritual marriage between God and His bride. The act of this Spiritual marriage is not ritual fornication in a temple, but the communion

---

sandwiched in between two notices of the unfitness of Esau's wives (27:46 - 28:9). Thus, it is because each woman in succession signifies the Bride, and each man in succession signifies the Seed/Lord, that cross-generational symbolic structures are appropriate. In one very real sense, the woman gives birth to her seed, who will grow up to become her deliverer, lord, and husband. The Bible strictly forbids any actual physical (sexual) acting out of this theology, thus reserving it wholly for the realm of symbol. In common life, the seed is the "bloody bridegroom" of his mother only in a symbolic sense, a sense fulfilled in Christ's redemption of the Church.

45. This can be seen from Revelation 1:10, but the worship pattern prevails throughout the entire book.

meal. Eve was said in 2 Corinthians 11 to have committed fornication with the serpent; what she actually did was eat the serpent's
food. Similarly, the act of marriage between God and His Church
is nothing more and nothing less than the Holy Eucharist.[46] Sharing the same food with someone else actually creates a more pro-
found "one flesh" relationship than does sex, since the same food
molecules go into the bodies of all eating the meal (1 Cor. 10:17).

Addendum on the Circumcision of Abram and Sarai

In Chapter 5, we saw that circumcision indicates the three zones
of salvation: justification, sanctification, and glorification.[47] We
called attention to Abram and Sarai. In terms of what we have found
in this essay, we can expand on that discussion and note the following. First, Abram's circumcision represents justification by encom-
passing both death and resurrection. It applies to Sarai in providing
a substitute for her: her token of virginity. Thus, the woman is justified in the circumcision of her husband and/or son. This sheds further light on why women were not circumcised in the Old Covenant.

Second, Abram is clothed with a new name in circumcision,
answering to glorification. Sarai's name is also changed, to Sarah.
Both names undergo glorification: Abram ("Exalted Father") to
Abraham ("Father of a Multitude"), and Sarai ("My own
Princess") to Sarah ("*The* Princess").

Third, Abram's hindrance to procreation is removed, answering to new life and sanctification. So is Sarai's. As a result, the
barren woman can conceive the Seed, Isaac.

---

46. We may also call attention to the parallel between the call of the bride in
Revelation and in Canticles: "Come swiftly." It is a call for the final and ultimate
Spiritual consummation of Christ's marriage to His bride. Cf. Rev. 22:17, 20 and
Cant. 8:14. The "marriage supper," which is the Holy Eucharist, is the weekly
consummation of the marriage. While Christ will return to end history some day,
His weekly meeting with His bride is the "swift coming" here invited. Christ feeds
his Bride, which is the Spiritual reverse and correction of Adam's being fed by his
wife (Gen. 3:6). In paganism, the fact that the festival supper is the Spiritual
form of the consummation of marriage was perverted and lost, so that sexual
relations were viewed sacramentally. The Bible nowhere teaches that sexual relations are sacramental. Physical marital relations are analogous to Christ's love
for His bride, and the Spiritual expression of that love is seen initially in the
sacrament of Holy Baptism (that is, New Covenant circumcision) and repeatedly
in the sacrament of the Holy Eucharist.

47. See in particular Chapter 5, footnote 9.

Appendix G

FOUR AND FIVE-FOLD RESTITUTION

> Exodus 22:1. When a man steals an ox or a sheep and butchers it or sells it, five oxen must he make whole for the ox, and four members of the flock for the sheep.

The difficulty in interpreting this law resides in the fact that the immediate context gives absolutely no indication of what the governing principle is, and unless we can come up with a governing principle, we cannot make any application of this law to any situation other than the particular one addressed in the very wording of the law. Why multiple restitution for these clean animals, but not for unclean (an inference we draw from the fact that the donkey is added in verse 4, but is not present in this verse)? Why four-fold for the sheep, and five-fold for the ox? Since the distinction between clean and unclean is gone in the New Covenant, into which category do we place swine? The immediate context is silent. Thus, expositors have been forced either to set aside the question of possible implications this text might have, or else to speculate (helpfully or unhelpfully) concerning what its implications might be.

The most common explanation is that sheep reproduce themselves, and when a sheep is permanently removed from the flock, this removes all its potential posterity as well. Similarly, the ox reproduces itself, and additionally is a trained work animal; thus the permanent loss of the ox entails the loss of much time and labor invested in training it. One problem with this view is that there is no corroboration for it anywhere in Scripture, so that it is pure speculation (as opposed to a Biblically-grounded hypothet-

261

ical explanation). Another problem is that it seems economically naive. In point of fact, the market price for any given sheep at any given time will include its reproductive potential, and so also for the ox. In terms of the training of the ox, its value will be proportionately greater depending on how it has been trained. Double restitution would be made in terms of the actual market value of the ox, and this value would reflect its training. Thus, the market price already takes into account both reproductive potential and training, and double restitution would be adequate if that were all that is in view. A third problem is that the donkey is also a trained animal, but apparently double restitution suffices in the event it is permanently removed.

Another explanation sometimes suggested is that the ox and sheep signify the tools of a man's trade. If a man stole a television set from a painter, for instance, he would owe double restitution; but if he stole that painter's pickup truck with all of his equipment in it, and wrecked the truck, he would owe five-fold restitution because he had destroyed the tools of his trade. Stealing the sources of a man's livelihood is more serious, according to this argument, than stealing a comparative luxury. One problem with this interpretation is, again, that the Bible nowhere corroborates it. Also, when speaking of what is essential to a man's livelihood, the Bible speaks of the "handmill or an upper millstone" (Dt. 24:6), not of sheep and oxen. Third, this explanation does not account for the difference between four-fold and five-fold restitution. If the pickup truck and tools are like the ox, what is like the sheep?

A third suggested explanation is that it costs the owner more effort to prove that his ox or sheep was stolen if the evidence has been disposed of. If the thief has kept the beast alive, it can be identified. The cost of recovery is relatively low. On the other hand, if the beast has been killed, eaten, and the remains buried, or if it has been sold to foreigners, then it becomes difficult to prove the suspected thief guilty. The owner may have to hire a detective agency, and put time and money into proving his case. Thus, multiple restitution covers the costs of proof in this situation.

Again, there are several problems with this view, and again the first problem is that it is wholly without Biblical corroboration. Second, this canon is valid for any beast, including dog or donkey: If the thief sells the animal, there will be additional costs to proving the case. Third, this explanation does not account for the difference between four-fold and five-fold restitution. Indeed, it is easier both to steal and to dispose of a sheep than of an ox, so that the cost of proof would be higher in the case of the sheep than in the case of the ox; thus, we should expect four-fold for the ox and five-fold for the sheep. Finally, though the cost of proof is a valid consideration in a case such as this, it can easily be covered by bringing an additional suit against the thief to recover any expenses involved. The thief could also be sued for the owner's loss of time (Ex. 21:19).

I should like to suggest a different line of approach. We need to see if the Bible itself gives us any clues to the meaning of these provisions, and then test our hypothesis to see if it finds corroboration in those passages which show the application of this law (2 Sam. 12; Luke 19:8).

Four-Fold and Five-Fold

When Israel heard this law, they had a background of Divine revelation consisting of the book of Genesis. What light, then, does the book of Genesis shed on the meaning of the numbers four and five? In Genesis 2:10, we find that the river of Eden split into four streams, and watered the earth. This signified that the source of life in the garden was extending itself to the four corners of the earth (Is. 11:12; Jer. 49:36; Ezk. 7:2; etc.). We can make an initial suggestion that the number four represents *comprehensive dominion*. A man may have dominion over a very limited space, but within the four corners of that space, he has comprehensive dominion. Thus, Abraham paid four hundred shekels of silver for a plot of land in Canaan, the only land he ever owned in the land of promise (Gen. 23:15f.). Thus, Esau came out to fight Jacob with four hundred men (Gen. 32:6; 33:1), signifying his continuing claim to the land of promise.

Before examining this further, let us consider the meaning of the number five. Five is four plus one. This trivial observation takes on meaning when we notice how frequently the Bible uses as a formula the literary sequence of a number and then the next higher number.[1] The most familiar occurrences are in Proverbs 30:15ff. and Amos 1:3ff. Glancing at the latter, it is clear that three transgressions are enough for God to judge a culture, and that four transgressions are more than enough. Similarly, a matter must be confirmed by two or three witnesses (Dt. 17:6); two witnesses are enough (John 8:12-20), but three are more than enough. If four is the number of dominion, then five, being dominion plus one, indicates some type of preeminence. Do we find initial corroboration for the hypothesis that five is the number of *preeminence?* Yes, in Genesis 43:34, Joseph gave five times as many portions of food to Benjamin as he gave to his other brethren. This indicated a singling out of Benjamin as preeminent. Obviously, Benjamin could not eat five times as much food; the action was clearly symbolic.[2] Similarly, when Joseph invested his brethren as fellow-officers in Pharaoh's court, he gave five times as many changes of clothing to Benjamin (Gen. 45:22). Since investiture indicates dominion, it is clear that Benjamin was being given a preeminence of dominion.[3]

Also, the number five is used in military organization. The expression in Exodus 13:18, "and the sons of Israel went up in *martial array* from the land of Egypt," literally reads "and the sons of Israel went up *five in a rank* from the land of Egypt."[4] This is platoon for-

---

1. This is surveyed by Wolfgang M. W. Roth, "The Numerical Sequence x/x + 1 in the Old Testament," *Vetus Testamentum* 12 (1962):300-311.

2. Joseph's design, of course, was to put Benjamin in the same position he himself had been in: singled out for favor. He wanted to see how his brothers would react this time. Would they enviously seek to destroy Benjamin, as they had him? Or would they offer themselves as substitutes to ransom Benjamin (Gen. 44:18-34)?

3. On investiture and dominion, see Gen. 9:20-27; 37:3, 23; 39:12-18; 41:42ff.

4. Brown, Driver, Briggs *Hebrew and English Lexicon* lists the Hebrew root *hmsh* meaning five, and another root *hmsh* having to do with armies. The problem is that there is no evidence whatsoever that these are two separate roots. Older commentators assumed that they were related. In fact, "five in a rank" is stand-

mation, five squads of ten men.[5] Thus, the number five is associated with might and power.

We also have to look at Genesis 14, the war of the five kings against the four. The Canaanite kings numbered five, and their opponents numbered four. At first glance, the symbolism seems reversed, so perhaps our hypotheses are in error. I believe not, however. The Canaanites manifested the sin of Ham, in attempting to seize dominion and preeminence (Gen. 9:18-27). They were overcome by the four-fold dominion of an alliance of Shemites (Chedorlaomer), Japhethites (Tidal), and non-Canaanite Hamites (Amraphel and Arioch). Since Chedorlaomer is preeminent (Gen. 14:4, 5, 17), the others are to be regarded as dwelling in the tents of Shem (Gen. 9:27). The Canaanites rebelled, seeking to assert preeminence, but were defeated. Possibly we should see Abram as a fifth to Chedorlaomer's four, especially since Abram defeated Chedorlaomer (note the language of 14:17) and thus has final preeminence in the situation. At any rate, in Genesis 14 we find some corroboration for our hypotheses.[6] All of this is background for Exodus 22:1.

---

ard military formation. Also, the supposed second root *hmsh* having to do with armies only occurs in one form, the form used in Ex. 13:18; Num. 32:17; Josh. 1:14; 4:12; and Jud. 7:11. The more obvious and simpler lexical explanation is that the number five is here used to refer to military organization.

5. In Exodus 18:21, we have elders over 10s, 50s, 100s, and 1,000s. Why not over 500s and 5,000s? The reason is that these elders would also have been commanders in the Israelite militia. Israel did not have a professional army until the time of the kings, and so the ordinary elders would have doubled as military leaders in times of distress. This system gives us squads of 10 men, arranged in platoons of 50. Two platoons give us a company of 100. Ten companies give us a battalion of 1,000, and ten battalions give us a brigade of 10,000. I have dealt with this more fully in an essay entitled "How Biblical is Protestant Worship?" *The Geneva Papers* 25 (February, 1984). This is available in exchange for a contribution from The Geneva Papers, P.O. Box 8376, Tyler, TX 75711.

6. The notion of four as the number of dominion is not strange. For further uses of the number five, indicating some type of preeminence, the reader should consider Joshua chapter 10 in its entirety, and the fact that there were five lords of the Philistines (Josh. 13:3 and many other passages), and the symbolic usages in Isaiah 19:18 and 30:17. When David confronted the giant Goliath, he selected five stones (1 Sam. 17:40), because there were in fact five giants, one for each of the five cities of the Philistine pentapolis (2 Sam. 21:15-22). The numbers four

Sheep and Oxen

The numbers four and five are associated with sheep and oxen respectively. (Both terms used to refer to sheep here can also be used for "member of the flock," including goats. Thus, goats are not excluded from view.) Do we find corroboration for the suggested meanings of the numbers four and five in their correlation with sheep and oxen? I believe so. These are the animals which particularly symbolize humanity in the sacrificial system. They are, thus, repeatedly set forth as preeminent analogies for men (cf. e.g., Lev. 22:27, with Lev. 12).

We should note here that the verb used in Exodus 22:1, "slaughter," is used almost always with reference to men. Ralph H. Alexander comments, "The central meaning of the root occurs only three times (Gen. 43:16; Ex. 22:1; 1 Sam. 25:11). The root is predominantly used metaphorically, portraying the Lord's judgment upon Israel and upon Babylon as a slaughter."[7] This again points to a basic symbolic meaning of this law.

A distinction between the two is set forth in Leviticus 4. In verse 3, if the high priest sins and brings guilt on the whole people, he must bring a bull as a purification sacrifice. Similarly, in verse 13, if the whole congregation brings guilt upon itself, it must also sacrifice a bull. On the other hand, in verse 22, if a leader sins and brings guilt only upon himself, he must sacrifice a male goat; and in verse 27, if any one of the common people sins, he is to sacrifice a female goat or lamb.[8] What this indicates is that the

---

and five figure preeminently in the dimensions of the Tabernacle and Temple, the number four generally concerning dimensions (four sides, four corners) and directions, and the number five generally having to do with thicknesses, lengths, breadths, and heights.

7. *Theological Wordbook of the Old Testament* (Chicago: Moody Press, 1980), p. 341.

8. Males were worth more than females, since the first male goat was always sacrificed (Ex. 13:12), so that there were fewer males than females, and because one male can perform stud service for an entire flock of females. Also, as mentioned in Chapter 10, male kids were frequently eaten; because they were not needed, they made a good meat dish. Thus, there were relatively few adult male goats.

bull represents the office-bearer, who symbolizes the whole community, while the sheep or goat represents the ordinary leader or citizen.

This is a bit different from what we said above concerning the numbers four and five. Concerning the number four, we said that it has to do with comprehensive dominion. We can readily connect this with sheep as symbols of ordinary people or leaders, in the exercise of dominion. Concerning the number five, however, we connected it with preeminence; yet the bull is not connected with preeminence (leadership) as such, but with the congregation as a whole (and its symbol, the high priest). The number five also seems to have this wholistic connotation, especially in its use in connection with the Israelite army. When Israel marched, they marched as the army of the Lord, five in a rank.

On the basis of this, I believe we can modify our original hypothesis concerning the number five. It indicates not only preeminence but power, and/or a special office in the community. The special officer represents the community as a whole before God, and also represents God's government to the community.

There is one other aspect to which attention should be called. While the ox is a beast of power, the sheep is an animal of weakness. R. A. Stewart has written, "Despite their harmlessness, sheep suffer from a lack of initiative amounting to weakness so that, like many human beings, they are easily lost or led astray (Jer. 1:6 and Matt. 10:6; Is. 53:6 and 1 Pet. 2:25; the parable of Matt. 18:12f., etc.). Without a shepherd, it is a helpless creature (Num. 27:17; Matt. 9:36, etc.; cf. Is. 13:14, and more strongly, Zech. 13:7). God's human servants are very frequently likened to sheep (Ps. 100:3; Ezk. 34:31; John 21:16f., etc.). This idea is elaborated with much beauty and richness in John 10. The animal's utter defenselessness before those who would steal its coat (Is. 53:7) or demand its life for their own ends (Is. 53:7 and Acts 7:32; Ps. 44:22 and Rom. 8:36; Jer. 12:3, etc.) is pathetic."[9]

Thus, the sheep can signify the poor in Israel, and the ox can

---

9. *New Bible Dictionary* (Grand Rapids: Eerdmans, 1962), article "Sheep."

signify the office-bearer.

Oppressing the Poor

The two instances in Scripture where the law of four-fold resti-tution is seen in operation both have to do with the oppression of the poor by a powerful man, who misuses his office to bring about harm to the dominion of a poor man. The poor man does not have much dominion, but he exercises comprehensive dominion over what he does have, and this is to be regarded as inviolable.

The first case is in 2 Samuel 12. Nathan tells David a story about a poor man who had nothing except one little ewe lamb, who was like a child to him. A rich man stole the lamb and killed it. David immediately states that this man is worthy of death, but that the actual penalty to be inflicted is four-fold restitution. Nathan then informs David that his stealing of Bathsheba from Uriah, and his murder of Uriah, correspond to the rich man's stealing and killing the ewe lamb. Four-fold restitution will be ex-acted from David (the death of Bathsheba's child, the death of Amnon, the death of Absalom, and the death of Adonijah).

The second case is that of Zaccheus in Luke 19:8. Upon his conversion, Zaccheus states that wherever he has defrauded anyone, he will make four-fold restitution. It is customary to see Zaccheus as going beyond the bare requirements of the law, which specify merely adding the fifth part in the case of voluntary resti-tution (Lev. 6:1-7). This understanding of the event raises a prob-lem, however.

If Zaccheus is going beyond the law, we should expect to see his generosity expressed in terms other than the particular re-quirements of the law. The Bible is usually quite particular in distinguishing among gifts, heave offerings, tithes, and so forth. We could reasonably expect to read something like this: "Half of my possessions I will give to the poor, and wherever I have defrauded anyone of anything, I will make it good by adding the fifth part, and also bestow upon that person a gift of such and such an amount."

This is a problem, and it directs us back to the text to see if we can find a better explanation. I think the proper explanation is this: Zaccheus sees himself as a thief apprehended and judged for his crime. Jesus is the Judge, and Zaccheus submits to the judgment. Thus, his restitution is not "voluntary," but rather a byproduct of his legal justification in the law-court of God. Furthermore, since his thefts resulted from his abusing power and oppressing the poor (cf. Luke 18:2, 8), he owes four-fold, not double, restitution. Thus, his action is in keeping with the law, and does not go beyond it, except in that he also offers to give half of his possessions to the poor.

The stories of David and of Zaccheus lead us to see a symbolic parallel between killing a sheep and oppressing the poor. If the sheep is found alive, only double restitution is required (Ex. 22:4). Thus, I suppose, if a powerful man stole from a poor man, but did not abuse his power in so doing, only double restitution would be required. If, however, a powerful man used his clout in the community, or his ability to hire gunmen, or his political office as a weapon against the poor man, then the act of theft would also be an act of oppression, and four-fold restitution would be required. After all, it is not simply stealing the sheep which is in view. The thief also either kills it or sells it (and either action is a capital offense when committed against human beings; thus David's initial response). It is theft coupled with violence, in this case directed by a man of power against a man of powerlessness, which is in view.

Revolution

If an attack on a sheep signifies an attack on the poor, then an attack on an ox signifies a revolt against constituted authority, or an attack on the entire congregation. This is an inference drawn from the general considerations detailed above. The Bible nowhere gives a single straightforward instance (that I can find) of five-fold restitution, so further corroboration of this thesis is difficult.

One somewhat oblique possibility, however, is found in 2 Chronicles 13, a narrative not found in the books of Kings. Jeroboam I of Israel made war against Abijah of Judah. Judah is stated to have an army of 400,000 men, while Israel is stated to have an army of 800,000, exactly double that of Judah. If we permit the numbers to take on symbolic significance, then Judah's is seen as the relatively poorer army. Abijah makes a speech, in which he expressly accuses Jeroboam of rebellion against his lord (v. 6), and in which he expressly states that the Lord God is the Head of the hosts of Judah (v. 12). Thereafter, Jeroboam attacks Abijah, and the army of Judah cries to the Lord. God grants them victory, and we are expressly told that 500,000 chosen men of Israel fell slain (v. 17). If we permit the numbers to speak symbolically, then we can see this as a five-fold penalty for rebellion, and for attempted theft. God had given Jeroboam the ten northern tribes (Israel), but Jeroboam was invading and attempting to take over (steal) the land of Judah (v. 4 with Josh. 18:22). Since this constituted rebellion against a superior, and an attempt to rob by force, the required restitution was five-fold. The Godly four-fold dominion of Judah (400,000) overcame the wicked, and exacted five-fold (500,000) restitution.

(Possibly also we have an application of this in 2 Corinthians 11:24, where Paul says, "Five times I received from the Jews the forty lashes minus one." The natural way to take this is that on five separate occasions, Paul was thus whipped. Possibly, however, Paul was seen as guilty of insurrection and of stealing members of the synagogues for the Christian faith, and so possibly he is referring to one occasion on which he was punished five-fold, perhaps whipped on five consecutive days. I offer this as a bare possibility only.)

Conclusion

If my explanation is correct, then we can readily apply this law to modern society.[10] The best explanation of Exodus 22:1 that

---

10. I am not totally positive that my interpretation is the correct one. I offer it to the Church as the best I have been able to do. There is, to my knowledge, no good study of Biblical numerical symbolism, and I have done my best with the numbers four and five. Studies of Biblical symbolism in general are rare, and

I have been able to come up with is that sheep and oxen here signify two types of men in God's field: the poor and the office-bearers.
A crime of violence directed by a powerful man against a poor one
must be avenged by the court, and if destruction of property is involved, the restitution exacted is to be four-fold. A crime of
violence directed against an office-bearer, who signifies God to the
people, is particularly heinous, an act of revolution, and if it involves destruction of property, the restitution exacted is to be
five-fold. Destructive theft, if committed between equals, would
entail double restitution.

The Bible, thus, sets forth special punishment for the man of
power who oppresses the poor. He is abusing his God-given office
and power, and his punishment is especially severe. The powerful
man who uses his power to steal and destroy something belonging
to a poor man should be required to make four-fold restitution.

At the same time, the Bible does not side with the poor against
the powerful either. The man who forms a conspiracy of envy to
attack and tear down the ruler among God's people is rebelling
against God Himself. To the extent to which revolutionary activity succeeds in destroying property, the conspirators must be
made to pay five-fold. Similarly, I suggest, a destructive attack on
the property of either state or Church should command five-fold
restitution, since such attacks are in the nature of the case acts of
insurrection, directed against authority and its symbols.[11]

Of course, rich people steal from rich people, and poor people
steal from poor people. Where neither rebellion nor oppression is
in view, double restitution is the rule.

---

mostly useless. It may be, of course, that I am absolutely correct, and that my interpretation only seems a bit strained to me because I am not sufficiently steeped
in the Hebraic-Biblical way of thinking about these things.

11. In Chapter 6, discussing the Law of Equivalence, I argued that a man's
status, rich or poor, should not be taken into account in meting out punishment.
This Appendix does not conflict with that position. I am arguing that it is the
conjoining of theft with either revolution or oppression which brings on the
infliction of five-fold or four-fold restitution. As I noted above, a rich man might
steal from a poor man without simultaneously abusing his power; in such a case,
simple double restitution would be in view.

Appendix H

ON BOILING A KID IN ITS MOTHER'S MILK

I should like in this appendix to look a bit more closely at the law prohibiting the boiling of a kid in its own mother's milk. My purpose is not to rehearse the information on this contained on pages 190-192 of this book, but to explore the line of argumentation used. I should like to make the methodology more explicit, both as an aid to students, and because I think that doing so can help alleviate psychological reservations on the part of the reader. My interpretation seems strange to the modern reader, so I should take space to defend it as best I can. Thus, I wish to take the reader through the stages of my own thinking on the matter, to show how I arrived at the interpretation found in Chapter 10.

First, we note that it is generally the case that laws regulating the behavior and treatment of animals find their application in the behavior and treatment of men. From the New Testament, we are aware that not muzzling the ox when it treads out the corn is applied to the payment of pastors. Not yoking an ox and an ass together is applied to the marriage of believers and unbelievers. Thus, we can reasonably hypothesize initially that not boiling a kid in its own mother's milk has application to a mother's killing and eating her own child.

This gives us an hypothesis which now we have to check out. Our method will have to involve four stages. First, we want to check out the *actual particulars* of the law: the kid, the mother's milk, the boiling. We want to see whether or not other passages that refer to these things tend to corroborate our hypothesis. Second, we want to look at the three occurrences of this law, to see

272

whether or not the *contexts* in which the law occurs tend to corroborate our hypothesis. Third, we want to look at *redemptive historical applications* of the hypothesis, to see whether or not it fulfills our reasonable expectations. That is, does our interpretation of this law
enable us better to understand the work of Jesus Christ? Fourth,
we want to look at *practical applications* of the hypothesis, because the
Bible is designed to be relevant to men in their historical context. If
our interpretation is utterly useless, it is probably also utterly
worthless. In other words: Can this doctrine be preached?

Now, if everything stacks up, then we can reasonably offer our
hypothesis to the Christian world, as a viable interpretive option,
and ask for criticism and interaction.

First, then, to the particulars of the law. We look to see what
the Bible says about kids. Our hypothesis assumes that they signify children. There turns out to be relatively little information on
this, and no particular verse which says, "Kids symbolize children." On the other hand, we are not in a position to dictate to
God how He must disclose revelation to us. The Bible does not
have to fit our preconceived (and rationalistic) canons of argument and proof. The Bible may teach that kids signify children by
a variety of "indirect indications" rather than by "explicit statement." We have to be open to this. We do find that a number of
passages *suggest* a connection between kids and children. We also
find that kids were used for food rather often.

Now we turn to mother's milk. We find that the weaning of
Isaac is an important occasion (Gen. 21:8ff). At this time, Isaac
leaves the protection of his mother, and thus is exposed to conflict
with Ishmael. Thus, Sarah's last act is to protect her child. We
also find in a more extensive way that a man is not said to leave
his father and mother until he takes a wife (Gen. 2:24). Thus,
there is a sense in which any unmarried man is "under age." This
sense is heightened in the case of a child not yet weaned. At any
rate, we find that Jacob is still being protected by his mother,
Rebekah, when Isaac wishes to steal the covenant from him. Additionally, we find in the New Testament that the early history of
the Church, before the destruction of Jerusalem, is likened to the

milk-stage of infancy. The destruction of Jerusalem is likened to
the casting out of Ishmael (Gal. 4:21ff.). What all of this corroborates and fills out is that there is a peculiar tie between a child
and its mother during the nursing years.

Then we look at the concept of boiling. We find twice that
when cities were under siege, women boiled and ate their own
nursing children (Lam. 4:10; 2 Ki. 6:28f.). This definitely tends to
corroborate our initial hypothesis, that the primary purpose of
this law is to regulate human conduct.

To summarize: What we have found thus far is nothing that
contradicts our initial hypothesis, and much that seems to corroborate it and fill it out.

We can now expand on the hypothesis and broaden our conception. Apparently, a child stayed with its mother until it was
weaned. The feast Abraham threw at the weaning of Isaac indicates that the mother presents the child to the father on that occasion. She has done her initial work. Now the child is ready for
"solid food" (Heb. 5:13-14). That a mother should devour her nursing child is, thus, not simply a horrible act of cannibalism, it is
also a consuming of her sacred trust. The child is not hers to
possess; rather, the child is in her stewardship. She is supposed to
rear him to a certain point, and then present him to her husband.

What our broadened conception points to is an analogy between weaning the child and paying our tithes and offerings to
God. In terms of the general teaching that we are the Bride of
Christ, we can say that all our works are like children. We are
supposed to present them to our Lord and Husband, once we
have developed them to a certain point. To consume the works of
our hands, without first tithing on them, is equivalent to eating
our own nursing children. That is our hypothesis at this point.

Now, we turn to the context of these three laws. What do we
find? We find that each time the law occurs in a context connected
to the Feast of Ingathering, when the tithe is presented (note contexts of Ex. 23:19; 34:26; Dt. 14:21). Again, this fits with the
overall hypothesis as it has developed. The positive injunction is:
Pay your tithe at the time of the harvest. The negative injunction

is: Do not consume the works of your hands until you have paid the tithe first.

Thus far, we have found that our initial hypothesis has led us into new and expanded insights, without contradicting any doctrine of the faith. We have found nothing that does not corroborate our hypothesis, even though some of the evidence is seemingly slight and/or indirect. What we have found thus far is, then, quite encouraging.

Now, however, we have to see if this hypothesis can reasonably be applied to Jesus Christ, since all Scripture speaks of Him. Again, using what we already know, we can say that Jerusalem is the mother of the Seed. We also see that Jesus Christ did not take His Bride until after His resurrection, and so was still under His mother's authority and rule — under the law. Even though there is no particular verse to indicate this, we might say that the teaching (law) of the mother to the child corresponds to her milk. Certainly the New Testament likens the Old Testament period to a time of infancy (Gal. 4:1ff.), and likens teaching to either milk or solid food, depending on whether it is basic or advanced doctrine (1 Cor. 3:2; Heb. 5:12; 1 Pet. 2:2).

Can we see an application? When Jerusalem kills her Son, can we say that the mother kills her kid? When we see that the Son is not yet married, and under the mother's special care, this also ties to our hypothesis. Finally, when we see that the mother perversely uses the law, which should have been life to her child, in order to put her child to death, we can see an analogy to boiling the child in her own milk. In other words, there is an analogy between:

> Mother boils her kid in her own milk.
> Jerusalem kills her Son using the law.

Well, we don't seem to be straining at any gnats or swallowing any camels in making these observations. We have an overall teaching that Jerusalem kills her sons, the prophets, repeatedly throughout history. We also have an overall teaching that Jerusalem perversely misused the holy law of God in order to put men in bondage (Pharisees), to corrupt the early Church (Judaizers), and to crucify Her Son (John 19:7, "we have a law, and by that law, He must die"). These teachings are familiar to all, and need no substantiation. Our hypothesis, we note, fits beautifully in with these common teachings, and adds a new dimension to them. That is what we should expect, if the teaching is true.

Finally, we want to know if the hypothesis enables us to preach to our modern situation. Times and seasons vary, and perhaps it would be difficult to find close analogies to child cannibalism in, say, certain more Christian periods of history. Today, however, we find no problem. According to "All About Issues," January, 1984, put out by the American Life Lobby, in an article by Olga Fairfax entitled "101 Uses for a Dead (or Alive) Baby," modern "collagen enriched" lotions, hand creams, shampoos, and the like are frequently made from the boiled-down substances of aborted children. Aborted babies are sold by the pound or by the bag. Dr. Fairfax mentions some drug/cosmetic companies which do not use human collagen, and some human collagen comes from placentas rather than from babies, but others apparently are using fetuses as a source. (Copies of a 40-page documented study are available for a donation from Dr. Olga Fairfax, 12105 Livingston St., Wheaton, MD 20902. The short article can be had for a donation from American Life Lobby, Box 490, Stafford, VA 22554. Similar data is found in William Brennan, *Medical Holocausts: Exterminative Medicine in Nazi Germany and Contemporary America* [Nordland Publishing International, 1980], and Brennan, *The Abortion Holocaust: Today's Final Solution* [St. Louis: Landmark Press, 1983], available from Geneva Christian Bookservice, P.O. Box 8376, Tyler, TX 75711.)

We have not yet seen widespread eating of fetal material by the women of America. But, the women of America are, as a group, boiling down their murdered children, and using the residue as cosmetics.

It seems that our hypothesis does indeed give us preaching material.

We've gone about as far as we can go. We've found a lot of reinforcement for our initial hypothesis, and we have not found any contradictions. Now we offer the thesis to the Christian community. Perhaps somebody out there will take issue with us, and prove us wrong, or at least give us pause for thought. On the other hand, maybe others will like the idea, and expand and develop it further, bringing in other lines of corroborative evidence, and making further applications. That is how the Body of Christ works.

INDEX OF HEBREW TERMS DISCUSSED

'ish, 252n.
ba'al, 252n.
ba'ar, 138
go'el, 36ff., 97n.
hamah, 38n.
hmsh, 264n.
hamas, 177ff.
herem, 154
haron 'af, 157f.
harats, 38n.
hathan, 249, 252n.
yalid, 55n.
yasha', 240n.
levir, 156
mohar, 43 (n. 22), 84f., 146ff, 156
mishpatim, 51

nagaph, 113n.
navah, 38n.
nakhah, 113n.
nasi', 162
nathan, 117n.
paqad, 227, 230
tsarar, 240n.
qoheleth, 152
qalal, 105n.
ribh, 110
regel, 250
shalam, 117n., 134
shoṭerim, 53n.
sheqer, 177ff.
tahath, 117

INDEX OF PERSONS CITED OR REFERENCED

(Not including Biblical personages; see Subject Index)

Aalders, G. Ch., vii, 30
Albright, W. F., 116, 118
Alexander, Ralph H., 266
Allis, Oswald T., vii
Anstay, Martin, 32, 44
Augustine of Hippo, 181
Bahnsen, Greg L., 6, 9, 20, 28, 126
Brennan, William, 276
Brichto, Herbert C., 105
Bush, George, 249f.
Calvin, John, 181, 244
Cassuto, Umberto, 63, 70 *et passim,*
    105, 136, 248
Chadwick, G. A., 246
Childs, Brevard, 163, 247, 248f.
Chilton, David, 192
Cole, R. Alan, 248
Courville, Donovan A., 43
Craigie, Peter C., 53
Dabney, Robert L., 91, 111
Daube, David, 33, 34, 39, 44, 113,
    117, 120, 125
De Graaf, S. G., 246
de Vaux, Roland, 146, 147, 150, 214
Delitzsch, Franz, 230, 246
Dooyeweerd, Herman, 213
Edersheim, Alfred, 233, 246
Ezra, Ibn, see Ibn Ezra
Fairfax, Olga, 276
Fensham, F. Charles, 110
Finkelstein, J. J., 123

Frame, John M., viii, xvii, 5, 67, 102
Gaffin, Richard B., Jr., 80, 181
Geikie, Cunningham, 247
Gemser, Berend, 72
Gesenius, 38
Gill, John, 246f.
Gispen, W. H., 152, 170, 246
Greer, Rowan, 245
Gregory of Nyssa, 243f.
Hamilton, Victor P., 191
Harrison, Roland K., vii
Hartley, John E., 240
Henry, Matthew, 245
Hodge, Charles, 111
Hoeksema, Homer C., 246
Hyatt, J. P., 247
Ibn Ezra, 160, 249
Ingram, T. Robert, 132
Jones, Hywel R., 247
Jordan, James B., 10, 20, 219
Kaiser, Walter C., 63 *et passim,* 113,
    199 *et passim*
Kaufman, Stephen A., 64, 199
Keil, C. F., 230, 246
Kline, Meredith G., 22, 59, 61, 254
Knight, G. A. F., 247
Knox, John, 181
Kosmala, Hans, 247, 250f.
Krabbendam, Hendrick, 199
Leibowitz, Nehama, 131, 157, 160, 173
Loeb, Meir, ben Yechiel Michael, 157

281

Maimonides, Moses, 157
Malbim, see Loeb, Meir
Maury, Matthew, 10
Mendelsohn, Isaac, 85
Mendenhall, George E., 228
Morris, Henry, 10
Morton, Jean, 10
Murphy, James G., 246
North, Gary, viii, xx, 41, 119, 138,
   140, 160, 163, 164, 172, 173
North, Robert, 84f., 147
Park, J. Edgar, 247
Paul, Shalom M., 63, 71, 72, 90,
   97, 104, 116, 123, 131
Pink, Arthur W., 246
Poole, Matthew, 245
Powell, Edward A., 207, 214
Rabinowitz, J. J., 138
Rambam, see Maimonides
Rawlinson, George, 246
Roth, Wolfgang M. W., 264

Rushdoony, Rousas J., viii, 19, 23,
   41, 95, 130, 147, 155, 172, 207,
   214, 215, 225, 238, 245, 258
Rylaarsdam, J. Coert, 247
Schoeck, Helmut, 33
Se'adiah ben Joseph (Gaon), 160
Sewell, Samuel, 154
Skinner, B. F., 174
Stewart, R. A., 267
Sutton, Ray R., viii
Theodore of Mopsuestia, 244, 245
Unger, Merrill F., 152, 153
Van Til, Cornelius, 5
Verdam, P. J., 74
Watts, J. Wash, 76
Wenham, Gordon J., 158
West, Jim, 20
Willeson, Folker, 55
Wines, E. C., 53
Yaron, Reuven, 33
Young, Edward A., vii

SCRIPTURE INDEX

(Bold face indicates a place where the verse or verses are discussed in depth)

OLD TESTAMENT AND APOCRYPHA

Genesis

1	187
1:5	94, 132, 137
1:8	132
1:10	132
1:26	24
1:27	3, 4
1:28	35, 100n., 155
2:7	100n.
2:10	263
2:10-14	256
2:11	15
2:15	49, 58, 133
2:17	96n.
2:18-25	155
2:19	94
2:19-20	132
2:23	132
2:24	19, 107, 273
2:25	63n.
3:1-5	59
3:6	260n.
3:7	63n., 76
3:10-11	63n.
3:14	56, 105
3:15	257
3:17	56
3:19	56, 100n., 165
3:20	132

Genesis

3:21	63n.
3:24	158
4	257n.
4:1	132, 164
4:3-8	94
4:10	37
4:10-11	99, 177
4:24	135n.
5	10, 21
6:2	35n.
7:2	51
9:4	37
9:5-6	112, 123
9:6	97
9:18-27	265
9:20ff.	35n.
9:20-27	264n.
9:27	265
10	190
11	10, 21
12	34n.
12:2-3	35n.
14	32, 51n., 265
14:4	265
14:5	265
14:14	92n.
14:17	30n., 265
14:18-20	209

Genesis

15:2-3	82
15:10-11	38
16	78
17	78, 79n.
17:12-13	76
17:12-27	82
17:14	78
18:10	35, 82, 256n.
18:19	51
18:23ff.	82n.
20	34n.
21:8ff.	273
21:10	44
21:22ff.	35n.
22:4	58n., 211
23	32
23-24	158n.
23:15-16	263
24:53	147
24:65ff.	160
24:67	258n.
25:1-6	256n.
25:2	40, 52
25:4	40
25:5	15
25:6	15
25:18	15, 256n.
25:23	251
25:28	35n.
25:31	251
26	34n.
26:5	51
26:8	62, 155
26:12-16	32
26:26ff.	35n.
27:4ff.	251
27:9	190, 191
27:16	190, 191
27:4-28:9	259n.
28:12	41n.
28:17	41n.

Genesis

28:20	210
28:22	234
29-31	34n.
29:15	33
29:30	78n.
30:22	78n.
30:25	78n.
31	33
31:12	33
31:15	147
31:39	51
31:39-40	33
31:41	33
31:42	33
31:43	34
32:6	263
32:31	137
33:1	263
34	35, 35n., 51
34:12	147
34:25	58n.
35:2	79n.
35:18	132
35:22	35n.
36:31	30n.
37:3	82n., 264n.
37:23	264n.
37:26	35n.
38	35, 51
38:17	**190**
38:20	**190**
38:23	**190**
39:12-18	264n.
39:19	157
41	34n.
41:40-44	82n.
41:42ff.	264n.
42:18	58n., 211
42:37	126
43:16	266
43:34	264

Genesis

44:18-34	264n.
45:18	35
45:22	264
46:34	35
47:6	35
47:7ff.	35n.
47:11	35
47:13-26	35
47:27	35
48:41ff.	251
49:5-7	51

Exodus

1:5	55
1:7	35
1:10-22	35
1:22	100n., 253
2:12	254
2:16	52
2:21	40
3:7	33
3:12	75
3:13-14	132
3:16	54
3:18	**41f.**, 75, 218
3:22	43, 152
4:14	157f.
4:21	255
4:22	37, 164
4:22-23	82, 82n.
4:22-26	38, **243ff.**
4:23	127, 218
4:24-26	82n.
4:25	212
4:26	80
4:28	255
4:29	54
5:1-3	218
5:6-19	53n.
6:6	37
6:12	79

Exodus

6:30	79
7:17ff.	253
8:1	218
9:16	127
10:2	214
10:7-11	**42f.**
10:10-11	34
10:25	43
11:1	**44**
11:2-3	43
11:4-7	39
11:7	38f., **38n.**
12	39
12:7	82
12:10	187
12:12	40
12:13	37f., 82n., 251
12:21	54
12:22-23	82
12:23	82n., 251
12:26	214
12:32	43
12:35-36	43
12:44	76
13:2	122n.
13:8	214
13:12	164, 266n.
13:13	122n., 164
13:18	264, 265n.
16:35	30n.
17:5	54
18	15, **52ff.**
18:10-12	52
18:12	40, 54
18:13-26	40
18:16	53
18:20	53
18:21	265n.
18:21-22	53
18:26	53
19	**55ff.**, 211

Exodus

19:1	55, 57
19:2-8	55
19:7	54
19:8-9	55
19:10-14	56
19:15	56f., 57n., 231
19:16	57
20:12	104
20:22-26	**62f.**
20:23	62
20:24	51, 62
20:26	62, 63n.
21:1	33, 46, 51
21:2	42, 75, **76**, 104
21:2-6	**76ff.**, 85
21:2-11	64 (outlined), 75ff.
21:3	42
21:3-4	**77**
21:4	34, 42
21:4-5	85
21:5-6	**77ff.**
21:6	141
21:7	**84**
21:7-11	**84ff.**, 147
21:8-9	**85**
21:9-10	**85f.**
21:10	7, 86n.
21:10-11	43, 44
21:11	**86f.**
21:12	64n., **97**, 104
21:12ff.	116
21:12-17	67f., **96ff.**
21:12-36	64 (outlined)
21:13	**97ff.**
21:14	**97**, 104
21:15	**103f.**
21:16	43, 89, **104f.**
21:17	**105ff.**, 105n., 161
21:18	68
21:18-19	103
21:18-27	**109ff.**

Exodus

21:19	124, 263
21:20	**90**
21:20-21	**112f.**
21:21	**90**
21:22	**113ff.**, **118**, 125
21:22-25	119
21:22-26	**128ff.**
21:23ff.	73n.
21:23-25	**115ff.**
21:26-27	89, 90n., 121
21:28	64n., **122ff.**
21:28-32	**121ff.**
21:28-36	68, 102
21:29	**90, 124f.**, 129
21:29-30	116
21:20	**125**
21:30-31	**90**
21:31	120, **125ff.**, 147n.
21:32	**127f.**
21:33	64n.
21:33-34	12, **129f.**
21:35	64n., 113n., **130**
21:36	127, **130**
22:1	viii, 64n., 117, 128, **261ff.**
22:1-4	**134ff.**
22:1-15	65 (outlined), **131ff.**
22:2	111, 112
22:2-3	**136f.**
22:3	89
22:4	129, 135, 261, 269
22:5-6	**137ff.**
22:7	135
22:7-12	**140ff.**
22:8-9	77
22:13	51
22:14-15	**142ff.**
22:16	65n.
22:16-17	68, **146ff.**
22:16-31	65 (outlined)
22:18	18
22:18-20	**152ff.**

Exodus		*Exodus*	
22:21	156	32	59, 195, 210
22:21-27	68, **155ff.**	32:2-4	62
22:22	65	32:6	62, 155
22:22-24	**157ff.**	32:10	157
22:24	65f.	32:11	157
22:25	**158f.**	32:19	157
22:25-27	66	32:20	145
22:26-27	72, **159ff.**	32:22	157
22:27	86	33:7-11	51
22:28	**161f.**	34:1	20, 46
22:28-31	**161ff.**	34:12-17	59n.
22:29-30	**163ff.**	34:13-17	62
22:30	164	34:13-18	154f.
22:31	66, **165f.**	34:14	33n., 145
23:1-3	**168f.**	34:18	59n.
23:1-9	66 (outlined), **167ff.**	34:23	229
23:2	178	34:24	185
23:3	160	34:26	**190ff., 272ff.**
23:4-5	**169ff.**	34:28	20
23:6-8	**171ff.**	35:1-3	75
23:8	31n.	35:3	153n.
23:9	156, 175f.	38:25ff.	231
23:10-13	**182f.**		
23:10-19	66 (outlined), 75, **181ff.**	*Leviticus*	
23:14-19	**184ff.**	1-7	51
23:17	229	4	266
23:19	viii, **190ff., 272ff.**	4:3	266
23:20-33	58, 66, **194f.**, 200	4:13	266
23:29	183	4:22	266
24:1-8	59	4:27	266
24:3	46, 51, 61	5:14-16	135
24:4	46	6:1-5	135
24:7	46	6:1-7	268
24:9-11	59	7:17	188
24:12	46, 61	8:23-24	80
25:16	22n.	9:24-10:2	153n.
28:42f.	63n.	10:2	158
30:11-16	126n., **225ff.**	10:11	213
30:12	227	11	51
31:12-17	75	11-15	56
31:18	20	11-24	201f. (outlined)

Leviticus

12	266
12:3	164
13-14	216
14:10	164
14:14	80
14:23	164
14:28	80
15	258n.
15:18	57
16	102
17:3-4	210
18	62, 258n.
18:23	153
19:9-10	135
19:15	167
19:18	22
19:31	18
20	62, 154
20:15	153
20:17	150
20:22-26	122
20:24-25	154
20:26	66
20:27	18, 152
21:9	154
21:13	257n.
21:19	120n.
22:11	76, 82
22:14	135
22:27	266
22:28	21
23:3	55, 182, 183, 211
23:5	58
23:7	58
23:10	58
23:10-14	188
23:11	58
23:15-16	58
23:15-21	189
23:17	186, 186n., 189 *bis*
23:39-43	190

Leviticus

24:10-23	53, 162
24:15	162
24:16	162
24:17	90
24:19-20	**116ff.**
24:20	120n.
24:22	90
25	100n., 156n., 183, 203
25:13	133
25:20-22	183
25:25	36
25:26	76
25:35ff.	135
25:39ff.	135
25:42	89
25:44	89, 105
25:44-46	76
25:45	89
25:46	89n.
25:47ff.	36
25:49	76
26	66, 194
26:34	183
26:43	183
27	210
27:1-7	127
27:4	149n.
27:30	210
27:30-33	221
27:32	210, 220, 230

Numbers

1	227, 230
1-4	203
1:4	54
1:16	54
3	101n., 164, 209, 251
3:12	40, 55
5	141, 145
5-6	204 (outlined)
5:5-8	135

Numbers

5:8	36
6	231
7:2	54
8:16ff.	55
10:29-11:30	52
11:11	52
11:16ff.	54
11:17	58
12:9	157f.
14:20-25	59
15:37-40	13n.
15:38ff.	161n.
18	210, 212
18:15	164
18:27	163
19	211, 229n.
19:11-12	57
19:22	14n.
20:22-21:3	99n.
20:28	35n.
21:1-3	35n.
21:4ff.	35n.
22:4	40, 52n.
22:22	157f.
24:20	206
25	158
25:6	40
25:8	86
25:11-13	86
26:10-11	126n.
27:1-5	54
27:1-11	53, 157
27:17	267
29:12-34	190
31	229n.
31:16	158
31:26-47	89
32:17	165n.
32:34ff.	30n.
33:4	40
35	93

Numbers

35:6	101n.
35:10-34	97ff.
35:16-21	97
35:19	99n.
35:21	99n.
35:24-25	98
35:25	93
35:27	99n.
35:31	97, 116
35:32-34	99
35:33	99n.

Deuteronomy

1:6-18	52
1:9	52
1:9-18	54
1:15	53
4:2	52, 52n.
4:8	10
4:9	214
4:13	22n., 46
5:1	80
6-26	199ff. (outlined)
6-11	200
6:5	21
6:7	214
6:20f.	214
7:13	210
10:4	46
12-13	201 (outlined)
12:17	210
13:2	27
13:5	153
13:6	27
13:12-18	154
13:13	27
13:16	231
13:17	162
14	190, 202 (outlined)
14:21	129, 165, **190ff.**, **272ff.**
14:22-27	211

Deuteronomy

14:22-29	210
14:23	210, 211
14:26	192
14:28-29	135, 211, 220
15	76
15:1-6	135
15:1-16:17	203 (outlined)
15:12	84
15:12-15	33, 76, 215
15:12-16	43
15:17	78
15:18	43
15:19-20	211
16:10	229
16:11	185
16:13-14	211
16:16	185, 229
16:17	229
16:18-18:22	67, 203 (outlined)
16:19	31n.
17:6	153, 264
17:8-13	174, 212
17:9	177, 216
17:12	104, 141
17:17	238
17:18	213, 216
18:6	211
18:10	18
18:10-11	153
19:1-22:8	203f. (outlined)
19:1-13	97ff.
19:2	239
19:11-13	178
19:12	98
19:14	**69f.**
19:15	22n.
19:15-21	168, **176ff.**
20:19-20	2n.
21:1ff.	102
21:2	54
21:10-14	79n., 89

Deuteronomy

21:17	164
21:18ff.	24
21:18-21	**106**
22	154
22:6-7	2n., 20
22:8	15, 129
22:9	163
22:9-23:14	204 (outlined)
22:12	161n.
22:13ff.	150
22:13-21	79, 257f.
22:24	112
22:25	149
22:25-27	**148f.**
22:28-29	51, **149**
22:29	148
22:30	161n.
23:2	150
23:9-14	132
23:14	229
23:15-24:7	205 (outlined)
23:19	158
23:20	158
24:1-3	150
24:6	262
24:6-13	**159ff.**
24:7	104
24:8-25:4	205 (outlined)
24:16	20n., 126
24:17	160
25:1-3	73
25:3	180
25:4	16
25:5-6	51
25:5-10	156
25:11-12	**118f.**
26:1-11	189
26:14	211
27:21	153
28	66, 194
28:17-19	163

Deuteronomy

31:9-13	213
31:10ff.	185
31:10-13	71
31:26	22n.
31:28	80
31:30	80
31:28-32:47	22n.
32:7	214
32:11	161n.
33:7	110
33:9	212
33:10	213

Joshua

1:14	265n.
2:3-5	20n.
4:12	265n.
5:3	83n.
5:5	247
5:5-7	59
5:9	79, 83n.
5:10ff.	83n.
5:13-6:5	228
7	126n.
9:16	58n.
10	265n.
10:21	**38n**.
13:3	265n.
15:16	147
15:18-20	147
18:22	270
24:14	36, 41, 62
24:26-27	22n.

Judges

1-2	194
1:6-7	80, 119, 116n.
1:17	231
4-5	191
4:19-20	191
5:2	231

Judges

5:24-27	191
5:31	137
6:19	191
7:11	265n.
9:6ff.	22n.
11:25	110
11:31	82, 82n., 256n.
13:15	191
13:17-18	132
15:1	77, 191
17	200
17:7	211
17-21	**218**
18:30	211
19:1	211
19:27	82n., 256n.
20:10	231
20:15	227
20:17	227
20:30	58n.
20:40	231
21:9	227

Ruth

1-4	158
2	135
2:12	161n.
3-4	156
3:4	80
3:9	66, 160, 161n.
4:14-15	258

1 Samuel

1:3	185
1:9	82, 185, 256n.
2:22	259
2:30	105n.
4-6	34n.
8	223, 238
10:3	191
11:8	227

1 Samuel

13:15	227
15:4	227
15:23	18
16:20	191
17:40	265n.
18:25-27	147
20:2	80
20:12-13	80
22:8	80
22:17	80
25:11	266
28	155
28:7	18

2 Samuel

5:22-24	229
6:17	236
6:22	105n.
7	209, 236
7:21	81
11:1	228n.
11:11	231
12	263, 268f.
12:26-31	228n.
13:11	149
14:4-11	101n.
15:27	82n.
16:14	183
16:16	82n.
18:1	227
18:18	30n.
21:1	126n.
21:1-14	126n.
21:15-22	265n.
24	126n., 226, **227f.**, 228n.
24:2	228n.
24:4	228n.
24:16	228n.

1 Kings

2:28ff.	98

1 Kings

3:16-28	53, 141
4:5	82n.
8:9	22n.
12:21-24	228n.
12:26-13:34	220
14:17	82n., 256n.
20:15	227
20:27	227
21	133
21:10	162
21:13	162
21:19-24	38

2 Kings

3:6	227
4:42-44	220
6:28-29	191, 274
9:22	153
12	230n., 232
12:4	230
12:18	230n.
20:5	58n.

1 Chronicles

7:20-24	55
15:16-24	217
17:25	81
23:4	216
25:1-7	217
26:29-32	216
28:3	228
28:11ff.	236

2 Chronicles

7:5	236
13	**269f.**
13:4	270
13:6	270
13:12	270
13:17	270
17:7-9	213

2 Chronicles

19:8-11	216
19:11	177
20:7	82n.
24	230n., 232
24:6	230
26:16ff.	236
31:3	236
31:7	211
33:6	153
35	187
35:7ff.	236
36:21	183

Nehemiah

8:9	213
10:29	237
10:32-33	233, **237**
10:34	237
10:37-38	211

Esther

5:1	58n.
8:2	82n.
8:15	82n.

Job

1:15	141
1:17	141
2:9	162
10:10	191
16:18	37
33:16	80
36:10	80
36:15	80
41:18ff.	157n.

Psalms

8:5	24
8:8	10
12:6	135n.

Psalms

19:4-6	137
19:5	252n.
22:12	128
22:13	128
22:16	81
22:21	128
40:6	81, **81n.**
44:22	267
58:7	79
58:10	98
68:30	128
69:20-28	37
78:20	86
78:27	86
79:12	135n.
82:1	77, 141
82:6	141
87:5	192
90:6	79
100:3	267
106:10-11	37
110	209
110:4	209n.
118:10-12	79
119:68	6n.
149:3	217
150:4	217

Proverbs

1:8	214
1:19	18
6:6	122n.
6:20	214
6:30-31	135
8:35-36	93n.
13:24	89
17:8	172
17:23	31n.
21:14	172
26:11	122n.
29:19	89

Proverbs

29:21	89
30:15	122n.
30:15ff.	264
30:19	122n.
30:24-31	122n.
31	238
31:1	214
31:26ff.	148

Ecclesiastes

12	254
12:3-4	82n.

Canticles (Song of Songs)

2:7	86n.
3:5	86n.
4:16	86n.
5:2	86n.
5:15	82n., 254, 254n.
8:2	86n.
8:14	260n.

Isaiah

11:12	263
13:14	267
14:2	88
19:18	265n.
26:21	37
30:17	265n.
41:8	82n.
42:20	80
48:8	80
50:5	80
53:6	267
53:7	267
53:8	81
56:7	231, 232
56:10	38n.
60:4-9	15, 256n.
61:5	88

Isaiah

61:10	252n.
62:5	252n.
63:1-6	98

Jeremiah

1:6	267
3:8	150
6:10	78, 81
6:29-30	231
7:11	232
7:34	252n.
12:3	267
16:9	252n.
25:10	252n.
33:11	252n.
34:19-20	38
49:36	263

Lamentations of Jeremiah

4:10	191, 274

Ezekiel

1	194
7:2	263
13:23	153, 155
16	18n., 63n., 145, 256
16:8	57n., 66, 160, 161n., 156n.
16:9	257n.
20:37	230
23:20	154
24:8	37
24:16ff.	257n.
34:31	267
40-48	236
45	238
45:13-17	**235f.**

Daniel

5:21	122n.

Hosea		Haggai	
1-3	256	1-2	224
2	18n., 145	1:1	237
6:2	58n., 211		

Joel		Zechariah	
2:16	252n.	1:18-21	96
		3:3-4	79
		13:7	267

Amos		Malachi	
1:3ff.	264	2:11-16	145
8:5	18	2:12	**86**
		2:14	7
Jonah		2:15	86
1:17	58n., 211	3:8	220
		3:8-12	208

Micah		Tobit (Apocrypha)	
3:2-3	86	7:13-14	150
6:8	6n.		

NEW TESTAMENT

Matthew		Matthew	
1:19	148	13:33	186, 186n.
5:17	60	17:24-27	**233**
5:17-19	11, 17, 19	18:12-13	267
5:21-22	65	18:23ff.	136
5:21-26	102	21:13	232
5:24	180	21:44	123
5:26	136	22:31	163
5:41	163	22:36ff.	19
6:26	2	22:37	21
6:30	2	23:23	91
7:16-18	6n.	24	36
9:36	267	24:28	38f.
10:6	267	25:27	158
10:29	2	25:51	26n.
10:35-37	212	26:15	128
12:33	6n.	26:51	81
13:24ff.	195	27:2-10	128

Matthew

27:46	4

Mark

7:9-13	106f., 161
9:49	115n.
10:18	6n.
10:19	20n.
10:42-45	232
13	36f.
14:47	81

Luke

2:37	158
2:41	185
3:38	24
4:25f.	158
7:12	158
12:58	180
14:26	108n.
18:2	269
18:8	269
19:8	263, **268f.**
19:8-9	135
21	37
22:15-20	197
22:51	81
23:27-31	37

John

1:51	41n.
2:21	82n.
5:21-29	57
5:25	57
5:29	57
6:53-58	197
7:37-39	188
7:38-39	208
8:12-20	264
10	267
10:1-9	82n., 256n.

John

10:22	185n.
15:14-15	82n.
17:20-21	5n.
18:10	81
19:7	276
20:22	189
21:16-17	267

Acts

2	189
2:1	58
7:24ff.	255
7:32	267
7:51	78, 81
10-11	14
10:1-2	256n.
11:3	256n.
17:29	24
23:3-5	162

Romans

2:14-15	45n.
3:19ff.	25
3:26	172n.
3:31	208
4	209
5:12	50
5:13f.	50
7:9ff.	25
7:12	6n.
7:16	6n.
8:17ff.	26n.
8:30	26n.
8:36	267
12:4	162
12:17-13:7	110
12:19	94
13:4	94
13:7	163
14:5	181

1 Corinthians

3:2	275
6:1-5	211
6:19	82n.
10:17	260
11:15	79n.
11:33-34	211f.
12	212
14:34-35	185
14:40	212
16:2	166, 210

2 Corinthians

11	260
11:1-3	63, 153
11:2-3	151, 257
11:24	**270**

Galatians

4	234
4:1ff.	208, 275
4:4	47
4:9-10	181
4:21ff.	274
4:26ff.	192
5:10	171

Ephesians

2:11-22	14
4:28	206
5:22-23	145
5:25	12

Philippians

2:7	81n.

Colossians

2:14	47
2:16	181
3:5	18

1 Timothy

1:8	6n.

1 Timothy

2:5	200
5:3	106, 106n.
5:16	106n.
5:17	10, 17, 106, 106n.
5:17-18	24
5:18	106n.
6:10	18

2 Timothy

3:16-17	3

Hebrews

1:6	40
5:6	209n.
5:12	275
5:13-14	274
6:13-18	96n.
6:18	102
7	209
7:1	40
7:3	209
8	xx
9:7	234
10:1-3	234
10:4	234
10:5	**81n.**
10:19-22	234
11:24ff.	255
11:39-40	234
12:29	158

James

2:10	18
2:23	82n.
2:25	20n.
3:1-12	167
5:14	216

1 Peter

1:8	234, 226

I Peter

2:2	275
2:25	267

Jude

9	162
12	212

Revelation

1:10	259n.
1:16	38n.
6:9-10	98

Revelation

9:13-14	98
11:3	22n.
17	192
17:17	192
19:7	259
19:7-18	39
19:9	259
19:15	38n.
19:17-18	39
19:21	38n.
22:17	260n.
22:20	260n.

SUBJECT INDEX

Aaron, 67, 99n., 157f., 251
Abel, 94
Abijah, 270
Abimelech, 34n.
Abiram, 126n.
Abortion, 113ff., 276
Abram/Abraham, 31f., 40n., 147, 258n., 263
   Chedorlaomer defeated by, 265
   circumcision of, 78, 78n., 79, 79n., 260
   household numbered around 3000, 54f., 92n.
   Midianites descendents of, 40, 52, 244, 256n.
   oppression/deliverance pattern, 34n.
   sanctuary for Lot, 51n.
   saved by faith in the New Covenant, 198
   sons of, 15, 78
   tithed to Melchizedek, 209
   weaning of Isaac, 192n., 274
Absalom, 268
Abuse, as grounds for divorce, 86f.
Achan, 126n.
Achsah, 147
Adam, 47, 50, 55n., 58 *et passim*, 127, 158, 164, 182, 188, 202, 258n., 260n. and Eve, 5, 63n., 79
Adonijah, 268
Adoption
   slavery and, 77, 81n., 82ff., 85

theological, 24ff., 82ff., 256
Adultery
   death penalty for, 148f.
   spiritual, 152ff., 158
   witchcraft as spiritual adultery, 18
Adversaries, dealing with, 66, 169ff.
Advertising, and calculating one's tithe, 222
Agape (see Love Feast)
Alliances, sinful, 194
Altar
   as hearth, 153n.
   as refuge, 98
Amalek, 206
American Life Lobby, 276
Amnon, 268
Amraphel, 265
Angels, 257n.
   Angel of Death, 37, 82n., 83, 101n., 126n.
   Angel of the Lord, 194
Animals
   clean and unclean, 56, 122ff., 164
   psychology of, 123n.
   social regulation of, 124f., 130
Antiochene exegesis, 244n., 245n.
Antiochus Ephiphanes, 185n.
Arioch, 265
Army
   mustering of, 227ff.
   organized by fives, 265n., 267
   versus militia, 228n.
Assaults, 109ff.

Asylum (see Cities of refuge)
Atonement
  atonement money, 126n., 147n.,
    226ff.
  day of, 102
  sado-masochism and, 95
  substitutionary, 37f.
Authority, 104
Avenger of Blood, 97ff., 252, 253ff.
  God as Avenger, 94, 146 (see also
    Angel of Death)

Baalam, 157f.
Babel, 41, 241
Babylon, 266
Balcony, requirement of, 129
Banking, fractional reserve, 160
Bankruptcy, 92
Baptism, 78n., 260n.
Barrenness, 194
Bastards, 150
Bathsheba, 268
Beating, as punishment, 73
Benjamin, 78n., 264
Bestiality, 153ff., 154n.
Betrothal, 148, 149f.
Bible
  church and, 8ff.
  devotional reading of, 9
  professional use of, 9
  purposes of, 1ff.
  redemptive-historical approach to,
    9f.
Bipolarity
  clean/defiled, 14n., 15n. (see also
    Clean/unclean)
  Israel/nations, 32
  special/general, 14n., 48n.
Birds, laws protecting, 2
Birth
  doorways (thresholds) and, 82n.
  symbolic, 256
Bishop, 54

Blasphemy, 94, 162
Blood
  calls for vengeance, 37f.
  issue of, 56
  pollutes land, 99ff.
  of wedding night, 257f.
Blood feuding, 100f., 103
Bloodshed, 37
Boaz, 258
Boiling kid in mother's milk, 190ff.,
  272ff.
Book of the Covenant, 46, 75, 83
  structure of, 61ff.
Booths, Feast of (see Festivals)
Borrowing, 142ff.
Breaking in (theft), 136f.
Bribes, 172ff.
Bride (of Christ), 256ff., 258n., 259n.,
  260n., 274
Bride price, 84f.
Bridegroom of blood, 243ff.
Burning of property, 120, 121, 138
Bystanders, laws protecting, 113ff., 117

Cain, 31, 41, 94
Caleb, 147
Calendar, 184ff., 193
Calf, golden, 59
Canaan (land), 55, 59, 66, 69, 83n.,
  99n., 100n., 186
Canaanites, 265
Cannibalism, 274, 276
Capital
  tithed?, 221n.
  taxed, 235, 238
Carefulness, doctrine of, 102
Castration, and circumcision, 78f.
Census, 226ff.
Chedorlaomer, 265
Children
  fights between, 111f.
  not punished for parents' sins, 125ff.
  of slaves, 77

Christmas, 185n., 193
Chronology, 32n., 44f.
Church
  infancy of, 13
  purpose of, 28
  state and, 26f.
  tithe and, 219ff.
Circumcision, 37, 59, 59n., 78n., 164, 243ff.
  Abraham and, 78, 78n., 79, 79n., 260
  adoption and (see three aspects, below)
  of Christ, 80, 81
  cutting off, 78f.
  dominion and (see three aspects, below)
  of ear, 77ff., 80ff.
  of foot, 80, 81
  glorification and (see three aspects, below)
  of hand, 80, 81
  justification and (see three aspects, below)
  of lips, 79
  Sarah and, 79, 79n., 260
  sanctification and (see three aspects, below)
  shame and, 83n.
  of slaves, 76
  of warbrides, 79n.
  of woman, 79f.
  three aspects, 78f., 80n., 260
Cities
  Levitical, 101n.
  of refuge, 93, 97ff., 239, 253f.
Clan feuding, 100f., 103
Clean/unclean bipolarity, 13f.
  animals, 56, 122f., 164
Cleansing, 56f., 102
Cloak, protective, 86, 160f.
Clothing, meaning of, 63n.
Cloud, glory, 161n.

Collagen, human, used in cosmetics, 276
Collateral, 160
Commandments, Ten, xix, 19ff., 46, 51, 61ff.
  related to Ordinances, 63ff., 199ff.
  two tables, 22
  Fifth, 67f., 104, 105f.
  Sixth, 93, 178
  Seventh, 145
  Eighth, 133, 159
  Ninth, 167, 178
Common grace, 83, 88
Communion (see Lord's Supper)
Compensation/composition, 97, 114, 116ff., 125, 134, 138
Consanguinity, 150
Conspiracy, 168f., 178f.
Contracts, 143
Cornelius, 15n.
Court system, 141
Covenant, 3ff., 21
  Adamic, 47ff., 50, 56ff.
  Book of the Covenant, 46
    structure, 61ff.
  blessings and curse of, 32f., 38f., 47
  Davidic, 209, 236
  definitive establishment of, 48
  law and covenant, 6
  Mosaic, 48f., 50
  New, 47ff., 57, 196ff.
    coming of, 50
  Old, 47ff., 50, 56ff., 100n., 187f., 196ff., 234
  provisional, 47f., 57ff.
  redemption and covenant, 46ff.
  Sinaitic, 48f., 50, 54, 56ff.
Covetousness, 33n.
Creation/fall pattern, 35n., 55ff.
Crop rotation, 183
Culture, extension of religion, 40f.
Curse, meanings of Hebrew terms for, 105ff.

cursing God, 161f.
cursing parents, 105ff.
cursing rulers, 162f.

Dathan, 126n.
David, 17, 236, 237
  Goliath and, 255n.
  numbers the people, 126n., 226,
    227f., 228n., 231
  saved by faith in the New
    Covenant, 198
  Uriah and, 268f.
Day, metaphorical meaning of, 137
Deacons (*shoṭerim*), 53n.
Death
  love of, 93
  symbolic, 56
Death penalty
  mandatory, 114
  not mandatory for adultery, 148f.
Deborah, 191
debt
  debtor's prison, 92
  slavery and, 76
Defenseless persons, 155ff.
Deliverance, 34
Dinah, 51, 147
Dirt, symbolic meaning of, 56
Discretion of court, 73
Disinheritance, 88f.
Dispensationalism, 17
Divorce, 86f., 88f., 148f.
  abuse as grounds, 86f.
Dogs, regulation of, 124f., 130
Dominion, 95
  circumcision and, 80n.
  law and, 24ff.
Doorways, and birth, 82n.
Doorposts, meaning of, 78, 81, 82f.,
  82n., 254ff.
Draft, military, 105
Dragon, 157n.
Drowning, symbolic, 78n.

Drunk driving, 115
Drunkenness, 106
Dueling, 110ff.
Dust, meaning of, 56

Ear
  circumcision of, 77ff., 80ff.
  piercing of, 77ff.
East, symbolic meaning of, 15
Easter, 193
Ecology, 2
Eden, 15, 31, 34f., 59, 240
Edna, 150
Education, and the tithe, 213ff.
Egypt, 33 *et passim,* 34f., 35n., 49, 55,
  60, 62, 75, 83, 83n., 100n., 127,
  176, 182, 186, 243ff., 251f.
Egyptians, 152
Eighth day, 58n., 164
Elders, 52ff., 53n.
  of the gate, 210f., 238
Elopement, 151
Enemies, treatment of, 169ff.
Engagement (betrothal), 148, 149f.
Enmity, 31
Enslavement (see Slavery)
Envy, 33n.
Equity of law, 16f., 18ff.
Equivalence, principle of, 115ff.,
  177ff., 192
Esau, 190, 256n., 259n., 263
Eucharist (see Lord's Supper)
Evangelism, by slavery, 83f., 88
Eve, 62, 153, 163f., 202, 257, 258n.,
  260
Evidence, 142, 177ff.
Exodus (event)
  law-giving based upon, 48f.
  legal foundation of, 39ff.
Extermination, principle of, 195

Fatherless, 65f., 156ff.
Faithfulness, laws of, 65f., 145ff.

Fall, of Israel at Sinai, 59 (see also Creation/fall pattern)
Familism, pagan, 103
Fat, meaning of, 187
Feasts (see Festivals)
Feet, circumcision of, 80, 81
Fertilizers, dangers of, 183
Festivals, 66, 184ff.
  Booths, Feast of, 163, 185, 190ff., 211, 229n., 274
  First-fruits, Feast of, 189
  Hanukkah, Feast of, 185n.
  Harvest, Feast of, 189
  Ingathering, Feast of, 190ff., (see Booths)
  Passover, Feast of, 58, 165, 186ff., 259f.
  Pentecost, Feast of, 58, 189
  Tabernacles, Feast of, 163, 185, 190ff., 211, 229n., 274
  Unleavened Bread, Feast of, 186ff.
  Vulture's Feast, 39
Festivity, 181ff.
Fetus, 113ff.
Feuding, 100f., 103
Fighting, laws against, 110ff.
Fire
  hearthfires, 153n.
  holy, 154, 231
  strange, 153n.
Firstborn, 39, 40, 55, 55n., 78n., 82f., 82n., 163ff., 209, 211f., 243ff.
First fruits, 58, 210, 229n.
Five, symbolic meaning, 264ff.
Flight, to avoid conflict, 112
Flood (Noachic), 31
  baptism and, 78n.
  recent, 44, 45
  science and, 10
Food
  laws, 165
  symbolic meaning, 4n.
Foreigner, 156

Fornication, 7
Four, symbolic meaning, 263ff.
Fracture for fracture, explained, 120n.
Fractional reserve banking, 160
Frustration, and violence, 94

Garden, concept of, 133
Genitals, punishment for attacking, 118f.
Gershom, 248 *et passim.*
Gethsemane, 81
Gifts, and release from slavery, 43, 76
Gladiators, 111
Gleaning, 183
Glorification, 24ff.
  circumcision and, 80n.
Glory cloud, 161n.
Gluttony, 106
God
  names of, 132n.
  personal character(s) of, 3ff.
  social character of, 3ff.
Gods
  Egyptian, 41
  false, defeated, 34, 40
  human office bearers called gods, 77
Golden calf, 59
Goliath, 265n.
Gomorrah, 35n.
Goring ox, 90, 116, 122ff., 130
Goshen, 34f., 41, 44, 55, 125
Gossip, 167, 168
Grace, and law, 6

Hagar, 44
Hair, as glory, 79n.
Ham (son of Noah), 265
  fall of, 35n.
Hamites, 265
Hammurabi, Code of, 125n., 131
Hand, circumcision of, 80, 81
Handmill
  not to be used as collateral, 160

symbolizes a person's livelihood,
160, 262
Hanukkah, 185n.
Harlotry, spiritual, 145, 157f.
Hatred, 93f., 95
of authority, 95
Havilah, 15, 32
Head tax, 225ff.
Hearthfires, 153n.
Heaven, 196
Hell, 102
covenantal character of, 4, 5
Helpless persons, 156ff.
High priest
death of, 98ff.
slave of, 81n.
symbolized Groom to the Bride,
163n.
Holiness, 165f.
Holy war, 230, 231, 237
Homeborn slave, 81ff.
House, and human body, 82n.
Husband, bloody, 243ff.

Idolatry, 154
harlotry and, 62f.
Image of God, 3ff., 111, 124n.
personal and social, 4ff.
Impartiality, 66, 167ff.
Incarnation, and slavery, 81n.
Inflation, 159
Inquisition, 153
Instinct, animal, 123n.
Insurance, 85, 148
Interest, on loans, 158f.
International relations, 171
Investiture, 82, 82n., 264n. (see also
Clothing)
Investments, 158f.
Isaac, 44, 190
conceived after Abraham's
circumcision, 78
fall of, 35n.

oppression/deliverance pattern,
34n.
seed, 15, 32, 260
weaning of, 192n., 273, 274
Ishmael, 15, 32, 78, 192n., 256n.,
273, 274

Jacob, 51, 258n., 263
descent into Egypt, 42, 55
enslavement of, 32ff., 50
oppression/deliverance pattern,
34n.
Rebekah and, 190f., 273
sons of, 35n.
tithe and, 210
Japhethites, 265
Jealousy
defined, 33n.
ordeal of, 145
wrath and, 157f.
Jephthah, 82n.
Jeremiah, 191
Jeroboam I, 270
Jerusalem
bride of the Lord, 257n.
destruction of, 14ff., 36f., 81, 191f.,
273, 274
heavenly, 102
kills sons, 275f.
Jethro
advised Moses, 52f.
believer, 15, 32, 40, 52f., 244ff.
descendent of Abraham, 15, 40,
52f., 244ff.
Melchizedekal office, 40, 40n.
taught Moses, 40
Jewelry, 146, 149
Jezebel, 153
Joab, 228n.
Joash, 230f., 230n., 231
Jonah, 32
Jordan River, 83n.
Joseph (son of Jacob), 35, 157, 264

influence on Egypt, 43, 45
savior of the world, 35n.
seed, 78n.
Joseph (husband of Mary), 148
Joshua, 240, 255
Jubilee, 70, 70n., 135f., 156n.
Judah, 78n., 190f.
Judaizers, 276
Judges, 53ff., 171ff.
Judicial procedure, 176ff.
Jury system, 232
Justice, 167ff.
Justification, 24f., 133
    circumcision and, 80n.
    resurrection and, 80n.

Keturah, 15, 32, 249
Kid (young goat), 190ff., 272ff.
Kidnapping, 67, 89, 104f.
King's Friend, 82n.
Kinsman redeemer, 36ff.
Korah, 126n.

Laban, 32ff., 34n., 258n.
Land, sabbath of, 183
Language, Biblical view of, 94, 167
    dominion and, 132f.
Law
    apparent incompleteness, 72f.
    applies today?, 48f.
    before Sinai, 50ff.
    binding nature of, 28f.
    case laws, 22ff.
    ceremonial, 16, 197
    changed in New Covenant, 12ff.
    changing and unchanging, 9n.,
        11ff., 11n., 73n., 74n.
    characteristics of, 68ff.
    civil, 117
    civil use, 26
    criminal, 117
    covenant and, 6
    coming of, 50ff., 50n.

common, 45
courts, 167ff.
death and resurrection of, 49
divine origin of, 70f.
equity of, 16f., 18ff.
Equivalence, Law of, 115ff., 177ff.,
    192
esoteric character of pagan law, 71
glorification and, 24ff.
grace and, 6ff.
"harshness" of, 27f.
hierarchy of, 19ff.
judicial, 68ff., 240, 242
judicial implications, 26ff.
justification and, 24f.
kinds of, 68ff.
motive clauses in, 71f.
not to be altered by man, 3
penal sanctions of, 73
public character of, 71f.
recorded at the exodus, 30
retaliation, 115ff.
revelation, 24
sanctification and, 24f.
spheres of, 69
state and, 26ff.
theology of, 1ff.
three-fold division of, 68ff.
to be read every seven years, 71
transcript of God's character, 6ff.
two tables of, 22
uses of, 24ff.
within the Trinity?, 7n.
written by Moses, 9f.
written constitution, 52ff.
Lawyers, and tithe, 217
Leah, 33f., 78n., 147
Leash laws, 125, 130
Leaven, 186ff., 192
Legalism, 8
Legs, and doorposts/pillars, 82n.
Leprosy, 216
Levi, 51

Levirate, 51
Levites, 230, 232
  ecclesiastical specialists, 212
  health and, 216
  replaced firstborn, family priests,
    55, 164, 212, 251, 253n.
  tithes, paid, 212
  tithes, received, 212, 220, 236
  work of, 218
Levitical cities, 101n., 253n.
Levitical tithe, 209ff.
Lex talionis, 115ff.
Liability, limited and unlimited, 129f.,
  130n.
Life, and death, 190
Loans, 158f.
  six year limit, 21
Lord's Day, 182
Lord's Supper, 259f., 260n.
  common grace and, 83
  consecration of elements, 187
  festival, 192, 211f.
  financing of, 211f., 235
  marriage analogy, 59n., 259f.,
    260n.
  presence of Christ, 48n.
  resurrection and, 59, 197
  sacrament, 188, 197
  sacramental theory, 218f.
  tithing and, 209, 211f.
Lot, 35n., 51n.
Love, 21
Love Feast, 211f.
Luke, 216
Lying, 20

Magic, 132f., 152f.
Magistrate, 69, 167ff.
Manasseh 153
Manna, 86
Manslaughter, accidental, 93, 97ff.
Marriage
  contract, 150

  covenant of, 6f.
  kinds of, 146ff.
  laws of, 65f.
  Marriage Supper of the Lamb, 39,
    59n., 259, 260n.
  one flesh concept, 19
Mary, 148
Masochism, 95
Mediator, 200
Medical expenses, owed, 110f.
Medicine, tithe and, 216
Melchizedek, 32, 40, 40n., 208ff., 236
Mercy, works of, 171n.
Metaphors, mixed, 258
Michael, 162
Midian, 40, 253
  Midianites, 15, 52, 52n., 243ff., 256n.
Milk, 190ff.
Millstone
  not to be used as collateral, 160
  symbolizes a person's livelihood,
    160, 262
Miriam, 157f.
Miscarriage, 194
Missions, financing of, 213
Mixed multitude, 176
Moabites, 52n.
Mob rule, 169
Morning (sunrise), significance of,
  187f.
Moses, 35, 50, 51, 67, 157f., 162
  head tax, 243ff.
  "levy of Moses," 230
  organized Israel, 52ff.
Multitude, mixed, 176
Murder, 93, 97, 110, 114
  attempted, 112
Muster, 226ff.

Naboth, 162
Nakedness, 62, 63n., 81, 202, 210f.,
  258n.
  circumcision and, 79

Naming, power of, 132f.
Nathan, 268
Nationalism, 193
Nazirite vow, 231f.
Negligence, punishment for, 93, 99, 102
Negro slavery, 91
Nehemiah, 237
Neighborliness, 142ff.
New Creation, 164
New Moon, 211, 212
New Year's Day, 193
Night, metaphorical meaning, 137
Nile, bloodied, 100n., 253
Nimrod, 41
Noah, 30, 31, 36, 44, 45, 51
Nostrils, God's, 157f.
Nursing, 191f.

Obed, 258
Occult practices, 152f.
Office, Biblical view of, 212
    office bearers, 266f., 271
    officers (shoṭerim), 53f., 150
Onesimus, 135
Open pit, 129f.
Oppression/deliverance pattern, 31ff.
Ordinances, 46, 75, 83
    structure of, 61ff.
Original sin, 127, 241
Orphans, 65f., 156ff.
Ox
    goring, 90, 116, 122ff., 130
    muzzled, 272
    symbolic meaning of oxen, 266ff.
    yoked, 272
Parachurch organizations, and the tithe 219
Parents
    attacking, 103f.
    repudiating, 105ff.
Passion, crimes of, 110

Passover
    event, 38f., 82f., 82n., 83n., 100n., 101n., 243ff.
    feast, 58, 165, 186ff., 259f.
Paul, 135, 162, 172n., 270
Peace offering, 62, 188
Pentateuch, platform for further revelation, 17, 30
Pentecost
    feast, 58, 189
    New Testament, 49, 192
Perjury, 179
Persecution, 35f.
Peter, 81, 234
Pharaoh, 33f., 35, 37, 127, 184, 218, 264
    fall of, 35n.
    God's war with, 39ff.
    law of God and, 39ff., 50, 75
Pharisaism, 8, 173f., 233ff., 276
Philemon, 135
Philistines, 32, 265n.
Phinehas, 86, 158n.
Pillars, and legs, 82n.
Pit, open, 129f.
Pleonasm, 96n., 106n.
Pledges, 159ff.
Poll tax, 225ff.
Pollution, 137ff.
Poor persons, 155ff., 268ff.
    tithe and, 211 *et passim.*
Pornography, 23, 23n.
Potiphar, 157
Prayer, house of, 231, 232
Pregnancy, 113ff.
Priests
    a nation of, 70, 71
    of all believers, 8
Princes, 54
Prison, 136
Private property, 70n.
Prizefighting, 111
Property, 131ff.
    familistic, 133

importance, 132ff.
laws protecting, 65
limits on owner's prerogatives, 129
private, 70n.

Rachel, 33f., 147
Rahab, 20n.
Ransom, 97, 125, 129
kidnapping for, 105
ransom silver, 226ff.
Rape, 51, 148, 149
Rebekah, 147, 190f., 258n., 273
Rebellion, 95, 106
witchcraft and, 18
Red Sea, 83n.
baptism and, 78n.
Redemption, 5, 36ff.
covenant and, 46ff.
Refuge, cities of, 93, 97ff., 239, 253f.
Regeneration, 95
Rent, 142ff.
Resistance to tyrants, 163
Rest, 181ff.
Restitution, 117, 129, 134ff., 142, 159, 177
multiple, 135, 261ff.
penal, 135
Resurrection, 82, 164, 196ff., 188, 189
baptism and, 78n.
double resurrection pattern, 57 (see also Eighth day, Third day)
first and second, 57
justification and, 80n.
third day and, 56ff.
uncleanness and, 56ff.
Retribution, 134
Reuben, 78n., 125f.
Reviling, penalty for, 107
Revolution, 95, 269ff.
Rumor mongering, 168

Sabbath, 8, 48, 57, 66, 153n., 187ff., 196, 211, 217,

slavery and, 75
year, 76, 83, 89n., 135f., 183
Sabotage, 138
Sacraments (as refuge), 101f.
Sacrifices, 37, 47f., 51, 57n., 62, 154, 266f.
peace, 62, 188
whole burnt, 231
Sadism, 95
sado-masochism, 89
Safekeeping, laws of, 140ff.
Salt, 115n.
Samaria, 191
Samson, 191
Samuel, 238
Sanctification, 24f., 133
circumcision and, 80n.
Sanctuary (refuge), 51n., 97ff. (see Cities of refuge)
Sarah (daughter of Tobit), 150
Sarai/Sarah (wife of Abraham)
circumcision of, 79, 79n., 260
death of, 258n.
drives out slave wife, 44
weaning of Isaac, 192n., 273
Satan, 151, 153, 227, 241
Saul, King, 126n., 147, 227
Scapegoat, 89
Seduction, 51, 146ff., 153
Self defense, 111f., 136f.
Senility, 108
Serpent, 56, 122
Sethites, fall of, 35n.
Shame, 63n., 79, 83n., 258n.
Sheaf, wave, 58, 188f.
Shechem
person, 51, 147
place, 51n.
Sheep, symbolic meaning of, 266ff.
Shelah, 190
Shem, 44, 265
Shemites, 265
Sickness, 194

Simeon, 51
Sin, original, 127, 241
Sinai, 251
Sisera, 191
Sixth day, 56ff.
Slaves and slavery, 34, 40ff., 75ff.,
  125, 158, 164, 182f.
  adoption and slavery, 81n.
  beating slaves, 88, 89f., 112f.
  blessings of slavery, 87ff.
  children of slaves, 77
  compared to animals, 127f.
  contracts for slave service, 85
  debt and slavery, 76
  disappearance of slavery, 105
  enslavement, 92, 95
  evangelism by slavery, 83f., 88
  female slaves, 84ff., 147
  freedom, might earn one's own, 76
  gifts upon liberation, 43, 76
  heathen slavery, 76
  Hebrew slaves, 76
  high priest's slave, 81n.
  homeborn slaves, 81ff.
  incarnation and slavery, 81n.
  Jacob as slave, 33f.
  Jesus Christ as slave, 81n., 127f.
  kinds of slavery, 87ff.
  law of equivalence concerning
    slaves, 121
  laws releasing slaves, 64
  liberation gifts, 43, 76
  man as slave, 95
  modern slavery, 90ff.
  Negro slavery, 91
  overview of Biblical doctrine, 87ff.
  price of slaves, 127f.
  purpose of slavery, 77, 83, 90
  redemption of slaves, 36
  risks of slavery 90, 127
  sabbath and slavery, 75
  sado-masochism and, 89
  six year limit, 33, 42, 76
  slave-wife, 33f., 43f., 84f., 146ff.
  sonship and slavery, 81n.
  Southern slavery, 91
  theft, punishment for, 92, 136
  trade, slave, 91f., 104f.
  voluntary slavery, 77ff.
  wife of slave, 77
Social security, and the Church, 173
Social pressure, 169
Sodom, 35n.
Sojourner, 156, 175f. (see Stranger)
Solomon, 31n., 216, 236
Sonship, 24ff.
  and slavery, 81n.
Southern slavery, 91
Sphere sovereignty, 213
Spirituality, 8
Standing (posture before God), 185f.
Statism, 240ff.
State
  avenger, 94f.
  Christian view of, 126
  Church and, 26
  purpose of, 28f.
Stealing (of men), 95 (see
  Theft)
Stewardship, 65
Stoicism, 174
Stones, symbolic, 123f.
Stoning, 123f.
Stranger, 16, 156 (see Sojourner)
Substitutionary atonement, 37f.
Succession, theology of, 55n., 164,
  258n.
Suffering, relief of, 171
Sunrise, metaphorical meaning, 137,
  187f.
Suppers, 38f.
Swearing, 94
Symbolism, sexuality and, 259, 259n.,
  260n.
Sympathy, as motivation, 175f.
Synagogue, 55, 211, 212

Tabernacle, 15, 51, 59, 62, 75, 77, 201, 231, 266n.

Tabernacles, Feast of (see Festivals)

Tamar, 51, 149, 190f.

Taxation
Biblical view of state financing, 225ff.
property, 221n.
resented, 95
taxing the Church, 172f.
temptation to withhold, 163
tithing and, 223

Temple, 209, 229ff., 237, 266n.

Thanksgiving Day, 193

Theft, 134ff., 141f.
enslavement for, 92, 136

Theocracy, 26

Third day, 56ff., 58n., 188, 197n., 211

Threshold, and birth, 82n.

Tidal, 265

Time, laws regulating, 66

Tipping, 175

Tithing, 159, 163, 185, 190, 207ff., 229n., 234 *et passim* 274f.

Tobias, 150

Tobit, 150

Torah, platform for the rest of Scripture, 17

Totalitarianism, 94

Transfiguration, 196

Transubstantiation, 218

Tree of life, 59

Trees, laws protecting, 2

Trinity, 5n., 7n., 19

Unclean (see Clean)

Uriah, 268

Veil, 160

Vengeance, 36ff., 94f.
covenant and, 46f.
God's, 29

Violence

laws regulating, 64f., 110ff.
nature of, 93ff., 241

Virginity, 147, 150, 257ff.
tokens of, 79f., 147n., 152, 257f.

Vulture's Feast, 39

Wages, versus income?, 210n.

War, 95
holy, 230, 231, 237
laws of, 2n., 20n.

Water, 188

Wave offering, 185

Wave sheaf, 85, 188f.

Westminster Confession of Faith, 69

Whipping (as punishment for crime), 73

Widow, 65f., 156ff., 160

Wife, of slave, 77

Wilderness, 31

Wine, 192

Wing (God's, imaged in clothing and architecture), 161n.

Wisdom literature, 17, 31n.

Witchcraft, 18, 152f.

Witnesses, 112, 168f., 177ff.
false, 177ff.
laws of, 66
malicious, 177ff.
mere witnesses versus accusatory witnesses, 178
two, 22n., 96n.

Worship, 183
centrality of, 10
formality in, 6
tithe and, 217

Wrath of God, 157f., 231

Zacchaeus, 135, 268f.

Zechariah, son of Jehoiada, 230n.

Zerubbabel, 237

Zipporah, 82f., 243ff.

Zoar, 35n.